COLLECTED WORKS OF
BERNARD LONERGAN

VOLUME 24
EARLY WORKS ON THEOLOGICAL
METHOD 3

GENERAL EDITORS

Frederick E. Crowe and Robert M. Doran

COLLECTED WORKS
OF BERNARD
LONERGAN

Early Works on
THEOLOGICAL METHOD 3

translated by
Michael G. Shields

edited by
Robert M. Doran and
H. Daniel Monsour

Published for Lonergan Research Institute
of Regis College, Toronto
by University of Toronto Press
Toronto Buffalo London

© The Jesuit Fathers of Upper Canada 2013
Toronto Buffalo London
utorontopress.com

ISBN 978-1-4426-4629-2 (cloth)
ISBN 978-1-4426-1434-5 (paper)

Library and Archives Canada Cataloguing in Publication

Lonergan, Bernard J.F. (Bernard Joseph Francis), 1904–1984
Collected works of Bernard Lonergan / edited by Frederick E. Crowe and
Robert M. Doran

Includes bibliographical references and index.
Contents: v. 24. Early works on theological method 3 / translated by Michael G.
Shields ; edited by Robert M. Doran and H. Daniel Monsour.

ISBN 978-1-4426-4629-2 (v. 24 : bound).   ISBN 978-1-4426-1434-5 (v. 24 : pbk.)

1. Theology – 20th century.   2. Catholic Church.   I. Crowe, Frederick E.
II. Doran, Robert M., 1939–   III. Shields, Michael G.   IV. Monsour, Daniel, 1958–
V. Lonergan Research Institute   VI. Title.

BX891.L595 1988   230   C880-933283- rev

The Lonergan Research Institute gratefully acknowledges the generous contribution
of the Malliner Charitable Foundation, which has made possible the production of
this entire series.

University of Toronto Press acknowledges the financial assistance to its publishing
program of the Canada Council for the Arts and the Ontario Arts Council.

Canada Council   Conseil des Arts
for the Arts   du Canada

ONTARIO ARTS COUNCIL
CONSEIL DES ARTS DE L'ONTARIO
50 YEARS OF ONTARIO GOVERNMENT SUPPORT OF THE ARTS
50 ANS DE SOUTIEN DU GOUVERNEMENT DE L'ONTARIO AUX ARTS

University of Toronto Press acknowledges the financial support for its publishing
activities of the Government of Canada through the Canada Book Fund.

Contents

General Editors' Preface

This is the third volume in the Collected Works of Bernard Lonergan concerned with tracing the proximate preparation for Lonergan's breakthrough in February 1965 to the notion of functional specialization. Volume 22 contains proceedings of three English conferences on method: Regis College, Toronto, 1962; Georgetown University, 1964; and Boston College, 1968. The last of these marked perhaps the first time he went public with the functional specialties. Volumes 23 and 24 trace the development that occurred in Lonergan's Latin courses and seminars on method at the Gregorian University, Rome, between 1959 and 1964. In the General Editors' Preface to vol. 23, I listed in chronological order all these materials plus other published documents that would have to be studied to gain a thorough grasp of this complicated development, both before and after the breakthrough. In addition, there are various notes on the archival website www.bernardlonergan.com, especially from folders 5 and 6 of Batch V in the Lonergan archives that contain relevant material, though the precise context of some of these notes remains to be determined. These notes begin at 45500D0L060 and extend to 47100D0L060 on the website. The breakthrough occurs in the document found at 47200D0E060, the first document in folder 7 in Batch V.

The present volume contains principally reconstructions that I have composed of Lonergan's two 1963 courses 'De methodo theologiae,' the first offered in the spring semester and the second in the fall semester. The second course extended to early February 1964. There are not available prose texts of Lonergan's notes for these courses similar to the text for the 1962 course of the same name, which is included in volume 23. Armando Bravo began work on the fall 1963 course, with a transcription made from Lonergan's schematic Latin notes. I edited that transcription for posting on the website, then translated it, and finally rewrote the translation in the form of a prose text, which is what appears here. The text is divided according to the divisions in Lonergan's notes, all of which are carefully dated.

A similar process took place in reconstructing the fall–winter course. Here I had the notes of Thomas Daly, who took the course, to help me with the materials. Michael Shields provided a helpful translation of Daly's notes. But again I worked just as much from Lonergan's schematic Latin notes, which again were carefully dated: first transcribing these, then translating them, and then correlating them with Daly's notes.

The results in each case are still schematic due to a lack of further material to work from. But I believe they reflect accurately these two courses, which I am convinced are important for following Lonergan's complex development in these years. I take full responsibility for any errors that may be found in my reading of Lonergan's notes.

Also included in the present volume is a lecture that Lonergan delivered in March 1964, about one month after the completion of the second of these courses. The lecture was entitled 'De notione structurae,' 'The Notion of Structure.' The material in the lecture mirrors some concerns in the first of the courses reconstructed here and points ahead to the article 'Cognitional Structure' written later in the same year. The translation is by Michael Shields, and the editing is shared between Daniel Monsour and myself.

As my work goes forward trying to identify and contextualize the notes from 45500DOL060 to 47100DOL060, I will attempt to include them in the volume in the Collected Works devoted to archival material (vol. 25). These notes too are important for understanding Lonergan's development towards the breakthrough in February 1965, but they require more work before they can be published.

ROBERT M. DORAN
Marquette University

EARLY WORKS ON THEOLOGICAL
METHOD 3

1 The Method of Theology Spring 1963: Editorial Reconstruction[1]

Does There Exist a Method of Theology? (8 February, 54200D0L060)

Does there exist a method of theology? It would seem perhaps that there does not, since theology is not one science but a combination or mixture of sciences, and so there cannot be one method. There must be a combination or mixture of methods. Theology today is a combination of (1) literary-historical studies of the scriptures, the councils, papal documents, the Fathers, the medieval, modern, and contemporary theologians, the liturgy,

---

1 This is an attempt to reconstruct Lonergan's spring 1963 course at the Gregorian University, 'De methodo theologiae.' This was the second time he offered a course with this title. See volume 23, *Early Works in Theological Method 2* for a much more extensive set of course notes that he distributed for the first course, in the spring of 1962. The reconstruction attempted here is based on Lonergan's handwritten notes, available in the Lonergan Archives and on the website www.bernardlonergan.com. The editor's decision is to present the material in each of the items that are included in Lonergan's course notes, even though there will be repetition from one class to the next. The subheadings given throughout this chapter are editorial constructions, based as much as possible on indications provided in Lonergan's own notes. The items are divided by date, and with each item there is provided the reference number on the website where the original Latin notes may be found. A great deal of help was provided by the work of Armando Bravo, s.j., who composed the first transcription of these notes and arranged them into a unified whole. Bravo's transcription appears on the website at 54200DTL060.

Christian art, the sociology of religion; and (2) philosophical, psychological, phenomenological, and social studies. Again, according to some there is the faith which believes, and there are the mixed conclusions that start with premises from faith and premises from reason, or premises from faith and premises from literary-historical studies, to yield theological conclusions.[2] Thus, it would seem, the method of theology is learned principally by learning the method of literary-historical, philosophical, phenomenological, social, etc., studies, and by adding what pertains to faith.

But there is another conception of theology that is possible and even probable. Everything depends on the conception one has of theology and of its principle. If things are learned by enumerating authors and by taking one's bearings on the basis of literary-historical studies, prescinding from the pre-predicative, pre-conceptual, pre-judicial realm, then one's principle is not real, that is, it is not the subject operating in such and such a manner; rather it is logical (the premises) or the given (the theological *loci*, the fonts); and since there are many premises, *loci*, and fonts, so also both theology and theology's method are a mixture; there does not exist one relatively autonomous science or method. On the other hand, for another conception of theology that is not only possible but also probable, there would exist a proper method for theology. According to DB 1795 (DS 3015) the principle is distinct from the object. The object includes everything that is known by reason and everything that is believed by faith, and so the principle is something real, namely, reason and faith, where 'reason' means the subject endowed with the light of reason, and 'faith' means the same subject endowed also with the light of faith; more precisely, according to DB 1796 (DS 3016) the principle of theology is a third, compound principle: *ratio per fidem illustrata*, reason illumined by faith.

---

2 Reference is made to 'A. Descamps, *Sacra Pagina*, vol. 1 (Paris: Gembloux, 1959) 132–57'; the reference is to Albert Descamps, 'Réflexions sur la méthode en théologie biblique,' *Sacra Pagina: Miscellanea Biblica Congressus Internationalis Catholici de Re Biblica*, 2 vols., ed. J. Coppens, A. Descamps, and E. Massaux (Gembloux: Éditions J. Duculot, 1959). This paper was frequently referred to by Lonergan after it first emerged in his notes little over a year previously; Descamps influenced Lonergan on literary-historical methods of scripture studies. It is quite possible that Lonergan's earliest reference to Descamps is in the spring 1962 course on 'De methodo theologiae.' See Lonergan, *Early Works on Theological Method 2*, vol. 23 in Collected Works of Bernard Lonergan, trans. Michael G. Shields, ed. Robert M. Doran and H. Daniel Monsour (Toronto: University of Toronto Press, 2013) 419, note 70.

Attending to this real principle excludes any extrinsicism regarding objective truth and regarding concepts. First, it eliminates extrinsicism regarding objective truth. Truth is not given apart from an affirming mind. There is only one eternal truth, that is, divine truth (*Summa theologiae*, 1, q. 16, a. 7). Truth is not given apart from the subject pondering the evidence, rationally judging, and reasonably believing. Second, it eliminates extrinsicism regarding concepts. Concepts detached from a real principle and floating as it were in the air are either Platonic Ideas or something derived from things without the mediation of intelligence. In fact, for every stage in the progress of understanding there are concepts that express understanding, and so there is a history of concepts of the same thing, and there is an understanding of this history and a crisis of this history. The three steps of lived history, understood history, and a crisis of the history and of the understanding will be key notions as we proceed in this course.

Attending to the real principle of reason illumined by faith will also direct us to the real problems. There do arise real problems, they are to be solved by us, and they will not be solved simply by pointing out and blaming the errors of our adversaries.

Theology is threefold: natural theology, the theology of us wayfarers ('theologia viae'), and the theology of our eternal homeland ('theologia patriae'). Again, there is theology as a particular science and theology as wisdom. The object of theology as a particular science is God and everything that is ordered to God. The principle of theology, when we are speaking of natural theology, is the natural light of reason; when the issue is the 'theologia viae,' the principle is the natural light of reason strengthened by the light of faith; and in the case of the 'theologia patriae,' the principle is the natural light of reason strengthened by the light of glory. As for mediation, natural theology is mediated by creatures, the 'theologia viae' is mediated by Christ and the church, and the 'theologia patriae' enjoys the immediate vision of God.[3]

The proper principle, then, is reason illumined by faith. Again, by 'reason' is meant the fundamental natural tendency or dynamism that intends being, everything about everything. The light of faith extends the field of this natural principle.[4]

---

3 Theology as wisdom is simply mentioned here. It is not treated at this point.
4 Or, as Lonergan was to put it in *Method in Theology*, 'the objects of theology do not lie outside the transcendental field. For that field is unrestricted, and so outside it there is nothing at all.' Bernard Lonergan, *Method in Theology* (Toronto: University of Toronto Press, 1990) 23.

Under 'proper object' three things are considered. First, there is *intelligentia mysteriorum*, the understanding of the mysteries achieved by one who inquires soberly, reverently, and perseveringly; this understanding is not reached by reason alone, since we are dealing with mysteries; and it is in process, precisely because it is understanding, not judgment. It is an understanding by analogy with what is known naturally; it is not a new mode of understanding through phantasms or a mode of understanding proper to the mysteries. It entails the connections of the mysteries with one another and with our ultimate end, but these are not connections that are naturally known.

Second, to understand a doctrine is to understand the history of the doctrine. Thus, we have what has been called the noblest task of theology (DB 2314 [DS 3886]);[5] and we have the understanding of the process mentioned in DB 1800 [DS 3020]);[6] the dogmatic end is that one understand, and the apologetic end is that one helps others to understand.

Third, there is the growth in understanding spoken of in DB 2314 [DS 3886].[7] It presupposes that one has already acquired some understanding.

Theology Has Its Own Proper Method – Mediation Materially Considered (12 February, 54300D0L060)[8]

If theology has its own proper method, it is not just a mixture assembled from other sciences. But to grasp this entails withdrawing *from* extrinsicism

---

5 'To show how a doctrine defined by the Church is contained in the sources [is] "the noblest task of theology" (DB 2314, DS 3886, ND 859).' Bernard Lonergan, *The Triune God: Doctrines*, trans. Michael G. Shields, ed. Robert M. Doran and H. Daniel Monsour (Toronto: University of Toronto Press, 2009) 7.

6 '... there is a *genetic* consideration when the apprehenders are placed in an order according to their dates and locales so as to show clearly that growing and developing understanding, knowledge, and wisdom about the faith which the First Vatican Council spoke of (DB 1800, DS 3020, ND 136).' Ibid. 9.

7 'Growth and progress cannot be limited on the side of the sources of revelation. The sources of revelation contain treasures of truth so many and so great that they can never really be exhausted (DB 2314, DS 3896, ND 419).' Bernard Lonergan, *The Triune God: Systematics*, trans. Michael G. Shields, ed. Robert M. Doran and H. Daniel Monsour (Toronto; University of Toronto Press, 2007) 43. The material on proper object is expressed more clearly in the next item, dated 12 February.

8 The notes for 12 February in part repeat material treated in the notes for 8 February.

with regard to both truth and concepts and withdrawing *to* the pre-conceptual, pre-judicial, pre-predicative realm, that is, to understanding, which is experienced just as much as are hearing and seeing. Then theology will have its own proper principle, which is not reason and not faith, but reason illumined by faith. Then too, it will have its own proper object, namely, the mysteries to be understood. This understanding is a function of reason inquiring soberly, reverently, perseveringly. The understanding achieved will be thematically appropriated as such; it will not be simply catechetical understanding. What such understanding is has been made thematic systematically in *Insight* and historically in *Verbum*. It has been systematically applied in *Divinarum personarum* and applied to the development of dogma in *De Deo Trino* [1961 'Pars analytica']).[9]

The growth of this understanding may be considered in two ways. DB 1796 refers to systematic understanding by analogy and by the connection of the mysteries with one another. DB 1800 speaks of understanding, knowledge, and wisdom growing with regard to the doctrine of the faith, in individuals and in everyone, in the whole church, and by stages over the centuries. To understand a doctrine and to understand the history of a doctrine are reciprocally related. When the process is understood, one can proceed from a given age or situation to any other age or situation.

The proper principle is reason illumined by faith. Reason is the subject as inquiring (What is it?) and reflecting (Is it? Is it so?), the subject as oriented to being (everything about everything), the one, the true, the good. Faith corresponds to 'we believe everything revealed by God to be true,' whether this be that which could have been naturally known or that which could not be known by us had it not been divinely revealed. Faith is not a new faculty or potency, but a determination within the intellect regarding an object

---

9 The references are: Bernard Lonergan, *Insight: A Study of Human Understanding*, vol. 3 in Collected Works of Bernard Lonergan, ed. Frederick E. Crowe and Robert M. Doran (Toronto: University of Toronto Press, 1992); Bernard Lonergan, *Verbum: Word and Idea in Aquinas*, vol. 2 in Collected Works of Bernard Lonergan, ed. Frederick E. Crowe and Robert M. Doran (Toronto: University of Toronto Press, 1997); Bernard Lonergan, *The Triune God: Systematics* is the Collected Works edition (vol. 12) of *De Deo Trino: Pars systematica* of 1964, which was an updated version of the earlier (1957, 1959) *Divinarum personarum*, to which he refers here. Material from *Divinarum personarum* that did not survive the revision is contained in an appendix in *The Triune God: Systematics*. Finally, *The Triune God: Doctrines* contains the material from the *Pars analytica* of *De Deo Trino*, 1961.

within being. Reason illumined by faith is not partly reason separated off and partly faith separated off but a new, composite principle.

The proper object is, first, an understanding of the mysteries, which is attained insofar as reason illumined by faith inquires soberly, reverently, perseveringly. This understanding differs from the understanding constitutive of faith itself and from catechetical understanding. As such an understanding it is distinct from faith, and as an understanding of mysteries it is distinct from reason. Faith adds truths whose 'exquisite' understanding theology as a particular science adds, and whose order with other truths theology as wisdom adds. This understanding does not occur through new, infused species but by analogy with what is naturally known. It is not through species proportionate to the object of faith. Thus, it is said to be 'obscure.' But this obscurity does not remove or do away with the understanding, which includes inverse insight.

Also included under 'proper object' is the fact that understanding a doctrine and understanding the history of the doctrine are mutually dependent sets of operations that illumine each other. Thus DB 1800: understanding, knowledge, and wisdom grow in the course of the ages; and DB 2314 regarding the noblest task of the theologian. Whoever does not understand mathematics, physics, chemistry, etc., cannot write a history of these disciplines or discover the principles and connections. And whoever does not understand the history of a doctrine cannot grasp exactly what needs to be developed, what is already complete, or the connection of the elements. Thus, we are speaking of an understanding of the process itself with its many internal intelligible connections that can be ordered in several ways: in accord with what is first dogmatically, or first apologetically, or first in terms of the science that is to be further developed and perfected, or first in regard to a controversy, or first in regard to preaching.

In mediation considered materially[10] the principle (reason illumined by faith) is applied, and through it theology proceeds to the object. The medium considered materially is twofold: (1) Christ and the church, the body of Christ, which provide the object to be understood; and (2) the revealed, preached, handed down, and declared word of God, which supplies the

---

10 Theological mediation can be considered materially or formally. *Mediatio materialiter* is contained in this set of notes, and *mediatio formaliter* in the next (54400DOL060). At this point Lonergan begins adding new material to what was covered in the notes for 8 February.

logical premises. (1) includes (2), since what Christ and the church are cannot be known without the word, and what the word of God is cannot be known without Christ and the church: and not only the *word* about the church, but the very sign itself lifted up among the nations, and not only the *word* about Christ, but the historical, crucified, and risen Christ himself.

Again, (1) adds a social, cultural, and historical context or surrounding to which theology necessarily turns in order to understand the word. Language, literature, and doctrine are not subsistent realities. They do not exist except within a community or society. They are not understood unless one takes on the mentality of the community. Thus, modern linguistic studies are concerned not with written words but with living speech.

(1) also adds other sources, other determinants: dogmatic facts, the sensible aspect of Christ crucified, of the Word become flesh, an artistic aspect, a personal, intersubjective, symbolic aspect, and a social ordering, so that the theologian is subject to the magisterium, to the legal requirements of 'ne doceat.'[11]

(1) opens the way to full mediation, the full function of theology as a wisdom that proceeds logically in accord with understanding. As the word is included in the church, so the church is included in the world; there is a dialectic between the church and the world. And theology is one science among many, and must take its place in relation to sociological, historical, psychological, etc., studies.

Mediation Formally Considered (15 February, 54400D0L060)

We move to mediation formally considered.[12] We have the material object, the proper principle, the proper object, and mediation. When the principle (reason illumined by faith) is applied to the medium (Christ and the church), there arise questions. When one proceeds from the principle through the medium to the object (God and all things in relation to God), there occur answers to the questions. The medium is the given. It is that about which one asks questions, in which one initially understands, and in

---

11 Lonergan adds 'sociologia cognitionis,' 'the sociology of knowledge.'

12 As *mediatio materialiter* was considered in the previous entry so *mediatio formaliter* is the first consideration here. At the top of the first page: Mediatio formaliter → datum. *Mediatio formaliter* entails a cognitional-theoretic analysis of theological procedures.

which one verifies. It is the given that precedes the scientific questions and answers, and that does not depend upon them.

Thus, we distinguish the empirical and the speculative. The empirical has to do with the data. There are no questions without the data about which one asks. To the data is added not some other, fictitious datum, but understanding. It is in the data that the understanding is verified. Hypotheses that cannot be verified are not scientific hypotheses. The speculative, such as 'pure reason,' is that which is not governed by empirical criteria.

Next there is considered the division of the empirical sciences. First, there is natural science. Here the given is the sensible qua sensible, constituted by the very fact that it is given, that it is sensed, that it appears, and by that alone. Next, there is human science, where the given is either sensible or conscious and is constituted not only by being given but also by the intelligence with which it is already informed. The data of human science are already included within a psychological, social, cultural, historical, religious field. But truth is not included in their 'formality' as data. The meaning with which they are informed may or may not be true. It is true that Socrates, Plato, Aristotle, Paul understood in such and such a way, but what they understood may be either true or false. Third, however, there is theological science, where the formality of the given is not only that it is given and not only that it is given as meaningful, but also that it is given as true. From this there arise theological *loci*. Finally, there is transcendental science, where the principle is applied to the principle itself, to give rise to a theory of science, a theory of methods, the objective theories of gnoseology, epistemology, ontology, logic, and mathematics. The principle in question may be either natural reason or reason illumined by faith.

The data of natural science are sensible realities as such. They are constituted by the very fact that they are given. They do not depend on any understanding, classification, hypothesis, or theory. Per se they can be seen, heard, etc., by anyone. For example, even if one does not understand a science, one can still see the place where a needle stands, or a column of mercury, or the color of a sheet of paper, or a point of light.

But natural science is not restricted to sensible data that are just spontaneously given. The data can be artificially or experimentally produced. Nor is natural science restricted to sensible data that can be observed without using instruments. Many very powerful instruments have been added to the procedures of natural science.

Whatever is received is received according to the mode of the receiver. In natural science that 'mode' is not one's passions, nor is reception achieved in just any act. The scientist is a human being not as social or practical or aesthetic or mystical, but as totally devoted to the theoretic goal, like Thales in his wonder at the stars.

Natural science reaches its object not through the data alone or through understanding in the data, but through understanding that begins from the data and is verified in the data. The object is being.

One does not proceed to the object without an a priori. The a priori is the very subject inquiring, observing, understanding, and verifying. In every science one moves from an a priori from above and from the data from below, employing a scissors action. The a priori of natural science evolved historically and continues to develop.

Natural and Human Science, Six Steps in Human Science (19 February, 54500D0L060)

In natural science the object is not intelligent; there is sought an understanding of what is not intelligent. In the human sciences the object is intelligent, but the understanding that is sought is not the understanding that the intelligent object itself has. A businessman understands an abundance of materials, say, of grain. He understands his status in the business and among merchants, and he understands other businessmen who are future buyers. But an economist seeks an understanding of economic reality, and does so in a way different from that of the businessman. He should understand businessmen, etc., but to understand them as businessmen is not his science. He seeks an understanding of the entire process, one that relies on systematic reasons and universal causes.

So there are economic systems – mercantilism, the physiocrats, mercantile mechanism (Smith, Ricardo, the Manchester School), direct economics, socialism. These theories are attended to, understood, discussed, expounded among economists. They undergo vulgarization, and thus have an influence on the common mentality, not because of their theoretical perspectives or in their totality, but in a fragmentary way, just as they are in fact understood: more or less, and in accord with their utility or their advantages for individuals and groups.

In this way the human situation, the object to be investigated and understood, itself changes. There occurs *die Wendung zur Idee*, which is a universal phenomenon. This change in the situation and in the object has an influence on economic science. Some principles and laws remain as they are. Others are purified and put forth more exactly. Others are eliminated by the events themselves, or because they are erroneous, or because of new techniques of solving problems.

Thus, there is a twofold understanding in the human sciences. There is (A) the understanding characteristic of the object of the science, that is, common sense, *Verstehen als exsistentiale.* And there is the understanding (B) of the subject of the science, the understanding that the scientist is searching for. There is a mutual influence between these two, for (C) in the very object of the science there is *die Wendung zur Idee,* and (D) in the subject of the science there is something like an experimental correction, in that history creates its own experiments. Historians (E) write about (A), (B), (C), and (D), and there are historical crises (F) regarding (A), (B), (C), and (D). This schema remains important through much of what follows, particularly as it is transposed to theology.

Thus, (A) there is the tranquil possession of the truth, the understanding of the faith at the everyday level, communicated socially and visibly; (B) there are authors, tendencies, and schools reflecting on and objectifying (A); (C) there may occur a great dispute, or a council, from which there emerges a change in the concrete situation (A); (D) there emerges a new generation of authors, tendencies, and schools in theology itself and in the history of dogma; ever since Petavius there has been history (E) with respect to (A), (B), (C), and (D), and also (F) crises in their regard. This schema is itself something a priori, heuristic, and evolving.

What is investigated concerning 'man' is the meaning of life, the human intentional order including that which is intended, the act of intending (sense apprehension, intelligence, appetition), and those who do the intending. The meaning of life may be undifferentiated, differentiated, or cultivated. When it is undifferentiated, it is also total and overdetermined; it is carried in symbols (G. Durand, Freud-Jung-Binswanger, Eliade), art (Langer, R. Huyghe), intersubjectivity (Max Scheler), and incarnate carriers (Marcel).[13] It is differentiated when there is a transition to a concrete mode of living and to actions that are to be directed, regulated, informed, or repressed, in the family, customs, society, education, the state, the law, the economy, technology. It is cultivated for its own sake in the arts, in myth, in languages and letters, in the religions, in history, in philosophy, in the sciences, and in theology.

13 For most of the references, see below, pp. 14, 17, 150, where Lonergan dealt with these figures a bit more fully.

There is a distinction between the undifferentiated and total meaning and the differentiated and specialized one. The differentiated becomes general and common insofar as in some way there occurs *die Wendung zur Idee*, insofar as there develop reflection, crisis, and expression. The distinction between undifferentiated and differentiated corresponds to a twofold human tendency: a tendency to the whole individual, who develops first and more efficaciously and more commonly in animality and sensibility, and a tendency to the intelligent, rational, and moral person who intends the universe (everything, being), who distinguishes, and who grasps the relations of the parts.

Linguistic meaning fluctuates under this twofold impulse or influence. There is the depth of undifferentiated consciousness, the real as ineffable, confused, obscure; and there is intelligence distinguishing and ordering, pursuing an ideal that seems almost unattainable. There results a variation of meaning like the continuous spectrum of colors.

Meaning (22 February, 54600D0L040)[14]

Regarding the six steps that we distinguished [in 54500D0L060], (A) is to (B) and (C) is to (D) as the implicit is to the explicit, *actus exercitus* to *actus signatus*, the *vécu* to the *thématique*, *verstehen* to *erklären*, the *existentiell* to the *existentiale*, life to theory, experience to experiment, the practical-dramatic subject to the theoretical subject, the perceivable world to the intelligible world. Historians (E) combine (A) and (C) into a history [(E₁)] of religion, of culture, of economic life, etc. They combine (B) and (D) into a history [(E₂)] of doctrine. And they combine (A) and (C), (B) and (D), into a history [(E₃)] of the total movement. And with (F) we encounter a crisis with regard to (E₁), (E₂), and/or (E₃). We have here a heuristic structure, telling us what is to be expected and anticipating a differentiation of methods. The a posteriori in this structure is from the fact of investigations, and these lead to the improvement of methods over the course of time. All this work becomes an a priori in relation to subsequent investigations.

What is investigated? Meaning. The formal element is the 'intentional': 'meaning' including what is intended, the very intending itself, and the ones who intend, both sense and intellect, each of which both apprehends and desires.

14 Some elements are repeated from notes for 19 February.

There is meaning as undifferentiated, total, overdetermined. 'Undifferentiated' means that distinctions are lacking between (a) sacred and profane – everything sacred is profaned and everything profane is sacralized; (b) the individual and the community – the individual does not think, judge, choose, act except as part of the community and within traditional structures; (c) the dramatic-practical and the theoretical – a theoretical interest is minimal, but myth and magic satisfy it in the dramatic and practical realms. 'Total' means that, because distinctions are lacking, there is a tendency to the whole, to everything, to being. 'Overdetermined' means that meaning is not restricted to one determinate meaning; it signifies this determinate thing in such a way that it also and simultaneously signifies a second and a third.

This indeterminate meaning occupies the whole life of man increasingly as we go back to the origins. Still, it is not eliminated in times of great civilization and culture nor does it remain only in the multitude; it is found also in the educated. It can be overlooked, as in rationalism, but then it is just devalued, not eliminated.[15] This undifferentiated meaning is symbolic (Durand), intersubjective (Scheler), incarnate (Marcel), artistic (Langer).[16]

Regarding the symbolic Durand correlated symbols with dominant reflexes – equilibrium, swallowing, mating – to which there are associated images, affects, values, and to which almost everything gets associated by likeness and analogy.[17] Thus, with St George and the dragon: St George represents all the good elements: light, erect position, sitting on the horse, armed, master of himself and of the horse; he does not fear, he is 'dexter et habilis'; he proceeds against evil. The dragon represents all the objects of fear, horror, repulsion, contempt. Or with Jonah and the whale: Jonah descends, is swallowed, but emerges none the worse after three days and three nights. The whale is a monster, but it is euphemized.

This indeterminate meaning is also intersubjective. Aquinas speaks of how the hand spontaneously moves to protect the head. So too we find the

---

15 Reference is made here to Mircea Eliade, *Images and Symbols: Studies in Religious Symbolism* (New York: Sheed & Ward, 1961). Lonergan comments that 'Paradise Lost' has degenerated into South Pacific, and the goddesses Artemis, Aphrodite, and Athena into movie stars.

16 Other names appear, divided from these by a vertical line: Freud-Jung-Binswanger, Cruchon, and Odier.

17 The reference is to Gilbert Durand, *Les structures anthropologique de l'imaginaire* (Paris: Presses universitaires de France, 1963).

same reaction in ourselves with regard to another human being.[18] There exists a level of experience where 'I' and 'you' have not yet been distinguished. The laughter of others makes us laugh; weeping makes us sad; horror makes us fearful.[19]

Theology, Differentiation of Consciousness and of Meaning (1 March, 54700DOL060)

Theology's proper principle is reason illumined by faith. Its object is an understanding of the mysteries. This emerges *in fieri* in the interplay of dogma and the sources, and *in facto esse* in systematics. The mediation of the object is through Christ and the church. In the method proper to theology Christ and the church are data, and the science is not a natural science nor a human science but a theological science.

Again, the structure of the object and the a priori functioning in the human sciences can be lined up in the six points already seen: (A) experience and understanding, the *vécu, actus exercitus*; (B) authors, tendencies, and schools: experiment, explication, the *thématique, actus signatus*; (C) *die Wendung zur Idee*; (D) a new generation of authors, tendencies, and schools; (E) the histories of (A), (B), (C), and (D); and (F) the crisis of things historical.

Again too, undifferentiated, total, overdetermined meaning characterizes constitutive symbols, intersubjective symbols, incarnate symbols, artistic symbols. Differentiated meaning is linguistic; it is indicative or constitutive or both. The indicative is distinguished into grammatical functions and dictionary meanings. The grammatical functions cover nouns, pronouns, adjectives; verbs, adverbs; conjunctives, subjunctives, prepositions. The constitutive dimension has to do with the meaning of life over against the absurd, the struggle for existence and the struggle for meaning; with the meaning of the love by which the beloved is loved; with the meaning of the family in accord with which a given family lives; with the meaning of democracy that

---

18 Lonergan narrates here an experience that he relates several times in lectures: while he was walking up to the Borghese gardens, a mother and her small child were coming down; the child began to fall, and automatically he reached out to protect the child from falling, even though he was too far away to be of any real help.

19 Two headings regarding this meaning are left without comment in the notes: the incarnate, and combinations.

makes a given society a democracy; with the meaning of religion in a religious person. This constitutive meaning develops from the global through differentiation to integration in the individual, in a given culture, in the human race. It is rooted in intentional human nature. It is communicated through common life and education. It is exhibited through humane letters and liberal arts. It is differentiated in accord with the individuality of a person, a people, a history.

The differentiation of consciousness may be schematized as follows.[20]

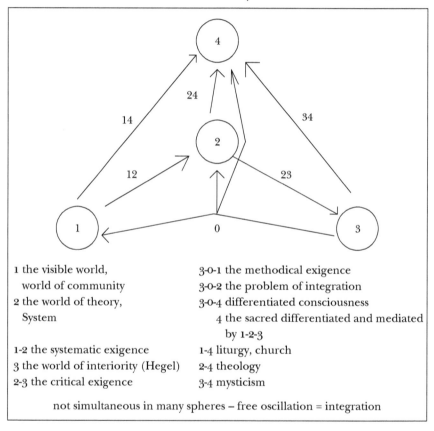

1 the visible world, world of community	3-0-1 the methodical exigence
	3-0-2 the problem of integration
2 the world of theory, System	3-0-4 differentiated consciousness
	4 the sacred differentiated and mediated by 1-2-3
1-2 the systematic exigence	1-4 liturgy, church
3 the world of interiority (Hegel)	2-4 theology
2-3 the critical exigence	3-4 mysticism

not simultaneous in many spheres – free oscillation = integration

Next, there is a distinction between meaning that is undifferentiated, meaning that is differentiated in ordinary language, and meaning that is

20 The graphic work here was done by Armando Bravo in his Latin reconstruction of this course. See General Editors' preface above, p. viii.

differentiated in technical language.[21] The symbolic includes a number of different markers. (1) Freud speaks of that which can be shown but is not appropriate. (2) To speak of overdetermination is to say that opposites regarding the same thing are not excluded. There is the ambivalence of love and hate, joy and sadness, desire and fear. (3) Because opposites are not excluded, there is no negation in the proper sense of the term. Poets negate, but they also evoke what is negated. Because it is negated, what is evoked is ambient, standing around. (4) Symbolic expression is not logical argumentation. There is repetition of various kinds. Lewis Carroll: 'I have said it thrice. What is said three times is true.'[22] (5) There is condensation: many themes are developed simultaneously. (6) Binswanger, *Traum und Existenz*,[23] speaks of preformation, dreams of the morning. (7) Jung and Eliade speak of homology. (8) C. Odier speaks of conflict.[24]

Four general points conclude this treatment.

First, the more one approaches the elementary and undifferentiated, the more there is attained a universal language, symbols that are intelligible to all, even the learned.

Second, elementary undifferentiated meaning is not at all to be considered in a materialistic fashion. 'Light' does not mean 'merely material light'; this would presuppose the development of a differentiation.

Third, the Greeks distinguished natural and rhetorical (poetic, story) speech, and proper and transferred meaning. For the classicist mind, *either* someone says what he means *or* he is using a literary genre. But the fact is that we all use literary genres all the time. Proper meaning is not something abstract, *per se notum*, but is that which is more common and more familiar in some determinate cultural and social milieu.

Fourth, there is a transcendental aspect, in that the interpreter can reach to the mind of another to the extent that one either experiences similar

---

21 There is a reference to 'Langer 242 ff.' The reference is to Susanne K. Langer, *Feeling and Form: A Theory of Art* (New York: Charles Scribner's Sons, 1953). The pages relevant to the points Lonergan is making here are 242–44.

22 Langer, *Feeling and Form* 243 quotes Carroll's Bellman: 'If I say it three times it's true.'

23 Lonergan's reference in *Method in Theology* (p. 69, note 16) is to the French translation: Ludwig Binswanger, *Le rêve et l'existence* (Paris: Desclée, 1954), which has a 128-page introduction by Michel Foucault.

24 The reference in Lonergan's notes is to C. Odier, *Les deux sources consciente et inconsciente de la morale*, Geneve, 1943.

things or can imagine them as experienced, can understand the 'thing,' the mode of understanding, and can understand the judgments and decisions of others. Nothing more is given on the written page than black marks on white paper in a certain spatial order.

Comparative, Organic, Genetic, and Dialectical Methods (5 March, 54800DOL060)

In human science the notion of *Aufhebung* will be retained, but not so that it is conceived as total or principal.

We have seen the six steps: (A), (B), (C), (D), (E), (F).

Constitutive meaning is what makes human reality, and it can be objective with regard to the family, mores, society, education, the state, the law, the economy, technology.

Undifferentiated meaning is more conformed to the laws of imagination and affect. Differentiated meaning is more conformed to the laws of logic.

For classicism, there exists a normal mixture. One uses nouns and verbs in their proper sense, includes expressions in phrases in an obvious manner, and thinks in a normal way. There also exist mixtures that depart from the normal. Expressions are used in a transferred way and are composed according to some literary genre. 'Literary genre' for classicists means an exception or quasi-exception. Either one says what one means (normal speech) or one says one thing and means another, and that is literary genre.

In romanticism, the laws of imagination and affect are vindicated, and stable forms are rejected.

For historicism, classicism is parochial. Each place and time has its own 'normative' mixture, and other places and times have their own 'normative' mixture. And we all use literary genres.

Historicism attends well to concrete data, and is open to everything, but it inevitably tends toward relativism, as is witnessed in Troeltsch. Classicism does well to want to salvage reason, absolutes, universal realities, in human life, but it uses a medium not suited to this end. Not only does it not apprehend the concrete data of the past, but also it is blind to the concrete data of the present. It conceives everything through universal ideals and normative laws, e.g., Mediterranean architecture, with its symmetry and elementary geometric forms; Gothic architecture, with its character of being vital, asymmetrical, exhibiting an elastic equilibrium.

Clarifications are in order regarding abstraction and transcendental method.[25]

There is abstraction (a) of the part from the whole: a man who lacks an eye or a foot remains a man; (b) of form from matter, e.g., of a circle from a circular thing, (c) of an invariant structure and proportion. Thus we have:

> the empirical element – potency – words
> the intelligible element – form – meaning
> the judicial element – act – affirmation, negation
> one knowledge – one being.

Regarding transcendental method, (a) the predicaments, the ten genera of being, are distinguished from the transcendentals: being, one, true, good; (b) the conception of the transcendentals varies: Parmenides, Plato, Aristotle, Plotinus, Avicenna, Aquinas, Scotus, Kant, Hegel; (c) whence practically everything changes; there is no deductive demonstration of realism or of idealism; premises are either taken in a realistic sense or they are not; if they are, the real and the ideal are not demonstrated but presupposed; if they are not, the real and the ideal are not concluded to. (d) The more accurately and coherently the transcendental position is formulated, the more easily it is reduced to a fundamental structure of the concrete subject. (e) It is not difficult to discern in these structures what is normative as well as aberrations and deformations.

More particularly, with respect to our six steps: (A) (the understanding characteristic of the object of the science, the common sense, *Verstehen* as *existentiale*) demands constant and intimate familiarity, the assimilation of the understanding of the common sense [of another time and place], and does not admit systematic exposition. E.g., Albright just by touching fragments and dust from urns at Qumrân was able to determine their age; or de la Taille was able to say, 'St Thomas never used such an expression.' It is as if there is acquired the common sense of another epoch, culture, author. Believe the experts, as long as they don't disagree. If they disagree, we have *F* (a crisis).

As regards (B) (authors, tendencies, and schools: experiment, explica-

----

25 The lecture 'De notione structurae,' presented in both Latin and English below, is relevant to this material.

tion, the *thématique, actus signatus*), there are four methodological steps: comparative, organic, genetic, and dialectical.

The fundamental step is comparative. It corresponds in human science to measuring in natural science. Otherwise, what is obvious is overlooked because one has not attended to the data, the differences and connections will not be known, and the questions will not come to light as to how things proceeded from one position to the next, or as to how what are not opposed actually cohere with one another. This work of comparison is very fruitful. The connections and differences in (A) lead to connections and differences in (B). One author is found to be very intelligent while a whole series of authors is found to be mediocre.

The next step is genetic, but it is based on connections (*complexa*). The connections that make up (A) lead to the connections that make up (B). For example, the question is not whether Nicea correctly arrived at *homoousion* but what precisely happened; not speculating a priori about causes but studying the texts a posteriori, as in 'gratia operans'[26] or in the question why the Alexandrians were imbued with Platonism.

The comparative is the first and fundamental step.[27] What measurement is in natural science comparison is in human science. One does not attend fully and exactly to the data without comparisons. And without comparisons differences are not known. Where the differences are found, scientific work can begin.

Next is the organic. Comparison reveals differences, which are successive, while connections reveal simultaneous interdependence and organicity.

A particular genetic study is not concerned with whether the process from (A) to (B) was taken rightly and truly, but with how it actually happened. How did Aquinas arrive at acknowledging actual grace? Why the movement from the naive realism of Irenaeus, Tertullian, Hippolytus, Novatian, to Platonism? Also, a particular genetic study moves from connection to connection.

Viewed globally, the genetic moves from differentiation to integration.

26 Lonergan is clearly referring here to his dissertation on 'gratia operans' in the writings of Aquinas. See Lonergan, *Grace and Freedom: Operative Grace in the Thought of St Thomas Aquinas*, vol. 1 in Collected Works of Bernard Lonergan, ed. Frederick E. Crowe and Robert M. Doran (Toronto: University of Toronto Press, 2000).

27 This material appears on a new page. It starts by repeating in other words what was said a paragraph above regarding comparative method.

First, there is the differentiation of consciousness. Where the *Wendung zur Idee* has not occurred, myth and magic flourish. And where there is no turn to interiority (the critical exigence), there is endless and fruitless dispute among systems.

Dialectic arises insofar as the issue is the intelligible, the true, and the good as contrasted with the absurd, the false, and the evil. As far as perennial philosophy is concerned, there are many perennial philosophies. There is perennial empiricism, confined to the data; perennial idealism, confined to the intelligible; and perennial realism, concerned with the true.

Major and Minor Criticism (8 March, 54900D0L060)

Differentiate (E) into (E_i), (E_j), and (E_k), where (E_i) means histories of the immediate data of everyday life $(A_1 \, A_2 \, A_3 \, ...)$, (E_j) histories of writers, schools, tendencies $(B_1 \, B_2 \, B_3 \, ...)$, and (E_k) the histories that integrate these.

To understand better (E_j), that is, histories of writers, schools, and tendencies, we may appeal first to degrees of descriptive science and degrees of explanatory science. In the natural sciences, instances of the first are zoology and botany prior to any evolutionary explanation, and instances of the second are biology once evolution has been acknowledged, Newtonian mechanics, Clerk-Maxwell's equations, special relativity, and quantum theory. So too in human studies, there are degrees of descriptive knowledge and degrees of explanatory knowledge.

First, then, degrees of descriptive knowledge in (E_j). There are manuscripts, and the question of the authenticity of their authorship must be determined; the works have to be examined and a critical text established; sources have to be determined; the intention of the work, its occasion, and its projected readers must be ascertained; the process of documentation and construction needs to be assembled, along with the chronology of works. There are both particular and general instances of such descriptive works. For a particular instance see Chenu's *Introduction à l'étude de saint Thomas d'Aquin*,[28] where the question is not what Thomas taught but what

---

28 Marie-Dominique Chenu, *Introduction à l'étude de saint Thomas d'Aquin* (Montreal-Paris: Vrin, 1950); in English, *Toward Undersanding Saint Thomas*, trans. A.M. Landry and D. Hughes (Chicago: Regnery, 1964).

must be known before one studies Thomas. For a general instance see Altaner's *Patrologie.*[29]

There are also degrees of explanatory work in (E_j). First, there is the discovery of a question, and not of a question imported from outside but one rooted in the data themselves. Second, there is the comparative method that studies connections and genetic sequences.[30] The connections should be homogeneous as regards time and author. Thus, Bouillard in *Conversion et grâce chez saint Thomas d'Aquin*[31] says that Thomas never speaks of an elevation of a faculty to an act prior to justification, whereas all modern theologians acknowledge the necessity of such an elevation; and therefore, he says, actual grace in the strict sense is not found in the works of Thomas. We would say, rather, 'Therefore, there is a difference,' but whether it is because of diverse meanings of grace demands a distinction. The moderns have two reasons for such an elevation: the supernaturality of the act and the theory of vital act according to which 'willing' is 'causing.' It does not seem that Aquinas departed from Aristotle to the extent of positing the theory of vital act.[32]

---

29 Berthold Altaner, *Patrologie: Leben, Schriften und Lehre der Kirchenväter* (Freiburg: Herder, 1958); in English, *Patrology*, trans. Hilda C. Graef (Freiburg: Herder, and Edinburgh, London: Nelson, 1960).

30 Among the examples listed are Artur Landgraf, *Dogmengeschichte der Frühscholastik* (Regensburg: Friedrich Pustet, 1952–56) and Dom Odon Lottin, *Psychologie et morale au Moyen Age* (Louvain: Abbaye du Mont César, 1942–60).

31 Henri Bouillard, *Conversion et grâce chez saint Thomas d'Aquin* (Paris: Aubier, 1942).

32 Compare the following from Bernard Lonergan, *Early Works on Theological Method 1*, ed. Robert M. Doran and Robert C. Croken (Toronto: University of Toronto Press) 189–90: 'Take Bouillard's *Conversion et grâce chez s. Thomas*, published some years earlier. In it, he holds that St Thomas has not got our notion of actual grace, that there is a basic difference. He does not mean the same thing as we do because he has no elevation of the faculty prior to justification. According to all the later theologians there is required some sort of elevation of the faculty for a supernatural act prior to justification. Why must there be this elevation of the faculty? Because the faculty produces the act; it is a vital act. But if St Thomas does not hold vital act, there is no sense in saying he does not hold the same doctrine regarding actual grace. What is true is he does not accept the principle of vital act in that particular meaning. I do not mean St Thomas does not admit the existence of living beings and the specific difference between living beings and non-living beings. That is not the point. It is a precise theory of what a vital act is. According to Aristotle, *quidquid movetur ab alio movetur*. According to Plato, the soul moves itself. According to 13th-century Augustinians, when they were forced to

So in explanatory work, there are comparative, organic, and genetic methods.[33]

There is also (E_i), that is, histories of the immediate data of everyday living: buildings, monuments, works of art. And there are the crises of these various histories (E_i E_j E_k). *Minor criticism* (F_i) may demonstrate that they have not adequately applied principles or have omitted this or that; there is, as it were, a spontaneous evolution of the science itself, to which there is joined a sort of spontaneous progress in method. So Hegelians gave rise to the Historical School: Niebuhr, Ranke, Grimm, von Savigny, and Droysen.

Major criticism (F_j) has two aspects. First, there are the fundamental terms in which the investigator thinks, the terms to which what is investigated is reduced. Second, there is the question whether issues regarding the true, the good, the false, the evil enter in the object to be investigated and in the judgment about the investigation.[34]

Description and Explanation in Human Science, More on Minor and Major Criticism (12 March, 55000D0L060)

The data proper to human science are data with meaning. They may be investigated descriptively (*quis, quid, quibus auxiliis, cur, quomodo, quando*) or in explanatory fashion (comparative in a way that the question arises from the data, organic, genetic).

Descriptive investigation suits what is best known by contemporaries, who are immediately involved with the things themselves. Explanatory investigation reaches what is rarely known by contemporaries.

---

acknowledge a real distinction between substance and accidents, substance and potencies, there are vital potencies, potencies that move themselves. That the potency moves itself is the doctrine of vital act. It is the opposite of *quidquid movetur ab alio movetur.* If you hold that view of vital act, then you have to have an elevation of a faculty to be able to produce its own supernatural act if it has not yet got the habit. But because you don't find that elevation of the faculty in St Thomas's discussion of acts prior to justification, it does not mean one does not find actual grace there. Of course, if you read St Thomas through the notion of vital act, you just do not get to the text at all.'

33 Lonergan gives nearly a page of relevant references from his 1941–42 articles on 'gratia operans,' under the heading 'series differentiarum.'

34 More is given regarding these two issues on the last page of the item, but it is repeated more clearly in the following item, and so is not recorded here.

As for human science and the question of truth, distinguish truth in the data themselves, truth at the descriptive level, and truth at the explanatory level. Regarding truth in the data themselves, the data are given, not suppressed or omitted, and they are to be explained either as fact or as conscious or unconscious fiction; the historian does not believe the data, as is shown by Collingwood with his detective story where all the witnesses are lying and all the clues are fabricated;[35] on the other hand, the historian also does not exercise Cartesian doubt.

Regarding truth at the descriptive level, slowly there is constructed an arrangement that is firm enough that nobody thinks of destroying it or of replacing it with something new. It is, however, more difficult to attain consensus when there are stronger motives for doubting.

Regarding truth at the explanatory level, in general the concern is not with the truth of what the author meant but with whether the author really meant it; the rules of hermeneutics apply equally well to Aquinas, Plato, Aristotle, and the Epistle to the Romans; specifically, there is slowly accumulated reliable information about the chronology of writings, the meaning of the vocabulary, the general connections, and what is known in particular questions. The more frequently and longer the work is cited, the better it is.[36]

Minor criticism treats the histories of the immediate data, of the writers, tendencies, and schools, and of the histories that integrate these. It yields judgments such as 'This was omitted,' or 'That was less clearly and exactly explained.' There is a quiet advance of methods, so that what once happened does not happen today except occasionally and out of ignorance. Experience is the best teacher. The art of history is learned in seminars under the best teachers.

Major criticism is grounded in minor criticism. It is hardly at all engaged in by historians. It poses philosophical problems. So we have the sequence: (1) the old Tübingen school, with its Hegelian dialectic in history; (2) the Historical School – Niebuhr, Ranke, Droysen, legal and political history; von Savigny in law; Grimm in popular literature: 'no philosophical presuppositions'; (3) the fact that there were philosophical presuppositions: from illuminism, Romanticism, Hegelianism. The positivist tendency eliminates

35 R.G. Collingwood, *The Idea of History* (Oxford: Clarendon, 1946) 266–74.
36 Lonergan gives the example of Gaston Boissier, *Ciceron et ses amis: Étude de la societé romaine du temps de César* (Paris: Hachette et Cie, 1865, 1908, 1941); in English, *Cicero and His Friends: A Study of Roman Society in the Time of Caesar,* trans. Adnah David Jones (New York: G.P. Putnam's Sons, 1925).

these and other presuppositions; but as Marrou says, it also logically leads simply to the editing of texts.[37] There are also relativistic or perspectivist tendencies. For relativists such as Dilthey, Troeltsch, and Rothacker, what is sought is not truth but correctness (*Richtigkeit*). For others, there are different conclusions for different presuppositions. For perspectivists, data are *materia prima*, so that from various points of view or standpoints things are variously illumined and everything can be 'objective.' The existentialist and transcendental tendencies distinguish what can be scientifically determined, *Wissenschaft*, from what can be mythically or existentially interpreted; the *existentiell* kerygma is what is to be responded to.

There is a problem that arises at least under the theological aspect, and it is concerned both with ultimate or fundamental or basic terms and with philosophical differences. Concerning ultimate terms, the problem is avoided in the paper by Descamps,[38] with his focus on the contingent and the commonsense mode, but it is assumed in different ways in Bultmann and in Thomism. The problem of ultimate terms can arise with respect to (A_i), that is, the data of ordinary life, (B_i), the writers, tendencies, and schools that treat (A_i), (E_{ijk}), the histories of the immediate data of everyday life and of the writers, schools, and tendencies, and of the histories that integrate these, and (F_{ij}), the crises that give rise to minor and major criticism. Concerning philosophical differences, it needs to be stressed that there is not one perennial philosophy but many, and they are opposed.

Major Criticism and Theology (15 March, 55100D0L060)

Major criticism enters into the theological field. There is the history of doctrine from the New Testament to Nicea, for example, and the writings, tendencies, and schools that emerged in that process. Then there is the modern process from Petavius to Daniélou and beyond, attempting to compose the history of doctrine and of the writings, tendencies, and schools. Someone today then comes along and writes a new history, choosing and selecting from the original process and the modern histories, and perfecting the latter; the new history contains and reveals material for minor criticism: 'This was omitted,' or 'That was less clearly and exactly explained,' and so

---

37 The reference is to Henri-Irenée Marrou, *De la connaissance historique* (Paris: Éditions du Seuil, 1954); in English, *The Meaning of History*, trans. Robert J. Olsen (Baltimore: Helicon, 1966).

38 See above, note 2.

on. But major criticism may note a different sort of problem in the new history itself, a problem which exceeds the method that moves from data to description and the various kinds of explanation (comparative, organic, and genetic): a problem of transposition or of basic terms, or a problem of dialectic intimately connected with transposition and basic terms.

Regarding transposition or basic terms, there is in the history a multiplicity: there are Judeo-Christians, gnostics, apologists, heretics, refutations of heretics; there are Petavius and all the moderns, Daniélou, Orbe, Bultmann, Jonas. What is it that enables these very diverse figures to be considered together, by reducing one to another or some to one? It happens tacitly, without any explanation or justification. But such a process is implicitly criticized, e.g., in Descamps. And the explicit consideration of this question is necessary for history and especially for Catholic dogmatics. DB 2314: the noblest task of the theologian is to show how a doctrine defined by the church is contained in the sources. If the same thing can be found in Nicea, Ephesus, Chalcedon, Trent, Vatican I as in the sources, then there is required the possibility of this identification being clearly and exactly apprehended. That is the problem of transposition and basic terms.

Concerning dialectic, the explanatory stage involves comparison, which reveals similarities. These are used to establish connections. Comparison also reveals dissimilarities, and these are the basis of genetic and dialectical method. Dialectic has to do with irreducible opposites, opposites that do not enter into connections and do not pertain to genesis or development. These opposites are so far from being eliminated that, once they have been overcome in one form, they return in another. We hear about *philosophia perennis*, but there is not one *philosophic perennis*. There is perennial empiricism, perennial idealism, perennial realism. We hear about one Lord, one faith, one baptism, but there are perennial heretics as well. This opposition, even if it is manifested in contradictory propositions, is still more deeply rooted in existential orientation itself. This is the reason it is perennial; this explains why it is found in the past process concerning which the history is written and in the histories themselves; this is why it is found between authors, tendencies, and schools, but also within the same author, the same tendency, the same school. It is found within the field of data, of description, comparison, connections, genesis. And it is found in the subject to whom the data are given, the subject who describes and explains. But it cannot be adequately investigated by an empirical or descriptive or explanatory method. It remains beyond the horizon of methodical consideration, since it deals not with predicamental realities as such, but with the transcendentals that are present in every category. It has to do with the openness of the mind, with being, with the true, with the good. And so it pertains not only to authors, tendencies, schools, and the histories that document these and the crises that arise, but also to the ordinary run of affairs in everyday living. Christ is the sign of contradiction: greater love over against hate, much fruit over against murder, 'that they might have life' over against death. On the law of transformation, see *De Verbo Incarnato*, thesis 17.[39] Dialectic, then, removes questions from the field of growing intelligence (description and explanation) to the field of judgment. It does not make a formal judgment: I must decide about my own existence. But it illuminates the act of judgment and reduces opposites to their principles.

Concerning fundamental or basic terms, there is no single connection of such terms. The fundamental terms are the transcendentals as preconceptual, as determining the dramatic-practical life, the theoretic life, the interior life, as manifested in various ways and in various cultural stages. There are as many opposed connections of these as there are oppositions, opposed positions, in dialectic. The same word appears with radically opposed meanings in the process of dialectic. The terms, the opposed meanings, exist not only in the logical or conceptual order, since this order is an expression of a fundamental existential orientation, and the issue is more existential than conceptual. Consciousness transcends any expression of itself.[40]

Dialectical Analysis, Horizon, and the Structure of the Human Good (22 March, 55200D0L060)

Dialectical analysis requires further treatment. What probability is there of major criticism when we are treating simultaneously minds so different in time, in their ways of speaking, and in their goals? The problem of radical

---

39 The reference is to the thesis on the Law of the Cross, the last thesis in Bernard Lonergan, *De Verbo Incarnato* (Rome: Gregorian University Press, 1960, 1961). A subsequent edition appeared in 1964.

40 A reference is made to Breton's paper in Edmond Barbotin, Jean Trouillard, Roger Verneaux, Dominique Dubarle, and Stanislas Breton, *La crise de la raison dans la pensée contemporaine* (Bruges: Desclée de Brouwer, 1960). Here Lonergan notes that Breton addressed the possibility of exactly formulating first principles. For Lonergan's review of this book, see Bernard Lonergan, *Shorter Papers*, vol. 20 in Collected Works of Bernard Lonergan, ed. Robert C. Croken, Robert M. Doran, and H. Daniel Monsour (Toronto: University of Toronto Press, 2007) 234–36.

opposition is not solved genetically. The opposition is such that what comes later simply repeats what came earlier but in a fuller and more accurate and deeper manner. Nor is it solved as the omission or overlooking of data are solved. The data are acknowledged but explained differently. The different explanations are a function of existential orientation.

Dialectical analysis moves from the opposition between actors and authors to its root, its cause, in any actor or author. This root or cause in general is very well known. Dialectical opposition arises from the data because it is not solved by appealing to the data. It arises because 'whatever is received is received according to the mode of the one receiving.' But this generic solution is useless until specifically, and in the individual cases, the modes of receiving are known and judged.

The mode of receiving can be coherent in itself, or self-contradictory; it can be coherent with what is received, or contradictory to what is received. The division of modes of receiving can be scientific and philosophic, on the one hand, or theological, on the other, insofar as what is received includes or does not include life in Christ and the word of God. Applying this division, we get positions and counterpositions in the ordinary run of affairs, in the writings, tendencies, and schools that arise out of the ordinary run of affairs, in the histories that engage in minor criticism, and in the critiques of all of these that engage in major criticism. Dialectical seriation is the process in which positions are advanced and counterpositions perpetuated.

What is the mode of receiving? It is the same as horizon. Horizon may be considered literally, where it means the circle at which earth and sky appear to meet. But phenomenologically it is the fact of attention, psychologically it is the efficacy of attention, and socially it is the utility and possible fruitfulness of attention. From the standpoint of cultural history, it has to do with clarity and distinctness in attending. From the transcendental point of view, it embraces what is worthy of attention. Existentially it is tied to orientation. In general horizon is determined by the pole and the field; the pole is that from which the field is attained; the field is that which is attained from such and such a pole. The field is contrasted with the formal object. The formal object is the object under the formality under which it is attained, while the field is concrete, the totality of objects. Pole and habit are related. Habit is the first act from which second act proceeds promptly, easily, expeditiously; the pole is the subject operating in such a way.

Literally, again, horizon is the bounding circle. The pole is the place where one stands, the point of vision. The field is the totality of visible things, those things that are selected by the pole.

Phenomenology's conception of horizon makes a move from ocular vision to de facto 'attention.' The field is what can be apprehended and desired, that to which attention is paid from a given pole. The shadow is in no way attended to; the penumbra is not seriously attended to (stereotypes, 'they'); the luminous center is fully attended to. The pole is concern, *Sorge*, interest.

Psychologically, horizon is the field of proximately possible operations, by reason of place, time, dexterity, intellectual habit, or volitional habit. By reason of place: I can make a journey, and after the journey something is proximately possible; but I cannot simultaneously make many journeys; I would consume my whole life in journeys. By reason of time: I cannot act on the past or immediately on the future or on what is awaited. By reason of dexterity: I can play the organ, and I can type, but I ought to learn art; it takes time, and I cannot acquire all skills. By reason of intellectual habit: I am able to learn the Hebrew language and mathematics, but much time is demanded, and unless I give myself totally, I will make little progress. By reason of a habit in the will: if I persuade myself, I will do it; but first I need to be persuaded.

Piaget speaks of operations that are undifferentiated, spontaneous, poorly adapted to objects, laborious, inefficacious, becoming adapted to diverse objects through differentiations. Through combinations of differentiated operations we arrive at a totality of combinations or a group, and at a group of groups. In contrast, Aristotle's distinction is more classificatory than explanatory. Piaget addresses the problem of the unity of a habit.

Socially, horizon has to do with the field of useful and opportune operations; the pole is the subject in a given social ambience. In this same context there is introduced the schema of the human good.

	Potency of subject	Act of subject	Social mediation	Object
I	need-capacity	operation	cooperation	particular goods
II	perfectibility	specialization	institutions	good of order
III	liberty	orientation	interpersonal	terminal values
		originating value	relations	

I. The particular good: a particular object de facto good for a particular subject; this dinner, this education of this person; operation, cooperation, Robinson Crusoe.

II. The good of order: materially: the people desiring, the series of cooperations, the series of particular goods; formally: the order itself, inter-connection, interdependence, conjunction, because of which de facto the series of particular goods is continued. This is not a question of an ideal order or utopia or of a juridical or ethical or theoretic order, all of which are a good of reason; it is a question of the order that de facto is found, from which de facto there is a series of particular goods.

Institutions include family, community, customs, education, the state, law, economy, technology, church. These are commonly acknowledged goods, and therefore are changed only with difficulty. To them speciali-zations are applied, in them cooperations take place; whence the generic determination and limitation of an actual good of order.

Horizon and the Human Good, continued (26 March, 55300DTL060)

III. The actual good of order is never the only one possible. The coop-eration of many and the continuous seriation of particular goods can be attained in several ways. Even within the same stable institutions, e.g., the family, education, the economy, there is a great variety in the actual good of order. And the institutions themselves can change and do change for better or for worse.

As for the orientation of freedom, conversion, originating value, noth-ing is *simpliciter* good except a good will. This is the point of application of ethical, juridical, social, historical doctrine. There is a dialectic between the converted and unconverted, giving rise to criticism. Negatively, there is the drifter, the inauthentic human being who wants what others want, while they similarly want what all the others want. Positively, one wills the good of order, which incorporates some ideal. Terminal value is objectified, incor-porated, in a good of order. Interpersonal relations are the concrete mode of apprehending institutions, specializations, and cooperations.

From the social standpoint, then, we may say that the field is the range of what is opportune, to which attention is usefully, fruitfully paid. The pole is one acting socially or acting socially under conditions. 'Opportune' means what can be done immediately or mediately.

More on Dialectical Analysis (26 March bis, 55400DOL060)[41]

The problems of transposition and dialectic arise from the data themselves,

---

41 This is a second set of notes dated 26 March.

and throughout the sequence of materials, whether in the ordinary course of events, or in writers, tendencies, and schools, or in histories, or in crises. There are irreducible oppositions in all of these. All the protagonists are human beings. They all hear, speak, and act. The problems affect not only documents and monuments, and not only interpretation, history, and doctrine, but also the subjects hearing, reading, inspecting, interpreting, narrating, teaching. All interpretation, narration, and doctrine proceed proximately from the experience, understanding, judgment, and decision of the interpreter, narrator, or teacher.

Thus, we distinguish *exercite* and *signate*, 'in practice' and reflectively or explicitly. *Exercite* refers to the activities of interpreting, narrating, teaching, precisely as experiencing, understanding, judging, deciding; *signate* refers to explicit interpretation, narration, doctrine. There is a transition from the opposition between what is *signate* in various authors, in Paul, Peter, John, Silvanus, etc., to a comparison between what is *exercitum* and what is *signatum* in individual authors. The comparison is twofold: in the same person the realms of *exercite* and *signate* may agree, and then we have a position; or they may be opposed, and then we have a counterposition.

Counterpositions are of two kinds. (1) Insofar as *exercite* means natural operations with determinate properties in a determinate structure, it is normative, concrete, existing, real, something which is signified in many ways depending on the diversity of place, time, and culture, but which in itself is the same because it is rooted in nature. Where *signate* is opposed to what is *exercite* normative, there is human inauthenticity. (2) Insofar as *signate* means the word of God, it judges a member of Christ who is interpreter, narrator, or teacher to whom the word of God is *exercite* in opposition. Whence we conclude – and it is a conclusion – to what *exercite* is in accord with the word of God.

Dialectical analysis thus discerns authors and the agents about whom authors write. It leads to what is *exercite* normative, erroneous, sinful, and this is transcultural, for in itself it is not signified but consciously lived. Thus, it grounds transpositions, through a regress to the *exercitum*, where there is revealed a likeness between positions and counterpositions in the first century, the fourth, the nineteenth, the twentieth, etc. This has transcendental implications: what is normative concerning experience, understanding, judgment, and decision also is normative concerning everything that is signified and everything that happens. This analysis thus helps to ground progress, in that positions are to be advanced and counterpositions reversed. And thus practical transpositions are also grounded.

Method and Horizon (26 March ter and 29 March, 55500DoL060)[42]

Method can be brought to bear on the question of horizon. There are data, and there is understanding both *in* and *from* the data. The understanding can be descriptive or explanatory. If it is descriptive, it tells who, what, how, etc. Explanatory understanding can be comparative, organic, genetic, or dialectical. Comparative understanding is with regard to the data as they are given and insofar as they are attended to in relation to all the differences that appear in them. Organic understanding with regard to the individual yields a psychological horizon, and with regard to the community it yields a social horizon. Genetic understanding studies individuals and communities of different times with respect to their cultural horizons, as the move is made from undifferentiation through differentiation to integration. Dialectical understanding discerns transcendental horizons in the individuals that have been investigated, in the communities that have been investigated, in the histories doing the investigating, and in the critical work, in accord with the developing complexifications of each.

There is a problem of irreducible opposition and a problem of transposition. Insofar as one has solved one's own existential problem properly, not notionally but really, one knows what a transcendental horizon is, how it is manifested, and what follows upon conversion. Insofar as one has developed culturally so as to inhabit the differentiated worlds of the sacred, the intelligible, the interior, as distinct from the profane, the perceivable, and the external, one has in oneself the capacity through the negation of differentiation to reconstitute prior undifferentiated stages. And insofar as one understands psychology and society, one can proceed from the relations by which one lives to other matters. All of the foregoing form a directive part of method from above, while the described data form the part from below, just as, in physics, mathematics from above and the data from below yield the empirical laws.

As for horizon in relation to cultural development, development is from undifferentiation through differentiation to integration. It is not from the unknown, but from global operations regarding objects to distinct groupings of combined operations with regard to clear and distinct objects. Differentiation *in fieri* is a breakdown of a previous integration. A stable new

---

42 These notes have the two dates of 26 March (the third set with that date) and 29 March. See also below, p. 36.

integration is not possible until complementary differentiations have been completed. Where these differentiations involve different states of the subject, integration on the part of the subject is through a sort of oscillation between one's practical life, one's intellectual life, introspection, and perhaps mysticism.

The fundamental differences in cultural development may be spoken of in terms of spheres or worlds: the profane world and the sacred world, the perceivable world of community and the intelligible world of science, the exterior world and the interior world. The profane world corresponds to the proper object of human intellect in this life. The sacred world corresponds to the formal object insofar as it exceeds the proper object.[43] The perceivable world of community corresponds to the dramatic-practical subject, whose common sense is concerned with the *quoad nos*. The intelligible world of science corresponds to the theoretic subject, whose scientific understanding reaches the *quoad se*. The exterior world is the world of 'objects,' and the interior world is the subject immediately present to self and mediated through human works or through other persons, and in relation to God and to moral and intellectual integrity.

Development *in fieri* may be considered spiritually, intentionally, temporally, in terms of freedom, and historically.

'Spiritual' means the negation of matter; the soul is neither material in itself nor intrinsically dependent on matter; positively the spiritual is the subject becoming known both immediately and mediately.

'Intentional' means not the thing 'in itself,' not the known in itself but the known in the knower; not the beloved in itself but the beloved in the lover; it is the spiritual positively intending, both in relation to what is intended and intending and in relation to what is intended and not intending.

'Temporal' refers to time as the number and measure of movement

43 Compare the following in Lonergan, *Early Works on Theological Method* 1, at pp. 149–50: 'Because of the fact that the formal object of any intellect is being, while the proper object of human intellect is *quidditas sive natura in materia corporali existens*, there is a difference between the two. There is a difference between what man naturally desires to know by his intellect, insofar as in his intellect he naturally desires to know everything, and what he naturally can attain, which is limited to the *quidditas sive natura in materia corporali existens* plus analogous knowledge of other things. The disparity between the proper and the formal objects of human intellect creates an opening, an openness, for accepting a divine revelation beyond what man can naturally attain.'

secundum prius et posterius (Aquinas, Newton, Kant, Einstein) and in relation to temporality (as in a symphony); the identity of the conscious subject through time, the memory, knowledge, anticipation, and deliberation of the subject above time, connecting the past and the future, the decision and act of the subject that is in time but in such a way that there remains always true what I myself have done and the fact that I am responsible for myself.[44]

'Free' means immunity from force and necessity and also something positively spiritual, where the total situation, all the determinations of the subject, and the subject himself or herself give rise to the act happening because I myself will it.

'Historical' refers to deeds of the past, outstanding examples, the education of political man; but also it means that just as I am responsible for myself, make myself, determine what kind of person I am, so collectively human beings make, destroy, and remake the human world constituted by meaning. All of this involves persons and things, what is opportune and what is out of date, *Existenz* knowing one's autonomy and assuming responsibility for oneself, and historicity, being a historical being inserted within a network of psychological, social, and cultural realities, acknowledging history and the human world as a human work, and assuming responsibility regarding this human work.

This development *in fieri* occurs in the world of interiority, where the subject is known through the subject and other things are known through the subject and in relation to the subject. This development is antithetically opposed, first, to the perceivable world, which is apprehended by the superficial and the inauthentic, either without much exaggeration as in historicism, or with exaggeration as in positivism.[45] It is antithetically opposed also to the intelligible world as the latter is apprehended in extrinsicism, whether in the extrinsicism of truth or in that of concepts. Third, it is antithetically opposed to the intelligible world as the latter is apprehended by scientists who are stuck in positivism, with its rejection of metaphysics, or in pragmatism, where the sole criterion is what works, or in secularism, which is confined to the profane world. It is easily put together with the world of the sacred, provided one attends to the interior life and not to dogma and propositional

44 The date in the same item and on the same page shifts to 29 March.
45 The meaning would seem to be that positivism is much more explicitly confined to the perceptible world than historicism.

truth (cf. Marcel).[46] The descriptions by which God is apprehended are not metaphysical but a matter of religious and social experience. God is a person, a subject. Before God we come to ourselves as subjects. Our life is not absorbed in time, but through our temporality we turn to and attain to the eternal. By the grace of God I am what I am, and without grace the sinner does not long avoid mortal sin. God is the Lord of history.

This development *in fieri* is particularly unfolded in an immanentist ambience: Kant, Hegel, Kierkegaard, Nietzsche, Dilthey, Heidegger, Jaspers.

This development is not a matter of a choice between fragments or of a mere combination of fragments, as in Bultmann, with his distinction between the Jesus of history, which is science, and the Christ of faith, which is myth and extrinsicism, unless it is demythologized for *Existenz*. It is rather a matter of the openness of the spirit, so that the inauthentic open themselves to the world of interiority, the intelligible world, the world of the sacred; the scientific open themselves to the world of interiority, to metaphysics, and to the world of the sacred; extrinsicists open themselves to the world of interiority, the perceivable world, and the scientific world; and immanentists open themselves to the intelligible world, the perceivable world, and the objective sacred.

This openness of the spirit can be grasped in two ways, one literary and the other analytic, systematic, and synthetic. The literary way is in the perceivable world but proceeds from interiority and aspires to the intelligible and the sacred. Augustine and Newman are examples. The *Confessions* express religious conversion, the *Contra Academicos* intellectual conversion, *De necessitate gratiae* moral conversion, *De Trinitate* God, and *De civitate Dei* history. The analytic, systematic, synthetic way is grounded in the world of interiority, and by way of method has an influence on the intelligible world, the perceivable world, and the world of the sacred.

The development that we now see *in fieri*, we experience in differentiations and in the problem of integration. Already it has been at play in a literary movement in humanism, the Renaissance, and modern languages and literatures; in a philosophic movement in the awareness of the epistemological problem; in the movement of natural and human science; in the opposition of church and state, and of church and sects; in industrialization, print media, radio, television, universal education. And where one locates a beginning, one can also find precursors.

46 See Lonergan, *Early Works on Theological Method 1* 77.

Thus, a prior differentiation is found in the move from primitive society to the ancient high civilizations.[47] The field of the proper object in the perceivable world continued to grow, and the affective sphere of myth and magic receded. An intelligible world is acknowledged within the perceivable world. A myth at once political, cosmogonic, and religious develops. Voegelin has studied this.[48] This then gives way to *logos*, both in the perceivable world and in the intelligible world.

The genetic dimension shows up in the problem of transposition. One may go back from integration to differentiations not yet integrated, and from these to the undifferentiated. Proceeding in this way is to be preferred to speaking, for example, of the Greek and Hebrew mentalities, which are not ultimate irreducible atoms.

Dialectic, Basic Positions and Counterpositions, Worlds, Horizon (22 and 26 March, 55600DOL060)[49]

We turn to dialectic, to basic terms, and to basic sets of antithetical terms, and in this context we treat first the real, knowing, and objectivity. Basic terms have to do with the real, knowing, and objectivity.

The real is assembled from the perceived (experienced), the understood, and the affirmed, while knowing consists of experience, understanding, and judging. If one stops at experience in one's account of knowing, one is an empiricist. Among those who stop at understanding are Platonists, Aristotle, Kant, and Hegel. Those who include judgment, like Augustine and Aquinas, are realists. And objectivity involves the assembling of the given, the coherent, and the posited, corresponding respectively to experience, understanding, and judgment.

Next, there are the different worlds: the world of community, the world of theory, the world of interiority, and the world of religion. They are negotiated by oscillating from one to another. They may be differentiated from

---

47 Reference is made to Karl Jaspers, *Vom Ursrprung und Ziel der Geschichte* (Munich: Piper, 1949; in English, *The Origin and Goal of History*, trans. Michael Bullock (New Haven: Yale University Press, 1952).
48 See below, p. 152, note 76.
49 The upper right-hand corner of the first page shows some confusion as to the date. '24' is crossed out, so that the date reads 'March 22, 26,' but there is a circled question mark under those dates. See also above, p. 32. Some of the material here seems to go back over that found in the immediately prior items.

one another and then find a higher integration. The alternative would be to mistake a part for the whole. Obscurantism, which can be either worldly or pious, would also block differentiation and integration.

The issue has to do with horizon. We distinguish literal, psychological, and transcendental meanings of the term 'horizon,' or more completely literal, phenomenological, psychological, social, transcendental, and methodical meanings.[50]

A horizon is determined by a pole and a field. The pole and the field are correlative: the field contains everything that can be attained from a given pole, while the pole is the subject operating in such a way as to attain a given field. The formal object of intellect in the concrete, the 'thing' itself and not concepts about things, constitutes the field; and the habits of the concrete subject constitute the pole.

Literally, horizon is *ho horizōn kyklos*, the bounding circle. Insofar as 'horizon' relates to visible things, the pole is the place where one stands, the point of vision, and the field consists of visible things insofar as they can be seen from such a standpoint.

Phenomenologically, the field has to do not just with visible things but with everything that can be apprehended and desired, insofar as attention is de facto paid to these. There is a shadow where there is no attention, no apprehension, no care whatsoever. There is a penumbra of surrounding things that are indefinitely apprehended, concerning which there is no serious concern. And there is the field, what is clearly and exactly apprehended, about which there is serious concern, some interest, some 'Sorge.'

The psychological contribution to the notion of horizon has to do with the fact and the genesis of habits. Here we may attempt an integration of Aristotle and Piaget. Regarding the fact of habits, we operate sensitively and corporeally, intellectually and volitionally, and we are able to operate both because of prime potency and because of second potency, which is first act, habit. There is the phase before first act or habit, in which we are able to operate if we acquire the necessary dexterity, if we learn, if we are persuaded; it is in this sense that the infant is able to walk, that one can play the organ, that one can type. And there is the phase after the development of first act or habit, in which we are able to operate because we have already acquired the dexterity, have already learned, have already been persuaded. The gen-

---

50 The first page in the item has 'literal,' 'psychological.' and 'transcendental,' while the second page has all six terms.

esis of a habit is a process from spontaneous, global, undifferentiated operations to differentiated operations adapted to objects, next to combinations of differentiated operations, and finally to a certain totality or group
of combinations. Piaget avoids the problem of the unity of habits and of
merely descriptive classifications because he proceeds from the concrete,
from our real mode of operation. The possibility of the attention that is the
focus of the phenomenological notion of horizon lies in the field attained
by such habits and the pole that is the subject adorned by such habits.

From a social point of view, the notion of horizon has to do with the
structure of the human good.[51] The particular good is this particular good
thing, this dinner or this beatific vision, for this person. 'Operation' is ex-
emplified in isolation in the primitive spontaneously taking the fruit he
finds, and again in Robinson Crusoe. But there is also cooperation. The
good of order materially consists in the people who desire, in a series of
cooperations, and in a series of particular goods. Formally, it is that order
from which de facto the series of particular goods flows. It is not a matter of
some ideal, whether utopian, theoretical, juridical, or ethical. All of these
are beings of reason, concepts. We are speaking rather of real, concrete
institutions, such as the family, the community, customs (not ethics), education, the state, law, economy, technology. These are commonly acknowledged bases that are slow to change. From them the good of order flows, in
them cooperations take place, and for them specializations are developed.

The actual good of order is never the only one possible. The cooperation
of many and the continuous seriation of particular goods can be attained in
many ways. Even within the same institution, the possible good of order is
multiple. But institutions can and do change for better or for worse.

The orientation of liberty has to do with originating value, as opposed
to the drifter, the inauthentic person. A given good of order is preferred
because it incorporates a certain ideal, whether it be aesthetic, intellectual,
moral, or religious. Personal relations can develop from institutions and
from orientation and are connected with the concrete mode of apprehending institutions, the good of order, and specializations.

From the social perspective, then, the field consists of the opportunities to which it is useful to pay attention, and the pole is the social actor.
What is proximately possible is determined by the 'what' and 'how' being
known, and by the presence of those who can learn quickly and be persuad-

---

51 See above, p. 29.

ed quickly. But there is also what is proximately not possible but remotely possible, given certain changes. Under this category were once such things as railroads, automobiles, and the invention of printing; or again, universal education comes under this heading as do the realities envisaged in *Rerum novarum* and *Quadrigesimo anno*, or again in *Deus scientiarum Dominus*. The church's liturgical change would be another example.

The transcendental aspect of horizon emerges when explicit attention is paid to horizons, and judgments and decisions are made in their regard. Such attention may reveal the deliberate omission of what lies beyond the horizon, which is omitted as not worthy of attention. Thus, from a practical standpoint one will omit what one finds useless, either in itself or because nothing can be done about it. From a metaphysical standpoint one will omit what one judges not real, beings of reason, myth, fiction, what is false, illusory, legend, deception. From a critical standpoint one will omit what one thinks is not knowable, a Kantian *Ding-an-sich*. From a scientific standpoint one will omit what cannot be scientifically determined by scientific method. From the standpoint of historical consciousness one will omit what one judges to be antiquated.

The transcendental dimension is present implicitly, as far as the *ratio* of horizon is concerned, even when no explicit thought is given to horizon, when explicit thought concerns utility, reality, knowability, opportunity, science. The radical fundamental transcendental aspect is grounded in the individual, social, historical development of the subject. This foundation is objectified in symbolic, philosophical, theological, methodical reflection. It asserts its effects in the phenomena of horizon either immediately or mediately in symbols, philosophy, theology, and method.

The pole of the methodical horizon may be diagrammed as follows.[52]

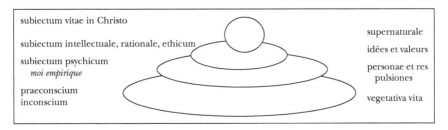

subiectum vitae in Christo

subiectum intellectuale, rationale, ethicum

subiectum psychicum
moi empirique

praeconscium
inconscium

supernaturale

idées et valeurs

personae et res
pulsiones

vegetativa vita

Rationalism would exclude faith and its mysteries as well as hope. It wants

52 Lonergan's Latin and French words are retained. The graphic design is the work of Armando Bravo.

charity but on a humanistic foundation. Materialism would reject any ideological superstructure. It can be collective or individual, dogmatic or skeptical, ontological or gnoseological. Reductionism always labors under the difficulty that it proceeds by pure reason. A closed reductionism is directed to what is below, while a closed aetherialism would be directed to what is above.

The pole itself may be engaged *exercite* or *signate*. The pole as engaged *exercite* is the conscious being that lives, knows, and chooses. The pole as engaged *signate* is the conscious being that knows himself or herself to live, to know, and to choose, that knows what the subject is, what the act is, what the objects are.

The development of the pole may be considered in its individual aspect, as when one reaches the age of reason or the autonomy of the adult. But it may be considered also in its socio-historical aspect, and there we may consider three stages: (a) the movement from a primitive stage to the ancient high civilizations; (b) the classical age, with its philosophy, science, and history, and with the emergence of individualism; (c) historical consciousness, where man acknowledges and assumes his own autonomy and historical responsibility.

All of this has to do with the spontaneous unfolding, but there is also a deliberate unfolding. Development is from the global through differentiations to integration. The center shifts from the 'subiectum psychicum' to the 'subiectum intellectuale, rationale, ethicum.' This shift happens either *exercite* or *signate*: it happens *exercite* in attending to objects; it happens *signate* when the subject's notion about the subject influences the development of the subject, that is, when the subject constitutes himself or herself not only consciously but also rationally and deliberately.

Development may also be fragmented. Differentiation out of undifferentiated operations needs complementary differentiations for integration to take place. Differentiations proceed from the pole *exercite* more easily in concrete matters, but they may proceed *signate* with erroneous knowledge and ineffective will, so that integration is not possible without a reorganization or revolution in the subject. The critical moment is reached when there is an opposition between the spontaneously functioning pole and the pole as *signatum*, as objectified.

The transcendental is the total horizon outside of which there is either nothing or nothing that I can know. From an absolute standpoint, horizon is transcendental; it affects everything. The meaning of being, one, true, and good is involved even if it is denied that there is any meaning in speaking of being, one, true, and good.

Finally, the methodical meaning of horizon materially consists of all transcendental poles and all transcendental fields. Formally, it can be considered heuristically or programmatically insofar as these are to be genetically or dialectically ordered; and historically, insofar as they have actually been genetically or dialectically ordered in some way or to some extent.

Transcendental Horizon and Conversion (29 March, 2 and 3 April, 55700D0L060 and 55800D0L060)[53]

We may expand on what we have said about transcendental horizon.

Man not only develops psychologically, socially, and culturally, but also is converted religiously, morally, intellectually. Psychological, social, and cultural development has conditions in man himself but is more determined from without: psychological development by education, social development by the society in which one is born or to which one has migrated, cultural development by the epoch to which one belongs.[54] Conversion has external conditions in education, society, and culture, but happens from the individual and in the individual, and it pertains to one's self-constitution; one makes oneself such and such a human being not *per accidens* and apart from one's intention but as present and knowing. Conversion is existential.

The horizon that results from psychological, social, cultural development is a relative horizon. It does not deny the existence, value, and knowability (scientific or other) of what lies outside the field. It simply de facto omits such things, whether because of a lack of acquired habits or because of the absence of opportunity in the existing society or because of lack of development on the part of the culture.

The horizon that results from conversion or non-conversion is absolute, transcendental. What lies beyond a transcendental horizon, as to existence, does not exist: there is nothing to be attended to; and as to value, it is of no value and so is not to be attended to; we should ignore it; to ignore it does

---

53 55800D0L060 is a typed set of notes on 'Horizon transcendentalis,' dated 'April 3 1963.' 55700D0L060 is a handwritten set, dated 'March 29 Apr 2.' It contains much the same material as the typed set, but also a good deal more. Both sets of notes are relied on in this section.

54 From this comment, it seems safe to say that these reflections on psychological, social, and cultural development are the source of Lonergan's later regular use of the triad 'education, socialization, acculturation.' See *A Third Collection*, ed. Frederick E. Crowe (Mahwah, NJ: Paulist, 1985) 181, 197, 217.

not conflict with perfect openness but directs it wisely; and as far as know-ability is concerned, it cannot be known and should not be inquired about. Whoever inquires about it, whoever speaks about it, whoever speculates on it, is under illusion, is deceiving himself, indulges in fiction and falsehood, believes myth, listens to legends; it is pseudo-science, pseudo-philosophy, pseudo-theology, ideology.

Consideration of transcendental horizon is complex because of two times, namely, before and after the question of conversion has arisen. Thus, we distinguish the originary and the existential pole, and correspondingly the field as it is *exercite, implicite,* and the field as it is *signate, explicite.*

The originary pole is common to everyone. It is the possibility that one can be converted, can constitute oneself. It is the very structure of human consciousness, where structure is arrived at by abstracting the whole from the parts, form from matter, the proportion among the elements or components.[55]

The existential pole is proper to each individual. It is the subject insofar as one has constituted oneself as such whether *per accidens* or deliberately, the subject who knows and wills oneself to be such or avoids and flees oneself and one's self-constitution.

The field considered *signate et explicite* is philosophy, theology, method. The field considered *exercite et implicite* is present and efficaciously influential through the way one operates; it orders one's inquiry de facto, through unacknowledged presuppositions, unformulated assumptions, choices, and acquired habits. It is manifested in one's judgments and decisions about the real, about values and ends, about what is possible, about legitimate methods.

By definition, pole and field are correlative. The field is what is attained by such and such a pole, and the pole is that by which such and such a field is attained.

The explicit field and the originary pole are correlative by intention. Method, philosophy, and (supposing faith) theology are not just the expression of a personal choice but intend to state that to which existential choice should be conformed, that which the originary pole demands.

From the nature of things the implicit field and the existential pole are correlative. What kind of person I am and what kind of world is present

---

55 See above, p. 19 on abstraction, and below, 'The Notion of Structure,' pp. 161–87.

to me are correlative. 'Qualis quisque est, talis finis videtur ei.' In the authentic the existential pole is in accord with the demands of the originary pole. Existential choice is sincere acknowledgment, faithful appropriation, assumption, acceptance of the originary pole in accord with the demands of the originary pole itself. In parallel fashion, the implicit field and the explicit field coincide or tend to coincide.

Inauthenticity may be either radical or derived, and derived inauthenticity is a function of rationalization or of obnubilation.

Radical inauthenticity is a divergence between the existential pole and the originary pole. Derived inauthenticity presupposes radical authenticity and includes it. It accrues to the field that implicitly corresponds to the radically inauthentic existential pole. Rationalized inauthenticity is false method, philosophy, theology: false in that it is in conflict with the originary pole. The explicit field is conformed to and expresses the implicit field that corresponds to an inauthentic existential pole. Inauthenticity by way of obnubilation is method, philosophy, theology that objectively expresses or corresponds to the originary pole but subjectively is reinterpreted under the influence of an inauthentic existential pole.

The originary pole is understood in terms of levels of consciousness or self-presence, the promotion of consciousness from level to level, the qualitative difference in the levels, and the unity of consciousness.

First, then, there are levels of consciousness. There is the consciousness of dreams; I am present to myself in dreams. Next, there is empirical consciousness; I am present to myself in sensitive actions and passions. Third, there is intellectual consciousness; I am present to myself as inquiring, understanding or not understanding, defining, forming hypotheses, constructing systems. Fourth, there is rational consciousness; I am present to myself as doubting, weighing evidence, affirming or denying. Fifth, there is self-consciousness; I am present to myself as taking counsel, deliberating, choosing, acting, disposing of objects, and disposing of myself.

Next, what 'present to myself' means is understood only from the experience of this presence itself, from seeing, hearing, understanding, etc. It is not local presence, like that of a statue in a room; it is not the presence of an object that is apprehended or desired; but it is the presence of the subject as the constitutive condition of oneself as apprehending or desiring. To understand what is meant by 'constitutive condition,' distinguish the spectacle and the spectator. The spectacle is present as an object. It has a presence to something other. The spectator is present as a subject, present to herself. Unless the spectator were present to herself, the spectacle could not be present to her, as would be the case if she were unconscious or asleep. The spectator is not present to herself in the same way as the spectacle is present to her. The spectacle as such is present not to itself but to another. The spectacle is not present as part of the spectacle: as the whole spectacle, so each of its parts is not present to itself but to another. The spectator is not conscious because she is part of the spectacle, for the spectacle is not conscious.

In radical rationalized inauthenticity, knowledge is like ocular vision, the known is like the seen, consciousness is a form of knowing, what is conscious is known and so like the seen, and the conscious and known ego is like the seen. At the very least, what is conscious is knowing, which is like seeing, which is like the spectator. If what is conscious were really like the seen, it would be per se unconscious.

In truth consciousness makes the subject known, but secondarily; primarily it constitutes the subject in act. It is not constituted through introspection or reflection. Rather it is presupposed by introspection and reflection. Unless one is conscious, one has nothing into which to introspect.

Third, consciousness is promoted from level to level: normatively from the first to the second by alertness, from the second to the third by inquiry, from the third to the fourth by doubting, and from the fourth to the fifth by asking what is to be done, what I myself will do about the object and about myself.[56]

Fourth, there is a qualitative difference in the respective levels. Each of us can experience them in himself or herself, and unless we experienced them in ourselves they could not be known. Sensitive spontaneity cannot be avoided; I see a large dog on the loose, perhaps ferocious, and this produces fear; I fear not because it is rational, but even if I know that fear is stupid and foolish. But there is something normative about the further levels. As for intellectual clarity, when there is understanding, consciousness itself by the power of intelligent consciousness forms definitions, hypotheses, explanations, theories. When it is grasped that the evidence is sufficient, consciousness itself by the power of consciousness grasping evidence posits a judgment absolutely. Again, when it is judged that something can and should be done by me, consciousness itself by the power of consciousness affirming an obligation, correctness, fittingness, excellence, makes a

---

56 Here the numbers of the levels reflect the scheme Lonergan is using here, where dreaming is the first level.

choice. The latter involves experience in the agent, experience of liberty, responsibility, and morality.

Fifth, there is the unity of consciousness. On the side of the object, we inquire about what we experience; we understand that about which we inquire; we conceive that which we understand; we doubt about that which we conceive; we weigh the evidence concerning what we have doubted; we affirm or deny that about which we weigh the evidence. The composition/ unity of the object comes about in this way: correlative to experience is potency; correlative to understanding is form; correlative to conception are form and matter yielding essence; correlative to judgment are essence and existence. Knowledge, abstractly, is any cognitive act, but properly it is the acts of experience, understanding, conception, judgment composed into one. Thus, consciousness is knowledge from the abstract point of view but not properly; it is the experiential part in self-knowledge.

The unity of the subject is a fact, not just a logical condition of possibility. I cannot inquiry about that which not I but you experience. I cannot understand that about which not I but you inquire. And so on.

Next, we will expand on the existential pole. The development of the human individual entails the emergence of an autonomous subject. The infant does very little for herself, determines very little for herself, knows very little for herself. She operates by a natural spontaneity that determines what she finds pleasant and not pleasant, consciously pleasant and consciously not pleasant. Gradually the small child, the boy or girl, the adolescent, is doing more for himself or herself; determining more for himself or herself, either in terms of enjoyment, as in play, or because one should; knowing more for himself or herself. The crisis of adolescence, which in some sense is the philosophical age, is that more or less ultimate questions are put, and mastery of self emerges, where one will do what one has determined to do, and one will determine to do what one has come to know for oneself. But this self-mastery is in many ways imperfect and incomplete. It is asked what this mastery, this emergence, this self-constitution as master of oneself means.

The subject insofar as one operates as poured out upon objects becomes what it becomes but *praeter intentionem, per accidens.* It becomes what it becomes since it acquires habits. But it does so *per accidens* because it is poured out on objects; it does not attend to itself; it makes itself what it is through habits that it has acquired.

The subject operating with regard to objects is mediated through the operations and objects. One reveals oneself as in a mirror operating with regard to natural things, on artifacts, with other persons, and before God. There arise practical, artistic, moral, religious, intellectual reflections.

The subject thus mediated passes from consciousness of self to knowledge of self. Consciousness of self is knowledge in an abstract sort of way but not in the proper sense of the word 'knowledge.' Knowledge in the proper sense adds understanding of man and of oneself, and judgments about man and about oneself. This knowledge of self increases one's self-consciousness. We are more conscious of those things that we clearly conceive and distinctly affirm about ourselves.

Self-knowledge moves on to a certain choice of oneself through which one freely constitutes oneself as master of oneself. The choice proceeds from *me*. I make use of a practical judgment as the principle by which there is spirated the volition or choice. 'Thus it shall be.' Consciousness is free, deliberate, responsible, unconditional. 'Man' is *esse-posse, Sein-Können*. Insofar as, poured out on external things, one does not think with the heart, one makes oneself, without really intending it, just the kind of person that, on reflection and self-knowledge, one does not want to be. One can seriously and sincerely choose to be other than one is, and discern the means towards this goal. But this present choice must always be preserved and renewed. Otherwise the chosen means are neglected. Neither here and now nor in some future here and now in this life can we enact those future renewals. Insofar as we seriously and sincerely now determine, we remain *Sein-Können*. Thus, I can apprehend, project, determine my life as a whole, myself as a whole, but in such a way that this determination is made only *per partes*, step by step. I am master of myself not as totally simultaneous towards something totally simultaneous, but successively with regard to individual parts. I have a problem of fidelity and perseverance, not only of moral conversion, but that I be a man, that I ex-sist. Here and now I cannot prevent that in the future I might will and not perform, judge that something is to be willed and not will it, or judge otherwise than I now judge.

Existential decision brings it about that per se, from my mastery of myself, I am such and such a person, but it does this in the way of intention, tendency, orientation, direction, and brings it about that what kind of person I am is something intended and freely chosen.

The existential pole is originary insofar as orientation and consequence are intended, freely chosen; and insofar as it understands and knows itself it freely constitutes itself as what it is. There is no absolute security or certitude about the goodness of the choice. I am not unconscious. I will to be a human being. I will the limitations that come with being a human being.

It is my decision. Otherwise I would not be a human being. I would be carried about by the wind. Perhaps if I had deliberated more fully or longer, I would have decided otherwise.

The existential pole in the concrete not only has structure, an orientation freely and responsibly chosen, but also content. It makes itself *such* in relation to *things* and to *persons* and to *God*. Its relation to *things* may be minimal in content, if one is poured out on external things, intending only maximization and domination. Its relation to *persons* may entail charity, friendship, love, intimacy, good works; it may also be indifferent; and it may be marked by anger and selfish desire, hate, suspicion, rash judgments, false testimony, injustice, injury, murder. Its relation to *God* may be equally diverse. In God's presence, through the grace of God, it may trust in God, pray, deny itself, find companionship with Christ. But it may ignore God in secularism or hold God in hate through ideology, militant atheism, and the declaration of absolute human autonomy.

The question of the true precedes existential election. The question of the true is not a decision. P → Q not because I decide, but because the evidence suffices unconditionally. The question of the true is not a matter of mere composition or hypothesis. It seeks an unconditioned positing on account of grasping the unconditioned.

The question about the true is a problem: a small problem from the nature of the problem itself, but a large problem under the existential aspect. It is intrinsically small: to know is to experience, understand, judge, and the known is an isomorphic composite. It is existentially a very serious matter whether 'the real' is 'being,' that which is, or rather whether experience, contact, vision corresponds to the 'really real.'

Thus, for Tertullian everything real is a body. Augustine held the same thing for a long time. For Plato, Scotus, Kant, Gilson to know is to perceive. Realism is devoted to that which is; idealism does not stop at that which is experienced or perceived; empiricism stops with that which is perceived in experience. There exists a problem of intellectual conversion. It pervades everything, not only epistemology but also history and hermeneutics.

Theological Mediation (23 April, 55900D0L060)[57]

Theology is knowledge about God mediated by Christ and the church. The-

---

57 Lonergan has a note 'restauruntur scholae,' i.e., 'classes resume,' i.e., after the Easter break.

ology is contrasted with natural and human science in terms of mediation. In natural science knowledge is mediated by data qua data; in human science it is mediated by data invested with meaning; in theology it is mediated by data as invested with true meaning.

The mediation of the object brings us back to the distinctions already discussed: human, religious, Christian lives; authors, tendencies, and schools; historical works; works written when crises arise. Mediation that touches on subjects in theology may be descriptive or explanatory. It is descriptive when one answers the questions Who, What, How, Why, etc. Explanatory mediation of the subject is comparative, organic, genetic, and dialectical. It is comparative when it discriminates similarities and dissimilarities; organic and synthetic when it points to coherence; genetic when it traces stages in organic growth and in developing synthesis; and dialectical when it reduces to radical oppositions. Such mediation is also judgmental: when dialectical method is employed the investigator is willy nilly committed. Otherwise, we would have to adopt the notion of science found in Bultmann.

The critical and judgmental functions bring us to the topic of horizon. As we have seen, pole and field are correlative; pole is either originary or existential, and either authentic or inauthentic; inauthenticity is either radical or derived; and derived inauthenticity is either rationalization or obnubilation. Relative horizons differ depending on psychological, social, and cultural development; absolute horizons differ depending on intellectual, moral, and religious conversion.

Horizon as in the object is a matter of categories to be determined from the data; horizon as in the subject is a matter of foundations, norms, methodical precepts.

Conversion: Intellectual, Moral, Religious (2, 5, and 23 April, 56000D0L060)[58]

We distinguished the originary pole and the existential pole. The originary pole is the standard for the inauthentic existential subject being converted to authenticity.

The first element in our discussion of conversion has to do with the differentiation of the transcendental horizon. What lies outside it does not exist, can only be attended to in myth, or through deception, illusion, false-

---

58 All of these dates are present on the notes.

hood, etc.; it is of no importance or value and should not be attended to; it is not knowable and so is not worth asking about.

Next, we are not talking about relative differentiation, which is psychological or social or cultural, but about absolute differentiation, where the field itself is changed and the pole exists in a new way.

Conversion is a threefold transformation of the existential pole: intellectual, concerned with being; moral, concerned with the good; and religious, concerned with God.

It is one thing to conceive what conversion is. It is something else to be converted oneself.

The *terminus a quo* of intellectual conversion is the *natürliche Einstellung*, the spontaneous orientation. It reflects on itself in many ways. As rationalized it becomes empiricism, as partly corrected it becomes idealism, and as obnubilated it becomes inauthentic realism, according to which it is manifest, obvious, clear, certain, indubitable to all, and can only be doubted by the insane, that there is given the 'already-out-there-now.' It is 'already': before any operation of the subject; 'out': not merely immanent; 'there-now': spatio-temporal. It is divided into the real and the merely apparent, and the merely apparent and the real are discriminated by vision, contact, perception, by the object revealing itself without any admixture of subjectivity. On this view, besides the immediate vision of the real there is given also mediated knowledge, whether certain or hypothetical. It may be (a) from principles, where the terms are abstracted from the real itself, or (b) if the principles are certain, the nexus between the terms is itself objectively perceived; and (c) if the principles are hypothetical, the nexus is not clearly and distinctly perceived, but if it is supposed, it becomes more probable the more it is verified. This horizon of (1) what are seen, (2) what are certainly deduced, (3) other things about which hypotheses are formed, and (4) what are not known, yields *die durchschnittliche Theologie*, the ordinary or mediocre theology that has been typical of the seminary ghetto.

The *terminus ad quem* of intellectual conversion has two steps: the opening of the mind, and the discipline of the mind.

The opening of the mind, of the horizon, of the field, occurs when one recognizes that what is attained by vision, perception, contact, by the object revealing itself without any admixture of subjectivity, is not the real but only a datum. The phenomenon is a datum; what is grasped in data by abstraction is a devalued datum. The real, by contrast, is that to which in its own way 'to be' belongs: the whole, the concrete, to be, being, the real, is that which is intended insofar as one proceeds beyond the data.

When the datum is given, I ask what it is. I am seeking something that is not given or perceived or seen or contacted or unveiled. I am not seeking some other non-datum that is to be given, some other non-perceived that is to be perceived, some other non-seen that is to be seen. I am seeking what lies simply beyond the field of data. I am seeking what cannot be known except by understanding. What is it to understand? Well, give me someone who understands, and he will experience what I am talking about. Whoever experiences understanding knows that understanding recurs in the intelligent and knows that seeing and perceiving occur very well in the stupid.

How large is the field of an open horizon? It is as large as the range of questions. But questioning is unrestricted, for when some questions are answered, there is achieved only a greater possibility of raising further questions. Do not confuse the field of questions with the field of responses that can be given *by us*. The latter is limited naturally, psychologically, socially, culturally. This is what is overlooked by those who want official philosophies and theologies, not so that there be a solid foundation from which ultimate questions can be asked but to discourage further questions from being put forward. This is obscurantism, obnubilation.

The field of an open horizon is the field of being, where 'being' is not of minimum connotation and maximum denotation, as in Scotus and Hegel, but of maximum connotation and denotation: *to pan, ta panta, omnia, totum, concretum*, everything that can ever be known about anything and everything, more than is known in the beatific vision of Christ and the saints in heaven.

Distinguish the notion of being, implicit conception of being, implicit knowledge of being, the idea of being, and explicit conception of being. Explicit conception of being is intended in questions, is reached in every conception, is known in every judgment: a unity which is different according to the proportion of essence and existence.

What is the discipline of the open mind, of an unlimited horizon? Our response begins by distinguishing the proper proportionate object of intellect and the formal object of intellect. The proper and proportionate object is intended beyond the data, but what is intended is not known except through the mediation of external and internal data. Intelligence, the act of understanding, understands in the sensible; we can understand nothing except by conversion to phantasm; and we cannot verify anything except in data. The formal object of intellect, everything about everything, includes natural knowledge of God and divine revelation.

What is the difference between the open mind and empiricism, and between a disciplined mind and idealism? The empiricist knows *because* he perceives. The idealist would know *if* indeed he did perceive. For the idealist everything is immanent. He does not know being *in se*. Empiricism is either rationalization or obnubilation. Either there is conversion or there is not, and if not the result is either rationalization or obnubilation. All the diverse criteria of knowledge, objectivity, and reality not only in philosophy but also in natural science, human science, history, exegesis, positive theology, and systematic theology are uncovered in the critique of empiricism.

As for moral conversion, it is one thing to know what it is, and it is something else again actually to be converted. We begin with some prenotes: (a) *actio* can mean 'act' as in 'intelligere est pati quoddam,' or it can mean the exercise of efficient causality; (b) insofar as a finite agent acts in the first sense, it is itself perfected; (c) this actuation pertains to the subject by nature and in accord with what is superadded; otherwise it is not a perfection of the subject; (d) this actuation has an end, a 'for the sake of which,' which is not this actuation or this act itself; (e) in rational beings this end is intended: not only *A* for the sake of *B* but *A* for the sake of an intended *B*; (f) we are asking about the end of the operator (*finis operantis*) in human beings as rational, which end is de facto intended and is something distinct from the very actuation of the subject.

The *terminus a quo* of moral conversion is myself as I am living, thinking, and judging, where my intended end is the very subject of the actuation, namely, myself. I am that for the sake of which I myself am perfected. My perfection is for the sake of me. My food is for the sake of me. My delight in eating is for the sake of me. My studies are for the sake of me. My good works are for the sake of merit, and merit is for the sake of rewards, and rewards are for the sake of me. If it is for the sake of me, there is no need to inquire further. I have a sufficient and efficacious motive for acting. Perhaps it may be added that an ulterior end for the operator cannot be given. The good is the desirable; for it to be able to be desired, it has to conform to appetite; where it conforms to my appetite, it conforms to me. To assign any other end is hypocrisy, delusion, vain speculation. The ultimate end is *my* happiness. Other things are chosen as means to attain this end.

Discussion of the *terminus ad quem* of moral conversion begins with a distinction of natural and elicited appetite. Natural appetite does not suppose knowledge in any way, or knowledge of the end to which it tends. Elicited appetite supposes knowledge whether sensitive or intellectual. The question about the end of the one operating (*finis operantis*) regards man as rational. It is a matter of the end intended by the rational agent as such.

This intended end is good in an absolute fashion, what is good by reason of itself, *value*. Natural appetite tends to what is good absolutely, and the elicited appetite intends what is good absolutely.

The natural appetite that is intellectual already is an appetite from which there is a tendency to the intelligible in the question *quid sit*, and to the true and being in the question *an sit*, and to what is good absolutely. This appetite as it were explains itself, reveals itself through operations, and grounds those things of which it is the condition of possibility.

An elicited appetite operates whenever we genuinely choose, whenever the object of our choice is genuine, what is just and fair, what should be or happen. As the criterion of the judgment about being is sufficient evidence, so the criterion of the judgment about the good is value.

What is good absolutely is a good not to be effected but to be participated. If it were to be effected, it would be a good not from itself or by reason of itself, but from the efficient cause. It is to be participated: our acts do not create values, but values render our acts genuine.

What is good absolutely is compared to other goods as the good in itself which diffuses its goodness to be participated by the others, or as what is principally intended, on account of which the others are intended.

The morally converted person intends as end and as that because of which he/she acts what is good absolutely. Matthew 5.6: blessed are they who hunger and thirst for justice; 5.13: blessed are they who suffer persecution for the sake of justice. The person who tends to the absolute good has a far more ample practical horizon than the one who tends just to the good for him/herself: 'Eat, drink, and be merry, for tomorrow we die.'

With regard to the notion of the good, there are particular goods, the good of order, and values. Because particular goods are only particular, they fall short of goodness or are fragments only. The good of order integrates the fragments, but by itself it surpasses egoism. The good of order grounded in egoism would be the organization of the universe around me as end. The good of order is the good of the human community. It is more a good for others than for me. It can demand sacrifices from me, even my life. Value selects between the possible goods of order. It configures the good of order as participation in the absolute good, as that which ought to be, must be.

With regard to the notions of end and means, the order between the end and those things which are for the end is twofold. When the end is a good that does not exist but is to be effected, other things are ordered to the end as means. When the end is a good absolutely, from itself, by reason of itself, it cannot be effected. Otherwise it would not be good from itself but from the one who effects it. Then those things that are ordered to the end are not means. They are from the end and on account of the end. They are compared to the good that is diffusive of itself as derivatives, as participants in the absolute, unlimited good.

Religious conversion is conversion to God. There is implicit conversion to God in intellectual and moral conversion. Historically and explicitly, religious conversion is the transition from the reign of sin to the reign of God. Romans 5.21: 'Regnavit peccatum in mortem.' What is implicitly intended is explicitly known by us through the mediation of the knowledge of God as the principle and end of all things.

Again, conversion to God is found implicitly in intellectual and moral conversion. It is found in intellectual conversion, since what is intended in questions is being: quid sit, an sit; and questions of themselves are not limited; they are endless. They include the question 'What is God?' Being of itself is not limited. Unlimited being is God. Therefore, the intention of being is the intention of God. And conversion to God is implicit in moral conversion, in that the intention of the good that is absolute is the intention of what of itself, by reason of itself, is good. Insofar as it is participated in human acts, it is called *honestum*, just, what must and should be, what is fitting; insofar as it is good from itself, insofar as it is not able to be effected, insofar as it is that from which all goods derive their goodness, insofar as it is not only the *category* of natural rational appetite, and the obligation of rational elicited appetite, but the *reality* of these, it is God. 'You have made us for yourself, Lord, and our hearts are restless until they rest in you.' 'Omnia Deum appetunt' (*Summa theologiae*, 1, a. 44, a. 4, ad 3m).

So we may conclude with regard to fundamental tendencies that the natural appetite of intellect, *intentio intendens*, intending the intelligible, the true and being, and the good, is a radical, natural, implicit tendency to God. Therefore, a tendency to God is constitutive of the originary, normative, exigent pole; it is the condition of the possibility of conversion and of the subject constituting oneself; it is the transcendental ego, man as he should be according to the *sempiternae rationes*, in potency.

Therefore, knowledge of God leads to knowledge of oneself, but knowledge of oneself also leads to knowledge of God; and denial of God leads to ignorance about oneself, and ignorance about oneself leads to denial of God; the separation of religion and philosophy reveals the inauthentic human being, and the alienation of philosophy from religion or of religion from philosophy also reveals the inauthentic human being; conversion to

God leads to the authentic existential subject, and the authentic existential subject leads to conversion to God; turning away from God leads to the inauthentic existential subject, and the inauthentic existential subject leads to turning away from God. In brief, the transcendental horizon, the religious horizon, and the philosophic horizon are in a state of mutual variation ('covariantur'). Wherever this mutual variation is at stake, there is an intrinsic connection. The Christian doctrine of God implies a developed Christian philosophy, and authentic philosophic development implies Christian apologetics. What was authentic in Hellenism was by that very reason the foundation of Christian apologetics, a *preparatio evangelica*. The authentic explicit development of Christian doctrine (the dogmas of Trinity and Christology) implies a Christian philosophy, which philosophy was distinct from Stoicism (Tertullian), Platonism (Origen), and rationalism (Arians, Sabellians).

Conversion and Authenticity (26 April, 56100D0L060)

Religious conversion is conversion to God, aversion from creatures; it is opposed to sin. Aversion from God is conversion to creatures. There is an implicit, personal, interior, individual aspect to religious conversion, and there is also an explicit, reflective (*signatus*), historical, and interpersonal aspect. We will call the first 'religious conversion *A*' and the second 'religious conversion *B*.'

As for religious conversion *A*, there is an implicit conversion to God and aversion from creatures, an implicit overcoming of the wound of ignorance and malice (*Summa theologiae*, 1-2, q. 85, a. 3), an implicit attainment of reason illumined by faith, that is given through intellectual and moral conversion. Intellectual conversion is from the perceptualist myth to the intelligible, the true, being, the good. Moral conversion is from what is good in a relative fashion to what is good absolutely. Anyone who undergoes such a conversion of the whole personality is *really* ordered to the end that is God and *exercite* is in relation to an end that is God. When we say '*implicitly*,' we are speaking about something that occurs even though one does not explicitly attain immediately to the recognition of God; we do not wish now to speak about proofs for the existence and reality of God; we wish to presuppose the philosophic materials and note the fact.

In intellectual conversion, there is left behind *die natürliche Einstellung*, and one adopts a tendency towards understanding everything, to being. The tendency to understanding everything is manifest in the fact that questions are not limited, even if answers are; but to understand everything would be to comprehend the divine essence, God. This is not attained even in Christ's beatific vision. The tendency is to being: *quid sit, an sit; quid faciendum sit*; what am I able to be, what should I be, what do I want to be. This 'to be' is what of itself is not limited. Limitation is of the essence of quiddity. Unlimited 'to be' is God.[59]

Moral conversion, again, entails conversion from the good in a relative fashion to what is good absolutely. It can be conceived as a category of the human spirit, as the categorical imperative, as the root of obligation and morality. In fact it is *exercite* conversion to God. Being and the good are convertible. The good that is itself good, good by reason of itself, and by participation in which other things have value, is God. 'You have made us for yourself, God, and our heart is restless until it rests in you.' See also *Summa theologiae*, 1, q. 44, a. 4, ad 3m.

There is a corollary to this, namely, that there is a mutual variation among (1) what has to do with the authenticity of the person, (2) religion, (3) philosophy, and (4) theology. For the originary pole is headed towards the intelligible (*quid*), the true (*an*), being (the real of the realists), and the good. The authenticity of the person is conformity of the existential pole to the originary pole. Personal authenticity is religious and moral conversion, and is implicitly conversion to God and aversion from creatures. Philosophy regards all of being. Its condition of possibility is the originary pole. Theology is reason illumined by faith, and faith illumines in two ways: by healing the wound of nature, and by elevating to divine mysteries.

This corollary is of great importance. It has to do with the absolute transcendental horizon, the total personality, the universe, in an absolute way.

There are some conclusions. First, regarding authenticity and religion, the acknowledgment of God leads to the knowledge of oneself, and the knowledge of oneself leads to the acknowledgment of God; the denial of God leads to ignorance of oneself, and ignorance of oneself leads to the neglect of God.

Second, regarding authenticity and philosophy, inauthenticity grounds philosophical errors, such as the view that 'to be' is of itself logical (Kant) or minimal (Hegel). It also corrupts true philosophy. Scholasticism becomes

---

59 The name 'Coreth' appears in the margin to the left of the statement 'esse illimitatum est Deus.' The reference is to Emerich Coreth, *Metaphysik: Eine methodisch-systematische Grundlegung* (Innsbruck: Tyrolia-Verlag, 1961; 2nd ed., 1964).

perceptualist, extrinsicist, partial. It does not ask about what is and seek to understand what is. It lacks interiority. Authenticity radically removes difficulties and obscurities. It is the light that shines in the darkness. It solidly lays foundations which cannot be shaken except by turning away from the intelligible, the true, being, and the good.

Third, regarding philosophic conversion and religious conversion, a philosophy that treats philosophic conversion also treats religious conversion, but implicitly. Religion regards life, philosophy the mind. Thus, we have the difference between existentialism and positivism: the question of God is either put, at least atheistically, in existentialism, whereas in positivism it is regarded as an absurdity and is not in any way even raised. Religious conversion is to the true God, not to an idol of the tribe, the market, the imagination, passion. It is homologous to philosophic conversion. The law, the prophetic word, the sapiential word, the word of the gospel all pertain to the order of the real good, of the true, of being as known through the true, and are opposed to the 'already out there now' and to the 'good for me,' the merely relative good. This is true even though religious conversion is not necessarily expressed in accord with differentiated consciousness, whether classical or historically minded. What the Greeks mean by *logos*, the Hebrews affirm in the word of God.

Fourth, regarding philosophy and religion, whoever regards philosophy and religion as alien to one another has departed either from authentic philosophy or from authentic religion or from both. Beyond the moment of conversion, philosophy and theology may diverge and there can be many aberrations of both. Not everyone will be able to discern between truth and error, but one who is not able can justly doubt and deliberate about taking up the theological task. Learning is necessary, but direction and orientation determine the fruit.

And regarding the Christian religion and philosophy, philosophic conversion is not a conversion to God through Christ, except implicitly, and conversion to God through Christ is not philosophic conversion, except implicitly. Still, implicitly, as the development of authentic philosophy, philosophic conversion is part of Christian apologetics. Whatever truth there was in Hellenism was *praeparatio evangelica*, so that the development and explication of Christian doctrine entails a Christian philosophy.

Fifth, regarding the authenticity of philosophy, the Christian religion and theology add the supernatural explicitly and historically. The principle of theology is reason illumined by faith. We arrive at reason through intellectual and moral conversion and through healing grace.

Transcendental Horizon, Authenticity, and Theology
(30 April, 56200DOL060)

There is a covariation of personal authenticity, religious conversion, philosophy (critical realism), and theology (reason illumined by faith), because the transcendental horizon is common to all of them. But it is one thing to have a common transcendental horizon, and quite another to arrive at a knowledge, an awareness, an appropriation of this horizon. Arriving at this is a matter of the development of dogmas and of theology.

The process begins from the word of God, which is spoken by the Son of God and heard in the Holy Spirit. This is the word of conversion from sin and to God through Christ in the Spirit.

The very handing on of the word manifests the principle 'quidquid recipitur ad modum recipientis recipitur,' that is, it manifests horizon. Horizons unfold through psychological, social, and cultural development and through intellectual, moral, and religious conversion.

The exclusion of heretics from communion eliminates inept and deformed modes of receiving and manifests the mode of receiving that is conformed to the word of God. Thus we have the development of dogmas. There were the Judeo-Christians, Gnostics, Marcionites, Adoptionists, Sabellians; the naive realists, Platonists, Arians. Nicea gave rise to Constantinople I and to Ephesus, Chalcedon, and Constantinople III. And from there we have the development of theology: (1) Abelard, *Sic et non*, with his 158 propositions; (2) Gilbert of Porrée, who taught that there is a question if and only if authorities and reasons are referred to in support of either side of a contradiction; (3) what is deduced from faith and reason is not theology but a theological problem; there is required an act of understanding to solve the problem; there is required wisdom, to order the problems and solutions, where what is first is what does not presuppose the understanding of anything else, and what is last is what does not presuppose anything except what has been understood prior. This order is manifest in the *Summa theologiae*. (4) Extrinsicism is not concerned with fostering and developing intelligence, but with terms, propositions, and syllogisms. Decadence sets in when theology is about conclusions – that is, it does not understand sources or theological principles; theology becomes a rhetorical exercise; theses from tradition are proved from the scriptures, the popes, the Fathers, theologians, and reason.

There is a way of withdrawing up to a point from such decadence. Commonly systematic theology is despised, because it is rejected or not known, but still we seek an understanding of the sources, and with great diligence attend to the psychological, social, and cultural development of the horizon; but at the same time attention to the intellectual, moral, and religious conversion of the horizon is feared. Everything can be asserted a priori about the authors: who, what, when, how, why, and with regard to psychological, social, and cultural details, since these matters are superficial and conform to conventions; but not a word is spoken about conversion of the transcendental horizon. An honorable exception is found in Bultmann and his followers. Still, they attribute intellectual conversion to a mythic mentality.

Anyone who wants to overlook this question is not able to speak or think seriously about method. Religious conversion without intellectual conversion leads to a radically confused theology. Intellectual conversion without religious conversion leads to clarity and distinctness without a soul.

Explicit Religious Conversion (30 April bis, 56300D0L060)[60]

Religious conversion *B* (religion under the explicit, historical, interpersonal aspect) is the transition from the reign of sin to the reign of God. Formal sin is what is said, done, desired against the law of God. It is aversion from God and conversion to creatures, as known and chosen at least indirectly. Sin is known through the law (Romans 3.20), but it is de facto conversion to creatures and aversion from God antecedent to any knowledge and choice. It is the wound of ignorance, malice, concupiscence, infirmity (Thomas Aquinas, *Summa theologiae*, 1-2, q. 85, a. 3). We are born without the virtues, the habits of good operation; until we acquire the virtues, we lack them, and whoever lacks the virtues lacks prudence, justice, temperance, fortitude, wisdom, understanding, knowledge; in individual cases one is able through inquiry, reflection, deliberation to know and choose the good, but one is not able in all cases to inquire, reflect, and deliberate. See St Thomas, *De veritate*, q. 24, a. 12, and compare *In II Sent.*, d. 28, q. 1, a. 2.

The reign of sin (sin reigns in the world, Romans 6.20) is omitted in classical philosophy, which treats of man as such and of that which is common to people whether asleep or awake, children or adults, wise or foolish. But the reign of sin is the *terminus a quo* of Christianity and of the New Testament (Romans 1.18–3.20). It is also the *terminus a quo* of apologetics, which

---

60 A second set of notes with the date 30 April.

wants to lead others to conversion. The reign of sin is a historical fact of the first magnitude; history that prescinds from sin prescinds from concrete fact; it is not out of humility but in truth that we pray, 'Forgive us our trespasses.' This has decisive effects under other aspects but especially under the religious aspect. Historians may prevaricate, being reluctant to judge or to incur anger, but the fact of sin is not omitted just because the principal element is omitted in a historical account.

What is the reign of sin? It is a dynamic scheme that excludes religious conversion and distorts psychological, social, and cultural development.[61] It enters into the determination of methodical categories, whether the method be comparative, synthetic-organic, genetic, or dialectical. It enters into 'horizon' understood developmentally and in terms of conversion. It distorts development. How does one attain to the synthetic-organic, and the genetic? By nature but also from data through inquiry, understanding, counsel, election, action, doing, whence at a given time the creative process starts over again on its own.[62] Insofar as sin enters into this development, there enters something unintelligible, irrational, absurd, contrary to right reason. Why did Adam sin? Why did the angels sin? If there were a 'why,' it would not be sin. There are apparent reasons and excuses, but there is no *reason* why sin is, since sin is precisely opposed to *reason*. There is a radical dialectical element, a contradiction between the rational and the irrational. Through sin there enters something absurd into the *human* situation. That is, the absurd is not found only in the inner acts of will but also in the consequent action and doing or making. The absurd enters into the human situation in a cumulative way: given the reign of sin, just as earlier so also later counsels are distorted by the absurd; in lieu of a progressive process there is had a process of growing absurdity. We do not need the writings of Kafka and Camus to observe this. We need simply to inspect those daily affairs that students and professors ask about, that the faithful ask about, and to acknowledge as absurd what is absurd. Ask and you will find sin, the probability of sin, the fear of sin and abuse. Thus, there are social, political, economic, bureaucratic, educational, legal determinisms. We are caught in snares, even after Christ, and even in priestly and religious life. How much more other workers, subordinates, administrators, in industry, commerce,

61 Lonergan refers to his 'Gratia Operans' articles and to *Insight*, chapters 6, 7, 18, 20, and Epilogue.
62 Lonergan refers here to Toynbee's 'Challenge and Response' as model, not as an empirical generalization.

medicine, the military, diplomacy, and the scientific world are caught. Not only is the human situation cumulatively penetrated with absurdities and distorted, but also human culture makes its own compromises. Culture is a kind of superstructure. The meaning that is embodied, not in daily practical actions but in art and letters, is not necessarily corrupted by the absurdity of the concrete situation; it can oppose the absurdity, and the higher it is, the more vehemently it will do so. But this opposition seems 'unreal,' in an ivory tower, separated and segregated from concrete life, from any possible concrete way of living. Then cultural works are regarded as 'idealistic,' whereas what is realistic is what displays man as he is, and what is approved is man who lives as best he can.

The Reign of Sin (3 May, 56400DOL060)

We pursue our discussion of the reign of sin. We are not describing a typical case. Positivists describe. We are exhibiting a model, a mechanism, causes, conjoined factors. Human life is constituted insofar *either* as it becomes absolutely the same as before, the primitive state of society, 'nasty, brutish, and short' (Hobbes) *or* as it becomes something different because of going from the data, through understanding and counsel, deliberation and consensus, to a change in the situation, whence new data, new understanding, emerge: a circle unfolding on its own. Given the reign of sin, there enters the absurd, the irrational, not only a stain in the will but the irrational in action itself, in the consequent situation, and in the data for future understanding. The absurd enters cumulatively. The font does not dry up, as long as the reign of sin obtains. Every element, even the least, of the human situation is penetrated and corrupted by the absurd. If there occur revolution, reformation, or renewal, even these are not without the absurd. The more radically it happens, the more profoundly does the absurd enter in. Once the irrational situation has taken hold, it practically forces sin to occur. Human solidarity is such that without heroic virtue we are not able not to act as others act.

This is interior moral impotence: without habits we cannot act well, because we are not able always to inquire, to reflect, to deliberate. Patience is easy when others are patient, honest, urbane, truthful, prompt to help and assist, but my moral situation is different if I want to be patient, honest, urbane, truthful, prompt to help and assist, while others are angry, dishonest, boorish, mendacious, egotistical: whether in the family, when husband and wife do not agree on morality; in industry, when workers and employers are mutually opposed; in commerce, when no one trusts anyone else; in law, medicine, the military, politics, diplomacy, the academy, the church. In the situation of the reign of sin the intellect is corrupted: (a) from the side of the will, which, experiencing its own moral impotence, joyfully accepts whatever moral, political, or economic teaching praises rather than reprehends this impotence; (b) from the side of the situation itself: data lead to understanding; per se this is an infallible process when the data are intelligible; but given the reign of sin, the data are penetrated with the irrational and the absurd; if no judgment, distinction, separation is made, if human nature and human iniquity are not distinguished, then the absurd itself is a datum to be interpreted, to be understood, to be considered in any taking counsel, and to be accepted in the formulation of principles. This occurs in two ways: in practical judgment, where 'primum est vivere' and morals and precepts of the church are good for people who do not know much about human life; and in a more speculative way. The more speculative way is manifest in *Realpolitik*, or in Machiavelli as he abandons theories about what is right in order to determine how to proceed efficiently in obtaining and holding on to supreme power, or in the empirical human sciences as they reveal in a mechanist-determinist way how to proceed efficiently towards ends that in themselves are praiseworthy, or in philosophies that move in this direction, or through the media of communication, literary works, newspapers, television, movies. There is a succession of ever less comprehensive syntheses. Because of church corruption, the Reformation took place through division; because of the wars of religion, rationalism insisted there was no positive supernatural religion; because of the disagreements of reason, liberalism and tolerance take over; because of the social ineffectiveness of liberalism, totalitarianism emerges, in which reason itself is proclaimed to be an ideology, a mythic superstructure.

Transition to the Reign of God (3 May bis, 56500D0L060)[63]

Transition from the reign of sin to the reign of God is aversion from creatures and conversion to God. The perfect aversion is death: death is the wages of sin. Death takes away not only visible things but sight; not only audible things but hearing; not only touchable things but touch. Although Christ neither committed nor had sin, he made his own the perfection

---

63 A second set of notes dated 3 May.

which alone is possible to us; not only did he die, he suffered and died. Hebrews 2.10: It was fitting that God ... should make the pioneer of salvation perfect through sufferings. Hebrews 5.8: He learned obedience from those things that he suffered. The Christian, before dying bodily, dies to sin so as to live for God (Romans 6.2–11, Colossians 3.1–4). As the epilogue of *Insight* argues, we may appeal to opposed forces: the depravity of intellect over against faith as healing and as elevating; the determinism of the will over against hope; the absurdity of the situation over against charity. 'An eye for an eye, and a tooth for a tooth' is justice bringing equality, but in an absurd situation, the perpetual absurd returns over and over again. See Matthew 5.38ff.

Method and Horizons (3 May ter, 56600DOL060)[64]

We have described horizon. It is differentiated relatively and absolutely: relatively in accord with psychological, social, and cultural development; absolutely in accord with intellectual, moral, and religious conversion. Horizon is found both in the object and in the subject. It is found in the object, whether this be the immediate realities of living or what the one being studied writes, the tendencies he or she exhibits in common with others, the schools to which he or she belongs, the histories he or she writes, or the critical judgments he or she passes on the histories. It is found in the subject, the one who treats the object, in the theologian, in me. As horizons vary, the field varies. There is authenticity and inauthenticity, and inauthenticity may be a matter either of rationalization or of obnubilation.

Method aims to determine horizons: the horizon of Christians, of writers and theologians, of historians, of critics.[65] This determination is factual; that is, it does not follow the way of empiricists or positivists, for facts are not known before the data are understood. The factual determination takes in everything that regards psychological, social, and cultural development. But this determination is also critical, since it takes in everything that regards intellectual, moral, and religious conversion.

This is the method of history, hermeneutics, positive studies. At the same time, it is the method which judges, discerns the sheep and the goats, re-

---

64 A third set of notes dated 3 May.
65 This sequence – Christians, writers, historians, critics – recalls the sequence of everyday life, authors, tendencies, schools, historians, crises used above. See the beginning of the next item, 7 May.

veals aberration and progress. It has an a priori element, which however is *ad utrumque*, ready for either alternative: either the same or different (comparative), either organic or incoherent, either developing or static, either position or counterposition. It discerns between what is of greater and of lesser moment to the theologian. The theologian especially considers the horizon as absolute, as having to do with conversion, and less the horizon as relative, as having to do with psychological, social, and cultural development. For example, from the New Testament to Nicea, the theologian does not study everything psychological, social, cultural, but those things that have to be known in order to distinguish positions from counterpositions.

Wisdom has been thought to reside in the speculative domain, prudence in the practical. But once historical consciousness has arisen, there is a need for wisdom regarding the concrete. Wisdom regarding the concrete is understood inasmuch as it is included in method. Method is open to everything; it is factual, critical, and evaluative. It does not bring it about that everyone thinks the same: there are as many ideas as there are horizons. It expects, explains, and judges differences.

Method in Four Steps (7 May, 56700D0L060)

There is a determinate horizon at each of the four steps: a horizon of Christians at the level of everyday living, a horizon of theological authors, a horizon of historians, and a horizon of critics. It is determinate descriptively, in terms of who did what, when, how, why, and where. It is determined in an explanatory fashion comparatively (same as and different from others), synthetically (organically connected or not), genetically (developing or static), and dialectically (position or counterposition). There is a relative determination of horizon in accord with psychological, social, and cultural development, and there is an absolute determination in accord with intellectual, moral, and religious conversion.

Method involves an a priori, which resides in questions and is ready for either alternative. It involves facts, since it responds to questions by judging facts. Facts are not the same as data; human knowledge is composite. Method also involves critical judgment determining positions and counterpositions.

Although there is a proper method that has to do with human science, still because it includes the transcendental horizon of intellectual, moral, and religious conversion, it automatically is a matter of theology. Theology discovers in the concrete both psychological, social, and cultural development, and intellectual, moral, and religious conversion, and these are not lived and expressed separately. What happens in psychological, social, and cultural development is like a garment, and is relative, but what happens in accord with conversion is what wears the garment, and is absolute.

Because method attends to the transcendental horizon, it attends not only to religious conversion conceived in some vague manner but to intellectual, moral, and religious conversion and their covariation. It is automatically theology, and in a comprehensive way. This method is radically opposed to any positivism, whether theoretical or practical. It is opposed to a theoretical positivism, where there is no valid consideration of the entire field, of the concrete field, of everything, no possible architectonic science. Positivism admits of method, yes, but not of transcendental method. This method is opposed also to a practical positivism, where only those questions are to be considered on which all agree, and where no question that touches on transcendental matters would be regarded as scientific.

We proceed differently. Transcendental consideration enters into our very method; the readiness for either alternative enters into our method; the diverse views of investigators are explained by their horizons; and diverse methods are explained in terms of authentic and inauthentic horizon.

Method exhibits unity in differences and continuity in development. There is a problem of categories and a problem of transposition. In every subject and every correlative object there are found an originary pole of experiencing, inquiring, reflecting, deliberating, which develops psychologically, socially, culturally, under influence from without but by assimilation and accommodation; an existential pole that is authentic or inauthentic in accord with intellectual, moral, and religious conversion; and a field, whether implicit or explicit, which is not created from nothing, but which passes from being conscious to being known when it becomes explicit. This unity and continuity are grounded in the transcendental element; if this element is removed, all that remains are the relative differences of psychological, social, and cultural development. Then there emerge those ultimate and irreducible entities like Hebraism, Hellenism, Gnosticism, dogmatism, Scholasticism, none of which is truly understood. There also emerge absurd demands, such as: (1) fidelity to divine revelation means putting on the Hebraic mentality, which seems to make the New Testament a contradiction; (2) the transition from the New Testament to the councils, the transition from an implicit to an explicit objective field, is impossible; (3) the living church assimilating the new and transforming it in a Christian way is overlooked.

Because the transcendental is included, there is also a radical critique. Biblical conceptions are one thing, but modern conceptions of biblical conceptions are something else. They are divided according to modern horizons, but the biblical conceptions themselves are not. Those who overlook their own horizons either do not know this, and are less scientific than they could be, or know it, and are less honest than they should be.

Horizon as Dynamic (7 May bis, 56800D0L060)[66]

We turn to the dynamic aspect of horizon. The problematic has to do with the interconnection of questions. Questions may be divided in several ways. First, there is a division according to material: physics, chemistry, biology, psychology, human reality, divine reality. Next, there is a division according to the way of considering the material. Classically, there is the division of speculative and practical, but today there are divisions of descriptive, explanatory, existential, transcendental, practical, hermeneutical, historical. Third, there is a division according to the way in which the question is put. It can simply be put; it can be put and expressed; it can be put, expressed, and justified.[67] The way it is put will vary according to the cultural and scientific situation. Fourth, questions are divided in accord with operations; thus, we have problems of understanding, with the questions 'What?' and 'Why?' and problems of fact, with the question 'Whether?' 'Is it so?' Fifth, questions are divided in accord with the connection of questions with one another. Some questions are quite independent of each other, e.g., those of physics and those of literature. Some are remotely connected in terms of the hierarchy of the sciences. And some are proximately connected.

Concerning questions that are proximately connected, several points are in order. First, some problems are not solved unless others are solved first. Sometimes, as soon as some are solved, this leads to the solution of others.

---

66 A second set of notes dated 7 May.
67 This corresponds to the division suggested in *The Triune God: Systematics* 21: 'Having treated the goal and the act in which the goal is attained, we must now consider the act in which we intend the goal before we attain it. This anticipation we call a question or a problem, and we can consider it either as it occurs spontaneously or as it is explicitly expressed or as it is put scientifically. A question occurs spontaneously in the experience of wonder that is the origin not only of all science and philosophy but also of all theology. A question is expressed explicitly when we say clearly and distinctly what it is that we want to know. A question is put scientifically when we add the reasons why this question ought to be put.'

Second, the task of wisdom is to order, to find that which is 'technically first,' that which when solved leads to the solution of a second question, so that when these two are solved, a third can be solved, and when these three are solved, a fourth can be solved, etc., etc. The task of understanding is to treat of principles by grasping the solution to the first question. The task of science is to solve what is explicitly consequent and connected.

Third, there is the development of systems. Connected problems and connected solutions lead to connected conceptions. Just as further solutions are derived from the first solution, so further conceptions are derived from the first conception.

Fourth, a technical terminology corresponds to systematic conceptions, as opposed to what is thought in a commonsense mode.

Fifth, there is a distinction between the way of analysis, which is followed before the system has been reached, and the way of synthesis, which takes over once the system has been reached. In the way of analysis, the order that derives from wisdom is not known. Beyond any intention, *per accidens*, one moves to the goal: it is a movement from whatever most excites one's wonder (that which is more apparent, commonly spoken of, solemnly believed) to that which is systematically first.

Sixth, there is the temporality of questions. Before understanding, that which we wonder about truly moves us. After we have understood, we are not so moved but express our understanding in an argument that offers a solution. The solution can become habitual, and when it does it is either an instrument of education, which proceeds in the order of teaching (the *via synthetica*) or an object of history, which follows the way of discovery (the *via analytica*, where the movement is understood from the term). The understanding of doctrine and the understanding of the history of doctrine are reciprocally related.

Also connected with the temporality of questions is the fact that a system that has been discovered can be rejected, can pass into oblivion, and can be renewed and perfected.

More on Horizon as Dynamic (10 May, 56900DOL060)

The dynamic aspect is intrinsic to horizons. The subject, the originary pole that asks the questions, is constituted as experiencing, inquiring, reflecting, deliberating. Questions are put in three ways: spontaneously, explicitly, and scientifically (where reasons for the question are assigned). The reasons are reduced to types: there are questions having to do with coherence, others having to do with understanding, and still others having to do with fact. Abelard's *Sic et non* is an instance of questions that were raised because coherence seemed absent. The Lombard's *Sentences* are largely concerned with displaying coherence that actually does exist. Understanding is by analogy with what we know naturally, and through the connection of the mysteries with one another and with our last end. Problems of fact may be put in many ways.[68]

The notion of systematic understanding includes connected questions, the order of the solution (a function of wisdom), understanding the principle, the knowledge (science) of conclusions, the concept of a formal system, and technical terminology. Instances are found in the commentaries on the *Sentences*, in the various disputed questions (*De veritate, De potentia, De malo, De virtutibus, Quodlibeta*), and in the *Summa theologiae.* The *Summa contra Gentiles* displays how systems are separate from the problem of coherence and shows how the sources that were the beginning of the way of discovery may be concluded to from the systematic understanding.

The fate of a system has to do with the differentiation of consciousness. The subject is different (as is portrayed in the story of Thales and the milkmaid), the apprehension of the world is different, the concepts are different, the language is different, the problems are different, the intelligible solutions are different, and the social community and culture, popular and academic, are different.[69]

We must distinguish differentiation of consciousness and separation of cultures. In differentiated consciousness, religion enters into and assumes its place in the world of theology. But by separation of cultures, theology is removed from the universities and taught in seminaries, the cleric has his own culture, and the lay person develops a different culture, so that the cleric is not understood by the lay person and the lay person is not understood by the cleric. To defend differentiation of consciousness is not to defend such a separation of cultures.

---

68 Note that this material is found also in section 3 of the first chapter of *De Deo trino: Pars systematica* (1964), a part that is quite new in comparison with the earlier *Divinarum personarum* (1957, 1959). See *The Triune God: Systematics* 20–31. The present notes may be the source of the material found there.

69 With respect to culture, Lonergan adds 'sensu anthropologico,' that is, culture understood in the anthropological sense, not in the normative sense typical of the classicist mentality.

There is the fate of system in the field of theology itself.[70] It grows through extension: Trinity, Incarnation, grace, sacraments, church. It also grows through organization: common principles emerge when philosophy is no longer some particular discipline but the reflection and expression of the mind itself, of reason itself. There is a covariation of rational psychology, epistemology, ontology, and natural theology similar to that of authenticity, religion, philosophy, theology. System not only grows but also is perfected through the more complete understanding of principles.

A system can be completely rejected. What 'to understand' means is not grasped. The problem of understanding is eliminated. Problems are restricted to coherence and fact. Systematic understanding is thought to be a new doctrine connected to philosophical dogmas. The systematic understanding of scripture, the Fathers, the councils, the better teachers is thought rather to be a rejection of these sources. Opponents of system may charge, for instance, that systematic thinking has made Augustine say something Augustine never meant. This can happen in the simplistic medieval sense of a Roger Marston, or in a modern and historical manner. One goes back to the problem of coherence and speaks about absolute necessities and absolute possibilities, or one goes back to popular culture.

With poor understanding, the understanding of the principle is not increased but diminished; conclusions solve problems imperfectly; there arises a new generation of problems, not simply from the fonts of revelation, the Fathers, the councils but from these along with a poorly understood system; there follow a new order for the less wise, new principles for those who understand less, and new conclusions for the less scientific; there follows also, not once but over and over, a multiplication of interpretations and schools, disputations, the imposition of uniformity from outside, and the triumph of the sociology of knowledge.

The problem of fact is found (1) in the old Protestants, with their works on grace, the sacraments, the church, (2) in the rationalists, who admit no positive religion and advocate a return to common principles, (3) in the liberals, who promote *living* religion and espouse the value of religion without dogmas and without propositional truth, (4) in the atheists, who acknowledge human values but maintain that religion is alienation, a projection of human excellence into the sky, and (5) in the historians, with

70 Note that this material on the fate of the system is also included in section 3 of chapter 1 of *De Deo trino, Pars systematica* (now *The Triune God: Systematics* 26–29).

their historical knowledge concerning the Jesus of history and the Christ of faith, their questioning of the value of the sources, their views concerning the gospels, the New Testament, and the Hellenism of the councils, their opinions concerning dogmas and systematic theology, and concerning the sources and systematic theology. There emerges a historical responsibility of systematic theology with respect to Christian culture and of Christian culture with respect to secularized culture.

Once the problem of fact has been posed, there is a transition from questions to be determined by systematic theology to theses to be proven from theological loci. Theological understanding is transmuted into theological reason; before this crisis occurred, connected problems led to systematic solutions; after the crisis, systematic solutions are construed to create a proof of fact. Systematic solutions do not prove facts unless they are contained in the sources, and to find systematic solutions in the sources is anachronistic. Paul and John are read as if they were disciples of St Thomas, and St Thomas is read as if he were a disciple of John of St Thomas! The fact that systematic solutions arise in time and develop in time (DB 1800, 2314) is overlooked.

Dogmatic definitions are not found in the sources. That is archaism. 'The same truth in the same sense' is affirmed in DB 1800, 2314, but in what way we have the same sense and the same truth is precisely the dogmatic and hermeneutic problem.

Next, there is the question of historicism, where the basic text is Karl Heussi, *Die Krisis des Historismus* (Tübingen: 1932).[71] Historicism is a historical and historiographical conception commonly accepted around the beginning of the twentieth century. It excludes the possibility of an objective structure of facts which the historian discerns and narrates independently of every philosophical operation. Thus we must ascertain (1) whether there exists an objective structure of facts, (2) whether the objective structure of facts is narrated, intended, in the sources, and (3) whether the historian discerns and narrates some objective structure of facts. This is the historical problem in its psychological, gnoseological, epistemological aspect. It is connected with the problem of biblical inerrancy.

Historical relativism maintains (1) that history is not yet finished; given past developments, great light is thrown on earlier events; so too with future developments; (2) that history is *materia prima*: it consists of data; the data

---

71 Karl Heussi, *Die Krisis des Historismus* (Tübingen: Mohr, 1932).

themselves have meaning, whether superficial or full and concrete; and depending on the different culture, nation, religion, education of historians that superficial sense is preserved in different ways, and the full sense is understood in different ways; (3) that history can be right, but whether it is true is not scientifically resolved (E. Rothacker).[72]

The existential victory of historicism and relativism is shown in the views that (1) the field of objective scientific inquiry is for those matters on which everyone is in agreement, (2) myth is found in a popular form, *Weltanschauung*, and in an erudite form, in systems, (3) demythologization, existential interpretation, is reduced to the orientation of the subject, and (4) what matters is interior personal response in the *existenziell* order of faith.

Development of Dogmas and of Theology (14 May, 57000D0L060)

Attention turns to theological problems, and the first is the possibility of the development of dogmas and of the development of theology. There are nine subheadings.

(1) Vincent of Lerins combined his 'quod semper, quod ubique, quod ab omnibus' with an insistence on the growth of understanding, knowledge, and wisdom with regard to the same meaning, the same dogma, the same statement, on the part of individuals and of all, of each person and the whole church, according to the degree proper to each age and time.

(2) The first of these ('quod semper ...') is more easily understood: Christ, the apostles, and the church successively preach the same truth.

(3) But what is more easily understood is also the only thing that is understood by the multitude, so that

(4) it would be anachronism to hold that if something is taught today by the church or by theology, it always was taught, if not explicitly, then implicitly. What is this 'implicitly'? What is required and sufficient that something be *always* taught but in such a way that it is *easily* understood? Such a way of proceeding yields a systematic misinterpretation of the sources.

---

72 The book by Rothacker to which Lonergan refers here and elsewhere is *Logik und Systematik der Geisteswissenschaften* (Munich: R. Oldenbourg, 1927, 1947). The book was reissued in 1965.

(5) And it would be archaism to hold that what is not contained in the sources is a later corruption or at least a superfluous addition; the dogmas developed later; they are not in the sources; theology presupposes not only faith but also doctrine, which is a Greek or medieval add-on; and so theological pronouncements are to be rejected or at least not paid any attention. From this there follows a threefold effect, clearly expounded by Newman: ignorance, since what is omitted is not known; mutilation of the whole (and knowledge is of the whole not in an additive but in a comprehensive sense); and distortion of the remaining parts: a vacuum cannot be tolerated, and so the other parts assume for themselves what once pertained to the omitted part. If matters whose explanation is juridical or religious or systematic are not going to be acknowledged as 'juridical,' 'religious,' or 'systematic,' then they will receive some other explanation. If philosophy and systematic theology are omitted, recourse is had to historical speculation.

(6) In terms of controversies, then, anachronists give a systematic misinterpretation or inexact interpretation of the sources (scripture, the Fathers, St Thomas), while archaists ignore a part, mutilate the whole, and distort the remainder. The material for controversy from these two sources is great.

(7) In terms of ecumenism, Christians are living in a laicized or secularized culture; they acknowledge precepts of charity, and pray for unity, but there is a diminution of the dogmatic spirit. There is some understanding of development. It cannot be said to be exact, and it is not needed by all. But there is a lack of understanding of dogmatic theology. Modern science attends to data very well, effectively promotes understanding, is most certain in its negations, and is incapable of positive certitude. People divide ideas into those that are opportune and those that have been superseded, rather than into true and false. The dogmatic theologian in modern culture is a stumbling block.

(8) One who wants a method of theology wants theology as a science in which a dogmatic element of judgment, of true or false, accrues to the understanding of the data without removing the understanding of the data. Such a person wants not only comparative, synthetic, and genetic study, but also dialectic,

and is not pleased, on the one hand, with the right, which does not think of data and understanding, and on the other, with the left, which does not consider judgment. Both left and right believe they know all there is to be known about method, and yet they do not know what is intended in a course 'De methodo theologiae.'

(9) The problem, then, is: in what precisely does dogmatic and theological development consist?

The Problem of Method in History (14 May bis, 57100D0L060)[73]

The second problem is history. The treatment accorded it in this item has five points.

(1) The first is existential history. Existential history is to the existence of the community what memory is to the existence of a given individual. If I suffered from amnesia, I would not know that I was (a) Canadian, (b) Catholic, (c) a religious, (d) a priest, (e) a professor of theology, (f) residing in Piazza della Pilotta. Perhaps I would do some strange things. Equally a community that has no memory of itself ceases to exist. There are taken away accepted modes of acting, the foundation of mutual understanding, of common conversation, collaboration, common deliberation, common decision.

(2) Next, there is narrated history. The larger and older a community is, the less does memory, the simple handing on from father to son, suffice, and the more the existence of the community requires a composed and narrated history that is either recited or written. This history does not intend merely or even principally a collection of facts, but has an existential goal: through the narrated facts it communicates a vision of the world, a *Weltanschauung*; it occupies itself with a task that is informative (what happened), explanatory (why did it happen), ethical (what is to be praised and blamed), prophetic (what is to be done), apologetic, and artistic. To this end it selects the facts and orders them insofar as they help bring these goals about.

(3) Third, there is 'critical' history.[74] It describes itself as follows. First, it intends to determine the past facts themselves, 'wie es eigentlich gewesen,'

---

73 A second set of notes dated 14 May.
74 Mention is made of 'Historismus' as in Heussi, *Die Krisis des Historicismus*.

what really happened. So it is not concerned with deep causes, ultimate reasons, but with events as we all know them in our daily life. Second, it admits no presuppositions, whether philosophic, religious, cultural, national, or any others; it is *Voraussetzungslos*. It does not deny that historians find it difficult to free themselves from every subjective influence, but it states an ideal of objectivity. Facts are real in themselves, and so are their interconnections, etc., and these real facts and connections the historian wishes to apprehend as they are on the side of the object. Third, since narrated history is not content just with the facts, it makes for a crisis of narrative historians. It seeks a supplement from all other remains of the past in order to narrate in an orderly fashion the facts, at least those of major importance, according to assigned times and places, persons, actions, and motives. Fourth, it seems obvious, sane, inevitable. Even today it is regarded as most evident and certain by all who do not think seriously about historical method. Inquiry about the facts is the principal element of the history to which all else is subordinate. If one cannot determine the facts, to that extent one knows nothing about the historical reality, the deeds that were done.

The fate of critical history is complex. It was rejected as methodically erroneous in Germany, according to Heussi, between 1920 and 1930. There was removed the presupposition concerning objective and structured facts to be inspected and narrated. It was thought that this is an error, not because there don't really exist persons, actions, and interrelations, but because knowledge is mythically conceived as perception. Data give way to understanding, and this leads to judgment. Presuppositions cannot be excluded concerning common principles; *quidquid recipitur secundum modum recipientis recipitur.* But this solution presupposes philosophy, and the commonly acknowledged philosophy leads to relativism, where presuppositions cannot be excluded but no criterion of solution is given in what is presupposed. There is a movement, then, from truth to correctness.

(4) The fourth point is historical relativism. It may be considered either on the side of the principle or on the side of the object. On the side of the principle, as we have just seen, philosophy cannot be excluded, and *Voraussetzungslosigkeit* is a myth. But between philosophies there is no sure selection, and so there results a transition from truth to correctness.

On the part of the object, there are description (who, what, when, how, why,) and explanation, where comparative, synthetic, and genetic methods are allowed, but not dialectical, for then there enters judgment, which is not a matter of *Verstehen* or *Entscheiden.* Judgment is not known by the

Greeks, by essentialists, by empiricists, by idealists, by existentialists. This element in the object is a very small problem. The synthetic and genetic are psychological, cultural, social, and affect horizon as relative. But truth and judgment are issues of dialectic, and affect horizon as absolute.

(5) The fifth point treats history and existentialism. Excluding presuppositions just means allowing many unknown and false presuppositions. Insistence on correctness leads to conventionalism. In Bultmann, (i) there is a certain inductive technique by which there is attained what is acknowledged by everybody everywhere: historical-critical method is extrinsic only, in the realm of exteriority, and mundane, in the realm of the world. The problem of the historical Jesus is *historische*. (ii) There are extra-scientific assertions in the order of *Weltanschauung*, ontology, metaphysics, dogmatic theology. If these are taken literally, they are myth; they may have the form of systematic conception, but they admit an existential interpretation which is reduced to the subject: the *geschichtliche* Jesus. (iii) There is the question put to me to which I respond in the *existenziell* manner, *Der kerygmatische Iesus*.

The entire question is whether there is given objective truth besides that which is attained by extrinsicist and mundane science. For the dogmatic theologian there exists a problem regarding the very method of history. If it proceeds in accord with what are commonly acknowledged, it proceeds in accord with (1) 'critical' history, (2) historical relativism, or (3) some form of existentialism. That is, without method, it does not know what it is doing.

Critical History (24 May, 57200D0L060)

'Critical' history claims to have no philosophical presuppositions; historically it is a reaction against Hegel. But in fact nothing can be said without philosophical presuppositions; as Heussi said, there is no clear line dividing historiography and philosophy.[75] Critical history proceeds in accord with common sense, which has presuppositions but does not know them. Consequently the method itself is radically uncritical, a perceptualism of facts and relations.[76] If this is rigidly applied, the historian will end

---

75 Lonergan refers to Heussi, *Die Krisis des Historicismus* 64.
76 Lonergan refers to ibid. 56.

up simply editing sources and indices.[77] If it is not rigidly applied, history becomes poetry.[78]

Historical relativism is exhibited in Erich Rothacker, *Logik und Systematik der Geisteswissenschaften*.[79] Truth in Fichte's idealism of freedom and in Hegel's objective idealism, as well as in naturalism, depends on the will. Correctness, though, is a matter of critically establishing data and making theoretical connections. Philosophy has the task of placing limits between what is scientific and visions of the world. In the contrary view espoused here, attention is to be paid to differences and connections according to psychological, social, and cultural development and to differences and connections in accord with conversion. If the second of these is not omitted or distorted by the counterpositions of the investigator, there is no problem proceeding in this way; but if it is omitted or distorted, that is the place for the critical function. Data are not enough. Even in physics there is a movement from above that entails differential equations, and one from the data below; the establishment of empirical laws is a function of both. Husserl shows in *Die Krisis der europäischen Wissenschaften* that the movement from above will either be conventionalism or entail a transcendental a priori.[80]

The existential history of Bultmann distinguishes *Historie* from *Geschichte*. *Historie* is technical history following the historical-critical method. It will at-

---

77 Lonergan refers to H.-I. Marrou, *De la connaissance historique* (Paris: Éditions du Seuil, 1954) 54–55. See Lonergan, *Early Works on Theological Method 1* at 245: 'one has in H.-I. Marrou, who is quite an eminent historian, in 1954, *De la connaissance historique*, the claim, put forth on page 54, that if one really follows the standard method in historical investigation and in writing history as set forth by Langlois and Seignobos, according to their prescriptions, the more you set aside all preconceptions, the more you attend simply and solely to the critically established facts, the more the historian is driven simply to edit texts with footnotes. Such a history consists of a book of blank pages.'

78 Lonergan refers to Gadamer on von Ranke, p. 199, cf. 206. The reference is to Hans-Georg Gadamer, *Wahrheit und Methode: Grundzüge einer philosophischen Hermeneutik* (Tübingen: Mohr, 1960).

79 See above, note 72. Lonergan refers to pp. 144, 149, and 157. See Lonergan's references to the same pages in *Early Works on Theological Method 1* at 246.

80 The reference is to Edmund Husserl, *Die Krisis der europäischen Wissenschaften und die transzendentale Phänomenologie: Eine Einleitung in die phänomenologische Philosophie*, ed. Walter Biemel (The Hague: Martinus Nijhoff, 1954); in English, *The Crisis of European Sciences and Transcendental Phenomenology: An Introduction to Phenomenological Philosophy*, trans. David Carr (Evanston, IL: Northwestern University Press, 1970).

tain what can be known by everybody. A universally accepted history is like a universally accepted mathematics, physics, or chemistry. *Geschichte* refer to extra-scientific affirmations in the sources: *Weltanschauung*, ontology, objective theology. These are myth, but they are given a true meaning by the subject, in *die existentiale Interpretation.* The *kerygmatic* proclamation puts the question to me about myself: this is *existenziell.*

The crisis of Bultmann's position is that existential interpretation and the kerygmatic posing of the question are reducible to the crisis of immanentism. Moreover, regarding the field of *Historie* there exists a historical field of questions and answers on which consent can be presumed, consisting of matters that do not transfer directly or indirectly into questions of truth and values: whether Brutus killed Caesar, whether Jesus of Nazareth suffered under Pontius Pilate. This field is extrinsic and mundane. Its extent is judged differently by different people. But besides the mediation of the past through historical worlds, there exists a mediation of the past through tradition. The church is a historical fact which testifies about historical facts. And according to Gadamer, the prejudice of the Enlightenment against prejudice is a means of destroying tradition.[81] The crisis has not yet been overcome; it is a deception to think it has.[82]

In hermeneutics the problem of knowledge is transposed into the context of the problem of interpretation. Either one must first solve the critical problem and then come to some conclusions regarding interpretation, or one will tackle the possibility of interpretation as a practical solution to the problem of knowledge. The issue of history versus nature entails a transformation of metaphysics, from considering it on the analogy of natural science to considering it on the analogy of human science. The issue is not 'quid' but 'quis,' not 'what' but 'who.' This will entail a transformation of theological categories.

History is about the past as such. It is also about the past as a temporal dimension in particular human sciences. The latter learn from history, which is assumed as a part of the problems of religion, art, literature, science, the state, the law. There arises the free subject who uses history. Again, history is about the past as a temporal dimension in Catholic life. Theology is related to human science but also to Catholic life, both in a technical sense and

81 Lonergan refers to p. 255 in Gadamer, *Wahrheit und Methode.*
82 Lonergan refers to Gerhard Ebeling, 'Die Bedeutung der historisch-kritischen Methode für die protestantische Theologie,' *Zeitschrift für Religion und Kirche* 47 (1950) 33.

with a view to Christian culture; here is where the kerygmatic dimension of theology comes into play.

The object of history is relatively fixed and relatively fluid.

History as Written and History as Reality (28 May, 57300DOL060)

Consideration of history is twofold. The gnoseology of history has to do with the writing of history, the metaphysics of history with its reality. As reality, history is what man does and makes, and what man undoes and replaces. To study 'man' according to development is to touch on destiny. To study 'man' according to conversion is to treat decision. History provides the highest level of reflection on human action and the concrete context of existential decision. The past sets the stage for the present situation; it provides the needs, exigencies, and opportunities of the present; it also provides collaborators and opponents. But it is the infinite labor of decision that meets the occasion.

The contrast of nature and history has to be presented in a non-Hegelian fashion. Perhaps the weakest feature of Hegel's thought has to do with the derivation of nature and the account of nature. Spirit, of course, is both transcendental and transcendent. Hegel missed the transcendental aspect and misconceived the transcendent. The issue really is nature precisely in the realm of spirit. This is what we have been calling the originary pole. But of course we must add the existential pole. The highest level of consciousness is neither speculative nor practical but *rational self-consciousness* disposing of self both speculatively and practically. In the highest level, intellect can and should lead to reflective understanding grounding a judgment of value, with these grounding acts of will. In the Catholic realm, this is faith that operates through charity.

Consideration of mediation is part of the topic of history. Mediation has to do with the relation of the parts with one another, and with the relation between the parts and the whole. The organism mediates itself, develops and maintains the parts by which it functions, and is a mediation of the species. In human beings mediation has psychological, social, and cultural significance.

Psychologically, we may distinguish immediate operations, mediated operations, and operations on the mediators, on language, mathematics, logic. A universe organized through technical terms is mediated through the natural, human, and theological sciences. The subject is mediated in a critical and methodical manner that illuminates one's existential destiny.

From a social standpoint, the whole is mediated and constituted by common apprehension and common consent.

In terms of culture, there is a mediated character of apprehension and a mediated motivation of assent.

But the Catholic is neither Jew nor Greek. A new principle has been introduced, a principle of transformation, rendering Jew and Greek subsidiary to something catholic, universal, and permanent.

Thus, there is mediation of the New Man in Christ Jesus, neither Jew nor Greek. We may treat this in three sections: in terms of undifferentiated consciousness, in terms of classical consciousness, and in terms of historical consciousness.

Undifferentiated consciousness yields a nontechnical mode of understanding in commonsense development, with a concern for both immediate and mediated communication; immediate communication occurs by way of example, preaching, summary statements as in creeds and catechism, liturgy, church discipline; mediated communication occurs in letters, documents, books, the Old and New Testaments, written official decisions, Christian literature both in sources and in present kerygma.

Classical consciousness moves towards a technical mode of understanding that defines terms and deduces conclusions; it adopts a mode of communication proper to a universal, perpetual church: neither Jew nor Greek. It has both a dogmatic and a systematic moment. Its dogmatic moment entails a transposition from the nontechnical to the technical expression of the same truth in the same sense but with different categories and context (DB 1792, 1800, 2714). The transition is from biblical to catholic categories and context. The systematic moment rounds out the field of technical statement with an understanding of the mysteries, *intelligentia mysteriorum*, by way of analogy with what we naturally know and in terms of the connection of the mysteries with one another.

Historical consciousness forces a move to method, to reflection on process, distinguishing positive, dogmatic, systematic, and kerygmatic parts and functions, assigning each its limits, determining the functions of each, relating each to the others, working out foundations, excluding radical errors, preventing confusions, mutilations, distortions. It turns to the subject, to interiority, to both the originary and existential poles in its search for the foundation of all that can be said and known. If for the nontechnical mind the issue is either Jew or Greek, and for the technical mind using catholic categories neither Jew nor Greek, for the methodical mind it is both Jew and Greek, and Catholic.

We turn, then, to the question 'What is a dogma?' Dogmas employ technical expressions such as *homoousios, duo physeis, duo thelēmata* in composing a creed, a solemn declaration, an anathema. But these technical terms are given a nontechnical understanding: *ousia* and *physis*, for example, are not given a scientific explanation. The requirement is that the same truth in the same sense be expressed in different categories and in a different context. There is a transition in this movement from biblical to catholic categories and context. Biblical writings express the mentality of a given author, in a given milieu, treating issues for particular purposes. Catholic expressions address a universal and permanent church, stating its doctrine for everyone, everywhere, so that they can know what is meant without a doctorate in scripture. The transition does not take place through Romantic hermeneutics, thinking oneself into the mind of Paul and John.[83] It is not a deduction per se, although some dogmas are, as is the case with Ephesus. Rather, what is entailed is a transposition. There is a sense in which it is implicit as a possibility, in the sense that the transcendental is always implicit in every mind – being and not being, nature, and so on – and in the sense that the less determinate is implicit. Dogmatic statements are less determinate than biblical: infinite and finite, absolute and relative, and so on.

The dogmatic process goes something like the following.

Is Christ the Son of God? Well, is it true[84] that Christ is (a) a man; (b) not merely a man; (c) not a creature; (d) not the Father; (e) from the Father; (f) given divine predicates; (g) Son in a singular meaning? Of these, (a), (f), and (g) can be found in scripture.[85]

The topic shifts, then, to the distinction of positive and dogmatic theology. At one point, as Congar makes clear (DTC 29) there was a distinction of Scholastic versus positive, and, within Scholastic theology, of dogmatic versus moral.[86] Then development came to be understood as a process of differentiation and integration. Differentiation occurs, is clarified, is understood and formulated, and then integration of distinct and complementary

---

83 Lonergan adds the names of Winckelmann, Schleiermacher, and Dilthey.

84 The word 'true' is underlined three times in Lonergan's notes.

85 This is what Lonergan's notes state. It must be said that at least in terms of mission (e) is also to be found in the New Testament. But it is likely that Lonergan is thinking of procession rather than mission here.

86 Lonergan's reference to Congar is to (Yves) M.-J. Congar, 'Théologie,' in *Dictionnaire de théologie catholique* (DTC) XV, 29, 341–502. [In English, *A History of Theology*, trans. and ed. Hunter Guthrie (Garden City, NY: Doubleday, 1968).]

functions becomes the task. A total method includes description and explanation, and under explanation it includes comparative, organic, genetic, and dialectical methods determining horizon both in accord with development and in accord with conversion. It includes the genesis of all dogmas and all systems, and the refutation of all heresies and all errors. It involves two types of operation: intelligence developing in commonsense fashion and in scientific fashion. The transcendental is implicit in common sense, which understands things as related to us, as related to Isaiah, Mark, Paul, John, Athanasius, etc. It does not attempt the swing over to things as related to one another, to patterns that are independent of the standpoint of Jew and Greek. With system, the transcendental becomes explicit, along with the understanding of the relations of things to one another.

Dogmatic and positive theology, then, differ in at least four ways. First, they differ in their respective modes of expression. Dogmatic expression is *oratio recta*: 'God the Son became man.' Positive expression is *oratio obliqua*: 'John said "Verbum caro factum est," and here is what he meant by that.' Second, they differ in object. The object of dogmatic theology is God and all things in relation to God. The object of positive theology is what *X* said and meant about God and other things. Third, they differ in their formal objects. The formal object of dogmatic theology is found in its own *Problematik*, its questions, terms, answers, and systematization; the formal object of positive theology is an author's concerns, language, horizon, synthesis, especially with regard to God. Fourth, they differ in their mode of understanding. Dogmatic theology moves to technical understanding and puts forth theory. Positive theology stays with particular works, authors, and cultures. Even technical writing is studied by a nontechnical type of understanding: understanding Aquinas is not a theory about Aquinas.

Despite these differences, there is an overlapping. The two ways of doing theology need not be in conflict. First, the inerrancy of scripture transforms *oratio obliqua* into *oratio recta*, and so does the infallibility of the magisterium. Second, in general there are not exegetical problems about the magisterium. It is not just clear enough so that it can be understood, but so clear that it cannot be misunderstood. Third, in scripture problems arise when differentiation is not understood. We may, then, consider both positive and dogmatic exegesis under four headings.

First, dogmatic exegesis argues from scripture. In Paul it finds faith without works, and in James faith with works. Problems of reconciliation are there from the start. Positive exegesis deals with scripture by parts: Mark, the Synoptics, Acts, the Great Epistles, the Pastoral epistles, the Catholic epistles. Problems of reconciliation are present usually to be settled later on.

Second, the dogmatic exegete raises his own questions, in his own terms, in his own context; they are the questions of one who learns from scripture about God; they are the questions that arise in contracting transcendental finality into dichotomy: for example, either Jesus is God or he is not; they are the questions that are answered in catholic categories, for a universal and permanent church that is neither Jew nor Greek. The positive theologian, on the other hand, raises the question of what Paul's or John's questions or concerns were, how Paul or John met his questions and concerns, and not what Paul and John should have considered, but what they did consider.

Third, a dogmatic question is not answered by finding its words in scripture. The contexts differ, and the categories differ; the dogmatic question is not answered by some Romantic penetration of Paul's or John's mind, but by analyzing the question into elements that *are* found explicitly in scripture. If dogmatic theology is done well, then positive theology will not disagree about the elements; it will acknowledge the validity of the dogmatic approach. The fact that the dogmatic theology learns from scripture will support the validity of the positive theologian's own approach, putting the elements together in the manner and measure indicated by the text.

Fourth, dogmatic theology refers to positive theology those who wish to learn about Paul's thought, while positive theology refers to dogmatic theology questions of the dogmatic type.

Dogmatic theology, then, entails transposition, from nontechnical to catholic statements, of the same truth, in the same sense, but now expressed in catholic categories and a catholic context. DB 2314 ('quomodo in fontibus contineatur') is a justification of this transposition. Three cases are distinguished. The first is represented in the movement from Nicea to Constantinople III, where the dogma is not reached through systematic theology. The second is found where dogmas are in fact mediated by systematic work: Florence, Trent, Vatican I. The third is manifest where given truths are clearly in scripture and very little definition, if any, is required. Examples are redemption and justification.

Dogmatic theology is not just an aggregate of catholic statements; it admits a certain amount of supposition and deducing of conclusions; the transcendental becomes explicit; it includes God under the formalities of true, being, good. It manifests a problem of coherence, due to the fact that what are being affirmed are mysteries. And it raises the problem of understanding mysteries. That understanding takes place through analogy and by grasping the connection of the mysteries among themselves. But that is a matter of systematics, not dogmatics.

The overlapping of positive and dogmatic theology may be addressed in another manner. Understanding the history of a doctrine and understanding the doctrine are reciprocally related to each other. We may apply the heuristic structure: description and the four modes of explanation (comparative, organic, genetic, and dialectical) as these determine a series of horizons both from the developmental viewpoint of psychology, society, and culture, and from the viewpoint of intellectual, moral, and religious conversion. Such a method includes the genesis of all dogmas and systems, a refutation of all heresies and aberrations, and an understanding of the history that puts doctrines in their concrete context.[87]

There exists a field in which positive studies are relevant only as material (secondary sources); a field which puts its own questions in its own terms with regard to historical process and uses secondary sources as an aid in making its own investigations; a field which arrives at its own results through its own methods, and that has criteria whose meaning lies beyond the horizon of merely positive investigation. Specifically, its results are not just a summary, synopsis, or encyclopedia of positive research. This field is history, the history of things done (*res gestae*), history as science (technical understanding) and as socially dynamic (as in liberalism, Marxism, and Catholicism). Non-recognition of this field results in its reappearance under other garbs, as when biblical scholars cease to be devoted exclusively to positive studies and set out to account for the existence of Christianity, to reform dogmatic theology; then they think they have a message for

---

87 Left out in the reconstruction is the following: '(3) Are Ibn K—, G.B. Vico, Hegel, Marx, Spengler, Sorokin, E. Gilson (*L'Être et l'essence*), Toynbee, C. Dawson, historians, sociologists/Msgr. Descamps: Biblical theology is not a total view of Old & New testament; some seem to think that is what it is mainly.

'(a) The questions exist

'(b) they arise when sufficiently broad & exact erudition present, compare, cultures, civilizations, epochs, periods. Arise on level of non-technical understanding over sufficiently broad field

'(c) the questions can be adequately put, defined, investigated only by a transition to technical & indeed methodical thought. Toynbee's inadequacy as a methodologist. (Walsh, Philosophy, 1963). Spengler, Sorokin (a sociologist but brushed aside: was dominant figure)'

mankind and for meeting the church's problems, when really they may be simply the source of wild opinions that will invite serious repercussions.

Illustrations may be given. The first is the theory of history as progress, decline, and redemption. The first vector is intellectual development, the second vector is sin, suffering, and death (see *Insight* chapters 6, 7, 18, and 20), and the third vector grace and resurrection.

Again, there is the illustration that runs from Tertullian's perceptualist account of the Trinity, through Origen's essentialist account where to be distinct the Son has to be another essence, through Arius's rationalist objection to the Trinity, to Athanasius's position on Christian realism. The Greek councils are the foundation of Christian realism, all without explicit advertence to the issue. The ultimate root is the connection to the word of God as true.

A third instance may be taken from development, where development means not just the new, mere expansion, multiplication, and mounting complexity, but the transposition of the problem to a higher level. In intellectual matters, we begin with nontechnical thinking. It leads to myth and magic, because nontechnical thinking is not good to the questions man raises. Technical thinking, though, leads to the Babel of philosophies and endless systems. Alternatives can be solved empirically and quickly in the empirical sciences, and in other realms they are solved empirically but very slowly; and this can lead to the death of civilization and of culture. Critical thinking builds a basic system on interiority, and insists that you may not assert what you cannot know.

A fourth instance is the relation of whole and part. Omission of a part leads to the mutilation of the whole and a distortion of the remainder. The part is difficult, obscure, disputed, has led to abuses; it is said to be so and so's opinion and to be not very important, not very useful, difficult to support universally because of divided views. It is maintained by a few with conviction, by others perfunctorily; it has to overcome even greater resistance; it is maintained in principle but generally dropped in practice; then it is dropped in principle; and finally it is excluded on principle. There is a vacuum to be filled, and there are functions to be performed; the other parts seize the opportunity; new parts are devised to fulfill the old functions; we do not give up looking for new devices; we are ready really to do anything but the impossible, namely, restore the part that was removed.

Fifth, the issue of whole and part, treated positively, leads to the principle of mediation. The technical does not replace the nontechnical or do its work. The intellectual does not replace or do the work of the technical.

But there is a mutual mediation of parts within a whole. So too, theology does not replace human science; human science does not replace natural sciences; but there is a mutual mediation, a setting of limits and functions, a differentiation and integration. Theology's history may be viewed as making a transition to the technical with the Fathers, watching the emergence of the systematic in the medievals, and reaching a technical understanding of history in modern times.

What, then, of systematic theology? Systematic theology has to move into the field of history as science, and it has to develop into the field of history as science. It must become personal, existential, psychological, social, cultural, historical. It will see the Old Testament as the prehistory of the church, and the New Testament as formative of the church. It will take seriously the history of doctrine and the history of the church. It will relate the church and the world, and to do so it has to use the human sciences of psychology and sociology, the resources of culture and history, as instruments of its own development in time. There is a historical doctrine illustrated by the bible and by church history, taught by the bible and by church doctrine, the Fathers, and so on. It gives rise to the dogmatic element and to the systematic element. The latter relies on the analogy of creaturely realities and the connection of the mysteries among themselves in order to fulfill its function.

There are several levels of communication to be considered. Dogmatic communication relies on the inerrancy of scripture and the infallibility of dogmas to express in catholic categories the same truth in the same sense as it was communicated nontechnically in another context. A technical systematic statement intends a field of presuppositions and implications. It includes questions of essence, as distinct from description. It adds hypothetical elements, with the use of analogy as systematic. The connection that it finds of the mysteries with one another is itself not revealed, but part of the hypothetical element of systematic theology. Dogmas may follow from a sound system, but systems do not follow from dogmas by logical technique without the use of intelligence. Systematics is an argument that does not prove. The best 'proof' of a system is that (1) it covers the field, and (2) it seems to be the only or best possibility.

May 28 bis (57500D0EL60)[88]

Contemporary problems arise on several levels. First, there is the level of

88 There is another item dated 'May 28' at 57400D0L060, which begins with the

nontechnical communication. There has been a vast enlargement first of the field of immediate communication through the mass media, and also of mediated communication through universal education. There has also been a relative shrinking of the impact of traditional channels.

Next, there are the relations between dogma, Scholastic theology, and church teaching. Dogma consists in what is proposed to be believed by all as divinely revealed, the same truth in the same sense as is found in the sources. Scholasticism is a scientific or rhetorical integration of dogma with the total field of human thought. The fate of Scholasticism is tied up with ambiguities regarding the notion of science, the decadence of much of Scholastic theology, the old rhetoric that it employs, and the new rhetoric called for today. Scholasticism is said to be antiquated, with the result that some are calling exclusively for a preaching theology, a *Verkündigungstheologie*,[89] or a *Verkündigungsphilosophie*.[90] Others are calling for Scholasticism to be developed. The base of a response will be found in the rational animal's mediation of himself or herself and of one's world and one's operations through knowing and willing. The church mediates its own life through theology. Initially, the church consists of Jews and Greeks, but these transformed. As to be transformed, they are Jews and Greeks, but as transformed they are Catholics. Then one concrete human being lives, understands, judges, chooses, precisely as Jew or Greek who has been converted. In the initial stage, the Jewish, the Greek, and the Catholic are not confused, but also they are not explicitly, technically distinguished. Later stages begin with the dogmatic movement among the Fathers. The church mediates itself. Technically, explicitly it determines what it is to be Catholic, and what is that reality that is said to be transformative, productive of conversion. Particular developments occur in the areas of reason, psychology, and social and cultural evolution. Then in the Scholastic stage, there is a systematic movement. A distinction occurs between the way of discovery and the way of teaching. The one divine revelation leads in the way of discovery to many dogmas, which are certain, technically expressed, develop-

---

numeral '4.' The material is related to what we have just covered and to what is presented in the current item, but there is not anything particularly new. Because of some uncertainty as to just where it belongs, it has been omitted here. But an English transcription is provided at 57400DOL060 on www.bernardlonergan.com.

89 Lonergan mentions H. Mühlen, *Der heilige Geist als Person* (Münster: Aschendorf, 1963).

90 Lonergan mentions Teilhard de Chardin.

ing over the course of time; and in the way of teaching to an understanding of the dogmas, to an understanding of what is certain, to a development of the technical terms, and to a systematic compendium. If the systematic part is omitted, the dogmatic part remains a multitude, technical but not understood and not learnable, a collection of items from different ages. The reaction is biblicism. But if the dogmatic part is omitted, there are no mysteries to be understood, and systematics turns to pseudo-problems and creates pseudo-systems. Thus we arrive at the most serious problem of contemporary theology. Experience and understanding are engaged in nontechnical ways. Judgment remains implicit. Matters are transmitted directly from both scriptural testaments to people of the twentieth century. The masses do not learn more than this. Many priests do not learn more than this. Judgment, which is fundamental, is not being formed. In spheres of both classical and historical consciousness the required differentiations are not occurring. The theoretic life of intelligence, science, wisdom, of the love of the universe, has become essentialist, deductivist, rationalist, idealist, concentrating on the per se, the universal, the abstract, the static. Or it is satisfied with *haute vulgarisation*. And the practical life of prudence, justice, fortitude, temperance, the cultivation of what is common to all and normative, has become simply juridical, legal, ideal.

2 The Method of Theology Fall and Winter 1963–64: Editorial Reconstruction[1]

Why Method? (30 October 1963, 50300D0L060)

Theology is about God and all things in relation to God. The method of theology is about theology and only indirectly about God

Why is there a question about method? The answer will take us to an investigation of what theology was like in an earlier period and to a statement about what the more manifest exigencies are today.

Aggiornamento provides us with three extrinsic reasons for a concern with method: historical consciousness, a new scientific ideal, and a new philosophical foundation.

---

1 This is an attempt to reconstruct Lonergan's 1963–64 course at the Gregorian University, 'De methodo theologiae.' This was the third time he offered a course with this title. See volume 23, *Early Works on Theological Method 2* for a much more extensive set of course notes that he distributed for the first offering of the course in the spring of 1962. An attempt to reconstruct the second offering, in the spring of 1963, forms the first item in this volume. The present reconstruction, like the previous one, is based on Lonergan's handwritten notes, available in the Lonergan Archives and on the website www.bernardlonergan.com. The 'reportatio' of Thomas Daly, s.j., who was a student in the course, was of immense assistance in this reconstruction. As with the previous item, the editor's decision is to present the material in each of the items that are included in Lonergan's course notes, even though there will at times be repetition from one class to the next. The items are divided by date, and with each item there is provided the reference number on the website where the original Latin notes may be found. Daly's notes appear on the website at 84300DTE060. The editor wishes to acknowledge the help of Michael Shields, who provided him with a translation of these notes.

First, then, historical consciousness. There are many diverse elements that have come together to give us historical consciousness. We are not dealing here with the history that is written, with books, but with the history that is written about, the various acts and deeds done. Historical consciousness is basically the transition of history itself from being implicit to being an explicit and thematized element in human awareness.

Among the diverse elements the first is the extension of the knowledge of human affairs. In terms of geography, since the fifteenth century new lands have been discovered, new peoples visited, diverse cultures written about and described. From an archeological standpoint, we know that ancient cities have been excavated and reconstructed, documents and ancient languages discovered and deciphered. Historical studies of the past have multiplied, whether social, cultural, psychological, or religious. Hebraic, Greek, and Roman traditions have ceased to be the only ones worth knowing or the only ones of absolute value; they have been relativized; each of them is but one among many; as for other cultures, which of them are better or more worthy of attention is a question to be investigated.

Next, there has developed a new way of investigating human activities: no longer, as with Augustine, according to the eternal reasons, but in accord with human beings as they are in the concrete: families as they are and not as they ought to be, economies and states as they are and not as they ought to be, and so on. Human studies now have an empirical foundation. It is not a matter of positing a definition and drawing conclusions, since there is a historical series of definitions, conceptions, and images to be narrated, and a historical series of systems, of *Weltanschauungen*, to be reviewed.

Third, the investigator himself or herself and one's method and system and *Weltanschauung* are no more than a standpoint. They do not stand outside the series but are in the series. If in fact they are anything more than this, this would have to be established, and it is not established by empirical methods. And so the experts in the various fields do not care much about this issue. They are expert in their own fields; everything else, including this question, lies outside their field, and so is just another specialization. Still, until the question of whether one's standpoint enables one to see the object clearly is resolved, there is a relativization on the side of both the object and the subject.[2]

---

2 Reference was made here to Husserl's *Die Krisis der europäischen Wissenschaften und der transzendentale Phänomenologie*, with its stress on scientific conventionalism. See above, p. 75, note 80.

Fourth, human reality itself is apprehended in various ways. The Greeks and the medievals spoke about human nature as something stable and well known, a metaphysical nature common to all. But that nature is common not only to the human beings who bring things about but also to infants, to those who are asleep, and to the insane. Besides this *esse naturale* there is the *esse intentionale* of those who intend, of their acts of intending, and of the world that is intended. There is an order of knowing and willing and of the known and chosen, and in that order the whole of human affairs and the whole of human history are included. The human soul will be judged according to its *esse intentionale*: what have you known, and what have you chosen? This is not just the opinion of idealists but a fact evident to realists as well. Human life develops not in infants and the insane but in the intentional order.

Fifth, there is increased awareness of human dominance. In order to subject nonhuman nature to human choice, science is necessary, as are the application of the sciences, the invention of machines, and the development of their use. But in order to subject human reality to human choice, all that is required are apprehension and decision; human realities belong to the intentional order.

Sixth, thus it can be seen what historical consciousness is. Everything that human beings do belongs to history, but implicitly and in practice, as it were, until historical consciousness comes on the scene. That is, unless the apprehension of history itself and a sense of responsibility with regard to history emerge – responsibility for which institutions are to be retained, which to be developed, and which to be jettisoned – and unless deliberate decision intervenes, the role of history remains implicit. But with these conditions met, such apprehension, sense of responsibility, and decision emerge, and history itself passes from the implicit and lived to the explicit and thematized.

Seventh, the question whether historical consciousness exists can be approached phenomenologically, by asking what 'isms' are. Apprehension, deliberation, and choice are placed in a larger context, with the result that this context itself also becomes an object of apprehension, deliberation, and choice, and so passes from the implicit and lived to the explicit and thematized. The object of apprehension, deliberation, and choice extends beyond particular concrete realities to a network of connections. Thus, feudalism was little understood in its own time, but now we understand it in relation to monarchy, parliamentary arrangements, political liberalism, democracy, progress, totalitarianism. All of these are apprehended consciously. The 'ism' is the context. Similarly, in economics there are mercantilism, laissez-faire capitalism, socialism, communism; in religion there are Catholicism, Protestantism, religious liberalism, agnosticism, militant humanistic atheism; in literature there are classicism, romanticism, symbolism; in art there are impressionism, cubism, abstractionism, surrealism; in theology there are the liturgical movement, the biblical movement, the catechetical movement; and finally in historicism, everything is located within a total historical context.

Theology is a particular fact: human, religious, Catholic, and from the twelfth and thirteenth century scientific. It is expounded in numerous writings, and imposed on everyone who aspires to the priesthood. But what does it do? What can it do? What should it do? What is its place, what is its task, not in the abstract but in that total process that we call history? It has an influence upon the lives of human beings both inside and outside the church. Here is where the question is put about the method of theology, where theology is a series of ideas, deliberations, and choices made concretely; the question is put so that theology may attain an explicit and thematized consciousness about itself, so that it may be apprehended, so that deliberations may be entered into in its regard, so that decisions may be made about it, and so that a critique of theologians may be pursued.

A second extrinsic reason why we are dealing with the method of theology is that a new ideal of science has emerged. The tremendous growth of the sciences in our time is known to everyone. But the very notion, *ratio*, essence of science has been transformed. The ideal that the ancient Greeks formed for themselves and that the medieval theologians adapted to theological exigencies has itself been profoundly changed by concrete modern methods. Theology is analogously a science, but a proportion is always to something, and the question is whether it should be conformed or proportionate to the Greek ideal or to the modern ideal of science. The *Dictionnaire de théologie catholique* is aware of the new ideal, but for a brief period of time it opted for the old ideal in theology, even in Congar's article 'Théologie.'[3]

In the Greek ideal, science is about the necessary. That it is *also* about the necessary, I agree. But principally it is about that intelligibility that de facto is verified. '$d_2s/dt_2 = g$' is not necessary, but it is understood and verified; accelerations are understood but not as necessary. Scotus viewed science to

---

3 On Congar, see above, p. 79, note 86.

be about the necessary, and it followed for him that theology treats only of every possible world. The result or corollary of this was voluntarism. The problem of nature and grace is an instance. Either the gratuity of grace is denied or nature and grace are in separate worlds, if the sole relation of intelligibility is necessity. But empirical intelligibility solves the question. Grace is not demanded but it *is* understood and verified in its own way. The argument in theology is from fittingness, an argument that does not prove. According to empirical understanding fittingness becomes a proper object of science and of theology.

Again, in the Greek ideal, science is about what is per se evident or can be deduced syllogistically from what is evident. Part of science *is* that, but not Euclid and not Newton. Deduction is principally from hypotheses, so that verification can be more complete.

Again, in the Greek ideal science is about the certain: *certa rerum per causas cognitio.* Of science *in facto esse* that is true, but science *in fieri* is a matter of the probable corrected by the more probable. Certitude is put off to a remote future.

Again, in the Greek ideal science is about the universal, and so history cannot be scientific. That science is *also* about the universal, I concede, but not that it is *only* about the universal. Prudence proceeds beyond universals and varies in accord with particular details, composing laws and applying them to particular cases. In like manner, history is about deeds that have been prudently or imprudently performed, and so history is intelligible in the manner of prudence. There exists a total field of intelligibility that is investigated by historical methods and that is not attained by any abstract and defined universality.

Again, in the Greek ideal science is about the unchangeable, the immovable, so that motion is understood only from its term. And again, that science is *also* about such realities, I agree, but in motion itself there is found intelligibility and law, as is manifested by d_2s/dt_2. There is development also in theology, where the term is understood from the motion. There are genetic and dialectical studies of development that regard a situation and understand it insofar as they understand motion. To understand dogmas one needs more than logical analysis. Dogma is the term of a development; just as terms are understood from motion, so dogmas are understood from the development of dogma. To understand a doctrine is to understand the history of the doctrine.

Again, in the Greek ideal science is about what is per se. But statistics discovers intelligibility in what is *per accidens*. History treats not only what happens in accord with the intentions of agents but especially how things happen beyond and even against the intentions of agents.

Again, in the Greek ideal science is through causes. This is valid today, in that science is not about brute facts or a mere collection of facts but about their constitutive intelligibility. But the notion of causality develops concretely. Efficient causes are known not in pure science but in applied science. Final causes in the human sciences are also a matter of application.

Thus, intelligibility in science is complex. There is the heuristic intelligibility of common principles, the systematic intelligibility that is had when intelligence employs defined terms in open and closed series – in theology, this is the intelligibility of the mysteries – and the positive intelligibility that responds to particular questions and that is also found in common sense. System is a matter of definitions and of a fundamental grasp determining mutual proportions.

The field of the sciences is greatly extended over time. Aristotle transposed the Platonic Ideas from their empyrean heaven to material things. The new ideal eliminates the Platonic element entirely. Things are not investigated inasmuch as they have necessity, intrinsic evidence, immediate certitude, universality, immobility, a per se status; all things are investigated as they are, whether natural realities or human realities. The intelligibility sought is empirical. It is difficult to grasp. It is probable. It resides in the particulars themselves, in what changes, in what is *per accidens*.

The changed ideal and the extended field of science invade theology and change it, causing both confusion and doubt.

First, there is a successive invasion of the changed ideal in scriptural and patristic studies and in the study of the theologians. Altaner's patristic studies proceed in accord with the new ideal.[4] The same is true of biblical and medieval studies.

Second, theology itself is radically and intrinsically affected, and this in four ways.

The first of these has to do with authority. Theology relies on authorities. What did so and so hold? An answer is awaited as the many documents are being read. Such studies do not work solely to prepare proofs for dogmatic theologians. They seek their own special understanding and ask their own questions. Thus, authorities themselves have become objects of the new studies. What they meant is not known except by pursuing the new stud-

---

4 See above, p. 22, note 29.

ies. And these studies themselves do not arrive at certitude but at hypotheses and probabilities, whether in the interpretation of scripture or of the Fathers or of Thomas Aquinas. Regarding Thomas, there have been the classical commentators, but today there is gradually forming a new body of knowledge about him and his work.

The second way in which theology is affected has to do with theological notions and systems. While once it was the case that a notion was defined and held to be true, now we are aware of a historical series of notions. For example, take the notion of the person. Once there was a fixed definition, but now there is a series of definitions. To avoid a mere multiplication and reach some unity, there is needed a method, which is something more than Aristotelian dialectic. As for systems, Scholastic opinions are hypotheses, and lack a method of verification. There is a multitude of systems, and each one of them is difficult. Recourse is had to pluralism, that is, to the notion that reality is so multiform and rich that it cannot be known except by many diverse notions and systems. Thus, the ellipse has explanations that are conic, or in terms of Cartesian coordinates, or polar coordinates, or elliptical functions. These are various ways of apprehending the same reality. With regard to the scientific ideal, see P. Boutroux, *L'idéal scientifique des mathématiciens*.[5] The Greek ideal was governed by aesthetic limits. The deductivist ideal found in Descartes and Leibniz culminated in Russell and Whitehead, *Principia Mathematica*,[6] and in Hilbert. Pluralism acknowledges diverse systems and notions, whether in the natural sciences or in the human sciences.

The third way in which theology is affected has to do with the latent ambiguity that surrounds the notion of science and its methodological foundations. Those who write about theology today are neither so conservative as to follow the Greek ideal nor so modern as openly to accept modern methods under every aspect, nor so bold as to try to think out a synthesis. The problem is that where the extremes are left in an indeterminate and confused state, implicitly and in actual practice theologians will vacillate. There is a collection of adaptations without clear determinations and rules. Theologians waver between the extremes.

5 Pierre Boutroux, *L'idéal scientifique des mathématiciens dans l'Antiquité et les temps modernes*, new ed. (Paris: Presses universitaires de France, 1955; Sceaux: Éditions Jacques Gabay, 1992).

6 Alfred North Whitehead and Bertrand Russell, *Principia Mathematica*, 3 vols. (Cambridge: Cambridge University Press, first ed., 1910–13; 2nd ed., 1925–27; regularly reprinted).

The fourth way in which theology is affected is that this ambiguity tends to eliminate dogmatic theology. 'Let us hear from the experts,' we hear; this means biblical exegetes in biblical studies, patristic scholars in patristic studies, medieval experts in medieval studies, and students of modern theology in more recent studies. There is no discipline that considers everything and does so *de iure*, as theology used to do. Then the only recourse in times of crisis is to listen to the magisterium.

The new historical consciousness and the new scientific ideal demand new philosophical foundations.[7]

Ernst Cassirer, *Das Erkenntnisproblem in der Philosophie und Wissenschaft der neuerer Zeit* (Berlin I, II, 3rd ed., 1922) (1st ed., 1906), III 1920, Yale UP IV 1950. The evolution of science is very closely connected with the development of modern philosophy. The questions of modern philosophers arise from the evolution of modern sciences, although they do not think of this.

Edmund Husserl, *Die Krisis der europäischen Wissenschafter und die transzendentale Phänomenologie* (The Hague: M. Nijhoff, 1954) with the best critical treatment of conventionalism, of people who think only about their specialty and not about the foundations of their own sciences, but also a way of thinking that is excessively dominated by the Greek ideal of science as rigorous and necessary.

Bernard Lonergan, *Insight*.

There is a very dangerous option before us, between the dead end of the necessary and the groundlessness of an uncritical historical consciousness and a superficial understanding of modern science without any notion of a rigorous method to guide and direct it. It is very dangerous to follow historicism without considering method.[8]

Foundations, Science, and Cognitional Structure
(5 November 1963, 50600D0L060)

The new science seeks and requires new philosophical foundations. An-

---

7 The references to Cassirer, Husserl, and Lonergan's own book *Insight* are intended as examples of attempts to come to grips with the foundational question in science.

8 Lonergan's notes in 50400D0L060 may be out of place. Those in 50500D0L060 begin by mentioning Macquarrie's *Twentieth-Century Religious Thought*, but the order of Lonergan's topics is not taken from that book but seems to be his own. The file is dated Oct. 30, but Lonergan adds 'non dicta,' i.e., he did not lecture on it. Thus, the next set of notes for the course is 50600D0L060.

cient science itself grounds a domain that is abstract, necessary, per se evident, universal, immobile, certain. But the sciences treat the concrete, the contingent, the hypothetical, the particular, the changeable, the probable. A new foundation, similar to what it grounds, is needed for this domain. New arts and techniques are to be discovered, developed, explicated, added. It is not a matter of subtraction. The old foundation should not be done away with. Rather, we must dig more deeply and be prepared to draw fuller conclusions. (We are using the words 'old' and 'new' as they are commonly accepted, and not as they have been erroneously appropriated. To remove the error would entail learning not what the manuals say but what Aristotle and Aquinas say, and also learning how the modern sciences really proceed and not opinions about modern science. Einstein himself admitted that modern scientists are not very astute in saying just what they are doing. Once these matters have been attended to, one would have to compare the genuine Aristotle and Aquinas with the genuine modern methods and discern where there is identity, where there is continuity, and where there is development.[9] This would entail an entire course.)

The new arts and techniques have to do with abstraction and structure. For Aquinas on abstraction, see Aristotle's *Metaphysics*, Z, and then Aquinas, *In VII Met.*, lect. 9–12, on the parts of the form and the parts of the matter; also Aquinas, *In Boet. de Trin.*, q. 5, a. 3.[10] Abstraction is not a question of common nouns; that is a linguistic problem. Abstraction is a question of the object of science in Aristotle's *Posterior Analytics*; it is about definition and the consequent demonstration or deduction. The issue is the abstraction of form from sensible matter, as of the circle from a cartwheel; or the abstraction of the whole from the parts of the matter. (A part cannot be abstracted from the whole; a foot cannot be abstracted from an animal – it would no longer be a foot.)

Structure is of the parts in a whole. It is known insofar as the relation of the parts among themselves and the relation of the parts to the whole are understood. It can't be known by those who don't care to work at understanding, or who don't want to understand something new, or who ask, What's the use of it? Structure is known not by subtraction but by the addi-

9 For Lonergan's own attempts along these lines, see 'Isomorphism of Thomist and Scientific Thought,' chapter 9 in *Collection*, vol. 4 in Collected Works of Bernard Lonergan, ed. Frederick E. Crowe and Robert M. Doran (Toronto: University of Toronto Press, 1988).
10 On abstraction and structure, see above, p. 19, and below, p. 161–87.

tion of understanding, the addition of an intelligibility that can be found in the thing known. It cannot be had except by turning to phantasms, without which we understand nothing at all. The structure exists not in itself and not apart from the concrete and the particular but in the concrete and the particular. It demands the concrete and the particular as a relation demands a base and a term, or as understanding requires phantasms. It admits not abstraction but precision. Even as we intend the whole we attend to certain parts. We do not say everything at once or attend to everything at once. Structure can be found not only in what is changeable but even in the very changes, as the interdependence of the movements. It can recur not in spite of many things but in many things. And once the structure of one thing is understood, we understand also the structure of some other realities without any new learning.

Structure can recur in various ways, as an invariance or constancy. Variation may occur according to a determinate law, as in series of structures. Or there may be series that differ from one another, where the difference itself may be because of a determinate law. It is not absolutely necessary that any particular thing have structure. It is a matter of empirical intelligibility. The structure has to be verified in fact. De facto things could be different. Structure is evident when it is grasped by understanding, and this requires work and earnest and astute seeking. But what is grasped by understanding does not exist necessarily. It is contingent, able to be or not to be. In itself it grounds a hypothesis, a theory. To determine whether things are such requires a judgment, and the judgment may be certain or probable. In the notion of structure are to be found all the elements that are present in the new ideal of science.We spoke of digging more deeply, and the structure that is uncovered is cognitional structure. Before conception there is understanding, but understanding emerges from wonder about experience. Experience and understanding together yield conception, which is a composition of the experienced and the understood. The intelligible is grasped in and added to the phantasms. This is abstraction yielding conception. St Thomas is not at all silent about this. He often speaks of the act of understanding, and very rarely about universals.

There is an analogy of proportion between those things that have a common structure. Matter is to form as the eye is to vision or the ear to hearing. As vision is to seeing, so the faculty of hearing is to actually hearing. *In IX Met.*, lect. 5, §§ 1828–29.

Cognitional structure is presented in detail in *Insight*. Here we can provide only very brief indications. The structure of human cognition is the foundation of method. It is found in our conscious operations, in the immediate data of consciousness. The relations between the operations are themselves conscious.

Generically, 'knowledge' is said of any cognitive act, whether it be *ipsum intelligere* (God), the beatific vision, angelic knowledge, human knowledge, or animal vision. But specifically human knowledge is structured. Experience without understanding is not knowledge but stupidity. Experience can be sensitive or external, or it can be the interior experience of the data of consciousness. We are moved from what we experience to understanding by wonder. We want to know what is, that is, being. To experience and understand without judgment is to consider, to speculate, to doubt, but not to know. Otherwise astronomy and astrology, chemistry and alchemy, history and legend, science and myth would be the same thing. To judge before one has understood is irrational. We are moved to judgment from experience and understanding by critical reflection, asking the question 'Is it so?'

The structure of human knowledge consists, then, of experience, understanding, and judging. All are conscious, as are the relations between them. Through wonder we are moved from experiencing to understanding; through critical reflection we are moved from understanding to judging. A single specifically human act of knowing comes to be through a structure consisting of many acts. There is an isomorphism between knowing and the known. As knowing is composed of partially incremental acts, so an object is composed of partially incremental objects: potency, form, existence.

We can ask, Is it so? regarding this structure, however. And we can answer not by comparing concepts or by grasping a necessary connection, but by interior experience. Each one can do it for himself or herself. If I ask, Is my knowing this sort of structure? I am doubting; and therefore I am rational. If I am doubting, I am doubting about something that has been understood. Otherwise, to judge would be irrational. If there is understanding, there is something that is understood, something about which we asked 'Quid sit?' We inquire about what is given in experience. Nobody says that never in his life has he judged reasonably. Nobody says that never in his life has he understood anything. Nobody says that never in his life has he experienced anything. If one did say this, he would not be speaking from any deep understanding, so nobody should listen to him.

Am I always like this? There are various patterns of experience, as is argued in chapter 6 of *Insight*. In scientific, philosophical, and theological matters, this is surely how I ought to be. It is an ideal to be learned by discipline and practice. While I am sleeping I dream: this is empirical consciousness, with a minimum of understanding and much less of rationality. But when I wake up, there is at least empirical consciousness. I can lie in the sun next to the sea and watch the clouds pass by without bothering about understanding anything, but I don't live that way all the time. I do understand, whether it be with respect to a work of art, where there is understanding in the aesthetic pattern, or with regard to what to say in a given situation, so that there is understanding in the dramatic pattern, or whether it has to do with what is to be done, revealing understanding in the practical pattern. The structure of the operations is such that they recur to a greater or lesser extent and more or less perfectly. They are occurring even when I utter contradictions and counterpositions, such as the view that to know is to perceive, the myth of trying to understand human knowledge by analogy with sense.

The concrete, a thing in all its reality, we do not know. We do not know anything in this way. Therefore it is unknown; it is not some abstract concept. To solve this, distinguish knowing from intending. We intend the concrete, being, which is not what is greatest in denotation and least in connotation but what is greatest in both denotation and connotation.

The New Foundation (6 November 1963, 50700D0L060)

In the immediate data of consciousness there are given the structured operations and the relations between them. The conscious subject who does not deny his or her rationality and who is not stupid about everything is the principle, not some logically prior objects, not questions about exact formulation and deduction, but the known conscious subject. The new foundation is that the principle, the conscious subject, is also known, being in its illuminated existence, categories that properly are categories, rendering all other categories secondary. Where a principle is affirmed to lie in a proposition or object, there arises a crisis of reason. See the essay of S. Breton in *La crise de la raison dans la pensée contemporaine.* For him the principles of sufficient reason and identity are accepted only in a formulation where all difficulties are foreseen; otherwise questions about formulation and deduction, conditioned by place and time, are endless.[11] Rather, the principle is had in the conscious subject, even if it is not perfectly formulated.

11 See Edmond Barbotin, Jean Trouillard, Roger Verneaux, Dominique Dubarle, and Stanislas Breton, *La crise de la raison dans la pensée contemporaine* (Bruges: Desclée de Brouwer, 1960).

Again, the 'concrete' is a thing taken in its total reality. Nothing is known by us in this way, and to the extent that something is not known by us in this way, it remains unknown. Nor can we abstractly conceive the concrete, for whatever we conceive abstractly is abstract, not concrete.

So how do we say 'concrete,' if neither the sensible nor the intelligible nor the abstractly conceived nor knowledge suffices? We must distinguish knowing from intending. Specifically human knowing is experience, understanding, and judgment, while by 'intending' is meant consciously tending towards an end by intellectual and rational consciousness. Besides 'quid sit' and 'an sit' there is simply 'sit.' '*Ens dicitur ab esse*, being is said from "to be."'[12] Being is the objective that we seek in every question; that objective is intelligible (*quid sit*) and unconditioned (*an sit*, where we seek what can be posited absolutely, what is independent of ourselves, what is without conditions). We never reach the end of our intending. What we intend is concrete. The concrete is the same as being. Everyone who intends the concrete intends being, the whole, everything. Outside of being there is nothing. Contrary to Scotus and Hegel, for whom being is the greatest in denotation and the least in connotation, for us being is greatest in both denotation and connotation.

Still, this intending is not knowledge. We intend the concrete whole, but we know only a part. In every judgment, we posit 'is.' In every concept, we posit what pertains to being: we think in order to judge. But there are many things that we do not conceive, and concerning many things that we do conceive we do not judge but doubt. We intend a priori, whereas we know a posteriori. We ask why because we do not know and are aware of our ignorance. This awareness *is* the agent intellect. We ask whether a thing is because we do not know whether it is. We do not yet know. This is ignorance and the awareness of being ignorant, and the light of agent intellect. But we know a posteriori, in that 'an sit' supposes something understood in data, and 'quid sit' supposes the data themselves. The data are simply given. They do not depend on us.

We also intend God a priori, but we know God not only a posteriori but also mediately. To intend being is to intend the unconditioned, the absolutely posited, what is independent and without conditions. But the unconditioned is either the virtually unconditioned, which has conditions that

---

12 See Thomas Aquinas, *Summa contra Gentiles*, 1, c. 25: 'nomen entis ab esse [imponitur].'

are fulfilled, or the formally unconditioned, which has absolutely no conditions whatsoever. What has conditions that are fulfilled is, but contingently. What has no conditions is in the fullest sense: God. The one who knows God, affirms that 'God is' is true, and this affirmation is the conclusion of a syllogistic reasoning from creatures.

From intending and through intending we proceed to knowledge. From intending: the question 'Quid sit?' promotes the mind from the experienced to the intelligible; the question 'An sit?' moves the mind from the intelligible to the unconditioned. Through intending: here we find the principle that is the foundation of all method, namely, that we know inasmuch as we answer questions. The answers are answers to questions. They are somehow precontained in the questions, and they somehow emerge from the questions. *Insight* shows this in mathematical and scientific examples.

The structure of human knowledge is both vertical – experience, understanding, judgment – and transverse and dynamic: from the intended as unknown to the intended as known, so that the intended as unknown has an influence on the very becoming of knowledge.

'Being' names the concrete whole that is intended and unknown, intended and to be known, intended and known. Insofar as 'being' names the 'to be known' it is a heuristic notion, the first, principal, fundamental heuristic notion, the foundation of all method.

Just as being as the 'to be known' is a heuristic notion, so metaphysics may be conceived as the fundamental heuristic structure. As 'being' names the concrete whole that is intended, that is to be known, and that is partly known, so 'act' names what is to be known insofar as we say 'is,' 'form' names what is to be known insofar as we understand, and 'potency' names what is to be known insofar as we experience. Metaphysics does not function as a science of particulars but anticipates the structure of what is investigated by the sciences of particulars.

The distinction between intending and knowing extends to a distinction between the intending itself and knowledge of the intending. Everyone intends being, whether Aquinas or Matthew, Mark, Luke, and John. Not everyone attends to the intention of being, understands what it is, and judges concerning its existence. In like manner, even if everyone intends being, not everyone knows metaphysics or ontology. Because of this radical intending, the categories of the various sciences and those proposed by a number of philosophers (e.g., Kant) are not categories properly so called. The categories that properly are categories have to do with the radical intending. As intending, the intention is the desire of intellect, the apex of the soul, the origin of questions, of wonder, of critical reflection. And as intended, the intention itself is the concrete whole, *ta panta, to pan*.

We have been seeking the philosophic foundations of modern science. We have moved from an abstract object to a concrete, structured object, from a *de iure* subject to a conscious, concrete subject that is consciously structured. We have not located the foundations of method in conclusions. We have located categories not in concepts but in questions, not in knowledge but in intentions. We have reduced the transcendentals – being, one, true, good – to something that 'quoad nos' is prior: the operations by which everyone operates, whether a metaphysician, a positivist, a conventionalist, an existentialist, a perceptualist, a realist.

Turning to Theology (12 November 1963, 50800D0L060)

Now we turn our attention explicitly to theology. There are several theologies. They are distinguished in accord with their end, their principle, and their medium. The end is to know God and all else in relation to God, but in natural theology, where God is known as the origin and end of all things, the principle is the natural light of reason, while in a theology that relies on revelation the principle is reason illumined by faith, and in heaven the principle will be created intellect strengthened by the light of glory. The medium in natural theology is found in created things in their natural mode of existence. In a theology where God enters our intentional order through revelation, the medium is the whole Christ, Christ and the church, the whole Christian fact, Christianity in all its aspects, the result of the Father sending the Son and of the Father and the Son sending the Spirit to establish the new law of grace. In heaven, there is no medium; God is attained immediately through the divine essence itself.

'Principle' here is used not in the logical sense of first propositions. Rather, it means some reality that is the source of all propositions. In theology there are not two principles, reason and faith, in some sort of mixture, but the one principle of reason illumined by faith. Reason illumined by faith is a sublation of natural reason[13] for the sake of understanding an entirely new field of investigation. Faith transforms life, including the life of reason, and so we have a single composite principle of theology.

---

13 Lonergan refers to Karl Rahner, *Hörer des Wortes*, 1942, for the notion of the 'Aufhebung der Philosophie.'

The medium is not restricted to propositions as true in various theological *loci*. Attention is paid rather to a complex historical reality in all its dimensions. There is an inadequate distinction between the principle (this particular theologian) and the medium (all theologians and all the faithful and the whole Christ). The principle is the theologian, but the theologian is also the medium, in that one knows in oneself what the Christian life is.

There are four uses of theology: expository-constitutive, sapiential, practical in the church, and practical outside the church; the latter includes apologetics.

The expository-constitutive use is theology as a particular science, the theologians' theology. As chemistry is about compounds and biology is about living things, so theology has its own field, namely, the supernatural order. Theology expounds this order, in an austere and academic fashion, whether this be the theology that has been acquired and is to be transmitted in the schools or the theology that remains to be acquired and perfected through progress in the doctrine of the faith. Two questions about method, therefore, arise: one concerning the transmission, and the other concerning the perfecting.

The sapiential use of theology has to do with its relationships to philosophy, the human sciences, the natural sciences, the humanities, the arts, history – in a word, the rest of the academic world. Formerly, theology was thought of as the 'queen of the sciences,' but now it is better regarded as at best a constitutional monarch. We can progress to theology as sapiential insofar as we have a deep knowledge of philosophy and the sciences.

The internal practical use of theology is for building up the Body of Christ and all things in Christ. The life of the faithful as it is actually lived ought to be known, so that theology may influence Christian life through catechetics, preaching, spiritual direction, liturgy, education, and the communications media, including theatre, books, radio, and television.

The external practical use of theology, through adding concrete knowledge of human life in all its forms, helps the church to be a beacon raised up for the nations, not a ghetto. In this way, theology may be a help to those who do not believe or do not believe as they ought. Here theology stands in service of the church in its function in human history. This includes but is not limited to apologetics.

In this course we are dealing mainly with the expository use of theology, which ought to be such that, by adding other bodies of knowledge, whether academic knowledge or knowledge of the life of the faithful or of human life in general, it may develop into wisdom and be practical both internally and externally. It has a potentiality to be connected and, once connected, to be enriched. And while expository theology is both theology to be transmitted (the work of scholars) and theology to be acquired and perfected (the way of teaching), we are paying more attention to theology as to be acquired and perfected, to theology not as closed but as open, not as static but as dynamic.

Attention turns next to the parts of theology. There is a twofold manner of dividing expository theology. The first is by material parts: the Trinity, the Incarnate Word, grace, the virtues, the church, and sacraments. The principle of division is the various 'things' that are treated. There are many difficulties with this division as it now exists.

A second manner of dividing theology is methodical, a division into integral parts. Questions are different because procedures are different. Questions recur in each of the treatises; they develop along with development in theology; they form a whole, just as in an organism eyes, ears, heart, and lungs each have their proper functions, which they perform for the good of the whole body. The totality of functions is required in order to have an organism. So too, in expository theology there are integral parts. No part by itself suffices.

What are the integral parts? Well, knowledge is composite, but the elements constitute one knowledge. The operations are experience, understanding, and judgment; their respective terms are the experienced, intelligible order, and truth. These can be improved upon with a different emphasis. That is, one can attend more to experience or more to the order of understanding or more to truth and certitude. In theology, specialization in experience yields positive theology, specialization in intelligence yields systematic theology, and specialization in certitude yields dogmatic theology. These specializations may be quite conscious. We can reflect on science and so develop method. We can reflect on philosophy and so develop transcendental method. We can reflect on theology and so develop a critical transcendental method. The method will be the same in each of the treatises, a matter of experience, understanding, and judgment.

Positive theology investigates single documents and monuments in order to ascertain what biblical theology, patristic theology, medieval theology, modern and contemporary theology mean. There is an instrumental part, which consists in editing the documents critically, preparing bibliographies, and so on. The systematic part is concerned with understanding the mysteries. The dogmatic part performs what Pius XII called the noblest task of theology, ascertaining how the faith of the church as expressed in dogma is contained in the sources. As chapter 1 of *Divinarum personarum* shows, the systematic part is *sui generis* and is not easily confused with the other two parts.[14] But the distinction between positive theology and dogmatic theology becomes more difficult. At the end of the sixteenth century they were the same. The distinction was between moral theology and dogmatic theology, and dogmatic theology was whatever was not moral theology. Biblical theology was used to furnish proofs for dogmatic statements, and so was a part of dogmatic theology. The same was true for patristics. But today positive theology has its own tasks. The study of scripture and again the study of the Fathers have their own proper ends, which are not restricted to the ends of dogmatic theology.

Positive and Dogmatic Theology (13 November, 51000D0L060)[15]

The external situation that provokes the methodological problem, as we have seen, is threefold: the development of historical consciousness, the modern scientific ideal, and transcendental philosophy. The situation internal to theology that likewise provokes the problem is specialization. What once was done in a unit by operations not clearly distinct from one another now is done only in parts, with each part having its own goal, its own object, and its own method. The methods are distinguished in such a manner that they are opposed to one another, and unless they are distinguished they tend to destroy one another. The part with the clearer method destroys the others. The parts in this instance are positive, systematic, and dogmatic theology.

What is positive theology? It researches the documents and material vestiges of the faith to determine their meaning. It is divided and subdivided in accord with subject matter: biblical (Old and New Testaments and their internal divisions), patristics, councils, papal documents, medieval theology, modern and contemporary theology. It considers both Catholic and heretical materials. It is theology in indirect discourse. The positive theologian does not directly speak of God and of other matters as they are related to God, but rather narrates what someone else once said and meant. It is

14 On *Divinarum personarum*, see above, p. 7, note 9.
15 50900E0L060 is a one-page entry on 'concretum,' the concrete. It is not dated, but it is related to other items in this set in that it emphasizes that we do not know, but rather intend, the concrete in all its details. Because its content has been treated already, it is omitted here.

about the theology of someone else: what Isaiah held, or Aquinas. It does not immediately state what is to be believed, but suspends that sort of judgment. It moves from the probable to the more probable, presenting the actual state of the question. Perhaps the question will appear in a different way in the future. Is it a science? Yes. There is a similar development. The conclusion is a personal interpretation from which a common opinion is derived. The positive theologian does not want to say what is to be believed in the church. In order to make a judgment regarding truth, wisdom is needed, and in supernatural matters a supernatural wisdom. It belongs to the church to judge about the true meaning and interpretation of scripture, not because it has undertaken special studies but because it enjoys supernatural wisdom from the Holy Spirit.

Positive theology may be spoken of in general and with regard to particular considerations. In speaking of it in general, we ask about questions, about intelligibility, and about judgment.

Positive theology treats questions that spontaneously and as it were immediately arise from the documents themselves. Who wrote what, under what conditions, where, when, how, and using what means?

The intelligibility discovered in positive theology must be what is found in the data themselves. There are various types of understanding. There is the understanding that can be strictly conceptualized, and there is another type that does not admit of universal definition or systematic formulation, but that occurs in a concrete situation. In a military battle, there are two generals with two battle plans, but the battle does not go according to the plan of either one of them, even though it does depend on these plans. After the battle someone reads the two plans and takes into account other circumstances to arrive at the understanding that is in the particulars, which is then related and described but not systematized. This is the sort of understanding that the positive theologian seeks to attain.

How is judgment made according to positive method? The intelligibility reached by understanding is corrected by the discovery of further data and the rearrangement of data in new seriations. It is not corrected by an appeal to the magisterium or to Denzinger or to the Fathers or other theologians. Such appeals may be correct, but they do not represent progress in positive theology itself. Only additional data or a deeper appreciation of the data will do. The question is not truth or falsity as such but the intelligibility inherent in the data.

Thus, positive theology, precisely as positive, is concerned with questions that arise from examining the data and comparing them with other data.

The intelligibility sought is one that emerges from the data themselves. And judgment is most effective if it emerges from a deeper examination of the data and from findings that may have been overlooked previously.

Some further points may be listed about positive theology, the better to determine its nature.

First, the positive theologian is not concerned with what is clear, certain, and common, with what is doubtlessly held by all the prophets, the Synoptics, John, and Paul, but with what is unclear, probable, singular, and in need of elucidation.

Second, the positive theologian works not to arrive immediately at the fullness of truth, but to do so gradually and in accord with the procedure of the proper positive method.

Third, the goal is that the mind of any given author or of all authors of a given period may be exactly determined in every aspect.

Fourth, we must distinguish positive studies from empirical human sciences such as economics, sociology, psychology, and linguistics, which also proceed from the data and seek an understanding in the data and are corrected through the data, since the latter sciences not only describe and narrate but also define and employ deductions and take on a systematic form, treating as they do laws, structures, and seriations that recur. A positive study does not proceed from hypotheses that can be explicitly affirmed and verified, but only from hypotheses that are inherent in particulars. Positive studies may receive help from the human sciences; thus, economics can provide help in understanding the crises in the Roman Empire. But their usefulness is in application to the concrete data of positive studies.

Fifth, positive studies are distinguished also from those explanatory inquiries that occupy a sort of middle position, where explanation is reduced to general principles, but these are discerned only over longer periods of time and as the result of many strictly positive studies. An example is Herbert Butterfield, *The Origins of Modern Science*.[16] Many advances were made between 1300 and 1800, but before 1700 they were contained in an Aristotelian context, so that science was neither self-consistent nor able to reply to objects. Only after the demise of the Aristotelian context did modern science really exist. The Aristotelian context opposed the newly emerging

---

16 Herbert Butterfield, *The Origins of Modern Science: 1300–1800* (New York: Macmillan, 1951); a revised edition was published by the Free Press (New York) in 1966.

context. The discovery of new facts scarcely touched the Aristotelian context for centuries. Something similar is true regarding the understanding of the development of dogma. It presupposes many positive studies researching particular developments over several centuries.

This intermediate form of study deserves greater attention. It emerges when what is explained is something particular. Modern science emerged only once. Every dogma was developed only once, nor is development the same in every instance. The principles are general but the matter is particular. The explanation is through systematic understanding. Questions arise in the field of positive inquiry that cannot be answered with the type of understanding that belongs to positive studies. This is especially true when the people being investigated accomplished more than they knew they were doing. Athanasius in no way wanted development in dogma, but he contributed to it nonetheless. To his way of thinking there was no dogmatic development at Nicea. Positive studies will reveal that there was development, but they will by themselves not be able to explain it. There is a totality that is inexplicable in terms of positive studies, which regard every attempt to understand it as mere speculation. Positive theologians will tend to say that such questions are insoluble, simply because they cannot be solved by positive methods. Or they will disregard those who attempt solutions, because the latter are not employing positive methods.

The dogmatic method is distinct from the positive method. Dogma, according to the First Vatican Council, is what is proposed by the church as divinely revealed and to be believed by all. And according to *Humani generis,* the noblest task of theology is to show how the doctrine defined by the church is contained in the sources in the precise sense in which it is defined.

The process from the sources to dogma is a process of universalization on the part of those apprehending. It is the process from faith in Mark and in John to the universal catholic faith. The process is from the apprehension found in preaching to the common confession of a common faith, and from that common confession to an account of what is necessary for such a common confession to occur, that is, what must be believed. What Christ taught is one. Among the people it becomes one that is common to many through preaching, and so it becomes universal in reality. The minds of the faithful profess in common what is believed in common. There is an abstraction from the singularity of apprehension. All this is the task of dogmatic theology.

The differences between dogmatic method and positive method start with the respective questions. For positive method, the questions are those that arise spontaneously from the data, while for dogmatic method the real questions arise after positive studies and comparative method have revealed the differences between scripture, the Fathers, the councils, and the theologians. Then the question emerges how the dogma defined by the church is contained in the sources.

Next, there is a different division of the materials. In positive theology there is a division into biblical, patristic, medieval, and so on, and there are subdivisions in each of these. Dogmatic theologians do not consider individual documents for their own sake but in order to find their connections, their implications, and their consequences. They have a different division of the materials. They must turn to various sources – scripture, the Fathers, the medieval theologians, and so on – in order to determine how the meaning defined by the church is found in the sources and develops over time.

Third, the consideration of the data is different. The positive theologian is concerned with what is doubtful, obscure, and singular. The dogmatic theologian knows that he will not reach the certitude of faith by starting where the positive theologian starts, and so he considers what is clear, certain, and common, and so areas that the positive theologian pays little attention to. And even when they do consider the same areas, they do so in different ways. The positive theologian wants to understand every aspect of the relevant data, whereas the dogmatic theologian is content with whatever can establish the dogmatic meaning taught by the church. Thus the expression 'No one knows the Son except the Father ...' will give rise in the positive theologian to the question 'What does the word "knows" mean as it is used here?' while the dogmatic theologian will be content to say, that whatever 'knows' means here, it does not exclude cognition.

Fourth, there is a difference in the categories. The positive theologian wants to express the same mentality as is expressed in the documents under investigation. The dogmatic theologian employs fundamental categories. Human nature and the human mind are one. If Mark were not intelligent, we would be unable to gather anything about him. Mark thought about being; otherwise he would have been thinking about nothing. The dogmatic theologian finds the transition from the implicit to the explicit. The basic categories of the human mind, the very conditions of the possibility of speech, and so on, are implicit in his authors, but he uses them to articulate the particular point he is trying to make.

Fifth, there is a difference with regard to singularity. The positive theologian is concerned with the singularity of the things apprehended and of the apprehensions themselves. John spoke in a particular way, Mark in a different manner, and both are important for the positive theologian. The dogmatic theologian does not at all remove the singularity of what he is studying, but he goes from the singularity of apprehension to a catholic apprehension.

Sixth, there is a difference in intelligibility. The positive theologian is interested in the intelligibility inhering in particulars, even if he is investigating something systematic. In that case, his interest will focus on the distinct mode of speaking in one system compared to another, on the fact that, for example, Scotus will define a certain number of meanings of 'action' and always use the word in one of those senses, while Aquinas will mention now two ways and now three, and the three will not overlap with the two, but he still makes sense. Thomas has system without the culture of logic. The dogmatic theologian does not seek the intelligibility that is so inherent in singulars that it cannot be stated in a general way. And in what we have called intermediate studies, singulars are investigated according to some general principles derived from the study of particulars over time but requiring something more than positive method for their articulation.

Seventh, they differ with respect to their relation to certitude. The positive theologian does not wish to arrive immediately at a complete explanation. He knows there will be further clarifications and perhaps corrections. His concern is collaboration over time, in fact over centuries. He is hardly perturbed if a question is left unsolved or if the solution is only probable. Rarely is he certain, except with regard to error and the exclusion of some possibilities. This is not so with the dogmatic theologian. Kierkegaard in his *Concluding Unscientific Postscript* speaks of the elderly New Testament scholar who, after a lifetime of labor, realizes that never once did he give a thought about the truth of what he was studying.[17] For religion certitudes are required. Faith is certain, with the assistance of the Holy Spirit. The dogmatic theologian cannot say with regard to his central problems, 'It is not solved.' Rather, he assigns theological notes to indicate the degree of certitude that has in fact been achieved.

Because of these differences, it seems inappropriate to say that the dogmatic theologian and the positive theologian do the same thing. There is

17 See Lonergan's longer reference to this passage in *Early Works on Theological Method 1* 178.

a differentiation of methods. To require of the dogmatic theologian that he use a positive method is to exclude the dogmatic part of theology altogether, while to require dogmatic certitude of the positive theologian is to exclude theology's positive part. An example is the question about Christ's beatific vision during his life on earth. It is erroneous to say, 'It belongs to the faith, and it is up to the biblical theologians to prove it.' It belongs rather to the dogmatic theologian to establish as well as he can that this truth can be derived from scripture. The paper of A. Descamps, 'Réflexions sur la méthode en théologie biblique,' *Sacra Pagina* I, 1959, presents an example of the concept of positive method entertained by the positive theologian.[18] As for dogmatic work, if the noblest task is to show how what is taught by the church is found in the sources, then the question is about the development of dogma, the nexus that is not logical but a matter of development.

Internal Aspects of the Movement from Sources to Dogma (20 November, 51100D0L060)

The movement from the sources to dogma, which is the focus of the dogmatic part of theology, has four internal aspects: objective, subjective, evaluative, and hermeneutical.

The objective aspect is twofold. First, there is the transition from one literary genre to another: for example, from a simple comparison between the gospels to the term of the dogmatic movement. The gospels move feelings, touch the heart, open one's eyes, affect the whole person. But dogma attends only to the austere truth. Second, dogma exhibits a different vocabulary from that of scripture. Dogmas are not scriptural concordances. The synthetic movement is expressed in technical terms, showing a transition from plurality to unity.

To understand the subjective aspect, we need to consider patterns of experience. See *Insight*, chapter 6.[19] For example, a person who is awake acts differently from one who is dreaming. In different ways consciousness urges practicality, experiences the aesthetic, knows mystical enlightenment, rejoices with friends, investigates scientifically. Each of these exhibits a distinct pattern of experience. In particular, there is a subjective division between undifferentiated and differentiated consciousness. In undiffer-

18 See above, p. 4, note 2.
19 Lonergan, *Insight* 204–12.

entiated consciousness, the whole person operates at the same time with virtually all one's powers. To the active person, the will, the intellect, and physical action present a single concrete goal.

There are connections among the patterns of experience. The dream state is hardly ever rational, but in wakefulness one state leads to another, in different ways. The fundamental difference is between normal undifferentiated consciousness and differentiated consciousness. In undifferentiated consciousness, an image represents a goal, the will chooses it, the intellect finds means and negotiates obstacles, and the whole person at one and the same time intends the one goal. This is not so in the intellectual pattern of experience. Here the goal is purely intellectual. One seeks a true understanding. Affectivity is more or less excluded. The imagination represents those things that will lead to a solution. It recalls those things that favor the goal, not other things, which would be a distraction. We must become trained through study and discipline if we are easily to enter this pattern. In the dogmatic part of theology the transition is from the gospels to the dogmas, which attend only to truth. For this there is required a transition on the part of the subject. Ordinary common sense will be baffled by talk, for instance, of consubstantiality.

The evaluative aspect of the movement has to do with the fact that we tend to make difficulties over such a transition. There is a development demanded in the subject, and it is one that we tend to resist. When we resist it, we will set ourselves against dogmas. Almost all popular religious movements are anti-dogmatic.

Normally, three objections are leveled against dogmas. First, they are obscure, while the gospels are clear. Second, in the scriptures the true religious spirit arises spontaneously, while dogmas are alien to that true religious spirit. And third, intellectual objections are presented.

As for the first objection, that regarding obscurity, we must ask to whom dogmas are obscure, and to whom are they clear. Scripture is clear to everyone except the exegetes. Intelligibility is inherent in the particulars themselves. The mind of St Paul is not the object of any definition. But clarifications may be attempted with the help of philosophy. Witness the role of idealism in nineteenth-century exegesis. Is an exegete prepared to override a philosophical movement?

Dogmas *are* obscure to many. But hermeneutics is not required to ascertain their meaning, no more than it is required when studying Euclid's *Elements.* After study, there is no question about the meaning. When one proceeds through definitions and axioms, the matter is either understood or it is not. Study is required, but no interpretation. There is clarity, and disputes do not arise. Scripture, it would seem, is clear to undifferentiated consciousness but obscure to differentiated consciousness, while dogmas are obscure to undifferentiated consciousness but clear to differentiated consciousness.

As for the second objection, that regarding the religious spirit – 'Dogmas are not very religious; we must go back to Hebraic simplicity' – we may say that it is not only among the Hebrews that antiquity was simpler. All peoples in ancient times were simpler. They little distinguished between the sacred and the profane. Categorization makes for distinctions that primitive peoples do not make. Without such differentiation, a deep, lofty, wonderful, and moving meaning is present within even common things, as Wordsworth captures so eloquently.[20] Thus, Congar distinguishes in his article 'Théologie' between the old Augustinian science and the science of Albert the Great and Thomas Aquinas.[21] According to the latter pair, science is science in its own proper right, with a dedication to truth. Where there is a religious atmosphere in everything, the interpenetration of sacred and profane, there are certain disadvantages, including a propensity to idolatry resulting from undifferentiated consciousness, and a tendency to render all sacred things profane.

With the development of consciousness, religion itself will develop as well. Religion is not a Platonic Form everywhere and always the same, whether in children or in adults. In more archaic societies, it might consist mainly in external cultic rites, but for Schleiermacher it is the feeling of dependence[22] and for Tillich the sense of being favored giving rise to gratitude.[23] It orders everything to God, whether a simple life or a complex one. To expel religion from intelligence is to invite secularism. For moderns, there is a need to order the intellect to God. The intellect judges all things, and when it finds that religion treats of emotion, it tends to say that religion is good for women and children. But dogma orders the

---

20 See William Wordsworth, 'Ode: Intimations of Immortality from Early Childhood,' in *The Poetical Works of William Wordsworth*, ed. William Michael Rossetti (London: Ward, Lock & Bowden, 1870) 357–58.
21 See Congar, *A History of Theology* 120–21.
22 The basic text is Friedrich Schleiermacher, *The Christian Faith*, ed. H.R. Mackintosh and J.S. Stewart (London and New York: T&T Clark, 1999).
23 One possible source is Paul Tillich, 'You Are Accepted,' chapter 19 in Tillich, *The Shaking of the Foundations* (New York: Charles Scribner's Sons, 1948).

intellect to God. What is found in scripture is taught precisely as true, for example, that the Lord is Messiah, etc., but there is a transition from the multiplicity of scriptural affirmations to the unity of the doctrine that the Son is consubstantial with the Father. And besides this objective aspect of the development there is the subjective aspect, where there is a transition from one pattern of consciousness to another. Wherever there is this kind of transition, there is some link, and in this case the unifying bond is truth itself. There is a different way of apprehending, conceiving, judging, and speaking, but the true does not become false in the process. Reflection on the dogmatic movement towards truth pays attention to the unifying bond of truth.

There is an analogy here, however remote, with mathematical transformations. The path of a Sputnik is measured first from the surface of the earth, then the central point can be positioned in the sun, the moon, and so on. The same truth is given in diverse systems or frames of reference. The geometry is always the same. Thus, it is one thing to conceive the Son as Son of God and another thing to conceive him as Son of Man. These are two different conceptions. The link is in the order of truth. Besides the order of apprehending and understanding, there is the order of judging. It regards the subject, but it enunciates an unconditioned. Insofar as it says 'It is,' it does not depend on the subject. When the question is about the forms of consciousness, it does not go beyond the essential order. Thinking is not the same as knowing, and one arrives at knowing when one arrives at the true.

As for the hermeneutical aspect, the general principle is *Quidquid recipitur ad modum recipientis recipitur,* Whatever is received is received according to the disposition of the receiver. But there are two kinds of reception, ancient and modern. The human mind is one and requires unity with itself. It is not a public forum into which everything has access. That would simply be a rendition of the principle of the empty head.[24] All human apprehension is selective. Selection means ordering, and ordering implies some judgment. Hence, *quot homines, tot sententiae,* there are as many opinions as there are human beings. An example of this is found in the various histories that are written about the same set of events. Another would be the so-called 'perennial philosophy,' for there are perennial materialisms, perennial idealisms,

---

24 A more familiar treatment of the principle of the empty head may be found in Lonergan, *Method in Theology* 157–58.

and perennial realisms. As for the mode of reception, we may learn something from the two processes that Piaget shows are involved when a person
learns something: assimilation, so that when one meets a new object one
uses habits already acquired, and adjustment or accommodation, the modification, often rather slight, that is required when a new object is added to
older operations. Time is generally required for such adaptations.

We can study the ancient modes of reception by attending to the ante-
Nicene movement. When Christianity was preached to Jews, many rejected
it. So did many Greeks when Paul preached Christ to them at the Areopagus. Yet his teaching was also received by a number of others. But in either case it was seldom received in its fullness. Thus, the Judeo-Christians
wanted to keep certain purely Judaic elements, and many Gnostics received
the gospel but wanted also to have some ancient Egyptian wisdom. The accommodation was incomplete.[25]

The traditional aspect is represented in Paul's 'what I in turn had received' (1 Corinthians 15.3) and in the sentiment that nothing new is to
be added to what has been handed down. But what is to be done when the
word of God is contradicted by heretics? Their way of asking the question
'Who is Christ?' called for a solution that required a transposition, including an adaptation of the subject. Philosophy had to be brought to bear. But
the Nicene solution was not something in the speculative essential order.
It was a rule about scriptural statements, about affirmations concerning
the Father and the Son. A series of thoughts is not the same as a series of
affirmations. Thinking pertains to the order of concepts, but the dogmatic process belongs to another order, namely, that of judgments, in which
one says 'It is' or 'It is not.' The ante-Nicene movement displays a twofold
development: a general movement regarding dogma and a specific aspect
regarding Christ. We are able to distinguish what they actually did (both of
these) from what they knew they were doing (the specific aspect).

Evaluative and Hermeneutical Aspects
(27 November, 51200D0L060)

The evaluative objections against dogma are that it is obscure, minimally
religious, and aberrant in different ways. We would address the accusation
of aberrancy from the standpoint of truth. Truth pertains to individual dog-

---

25 See Lonergan, *The Triune God: Doctrines* 54–82.

mas. It has to do with both the objective aspect of development, where it is based in scripture itself precisely as true, and with the subjective aspect, where it is the bond of union between diverse patterns of experience, so that a change in a pattern, which entails a different mode of apprehending, understanding, conceiving, and speaking, does not transmute the true into the false but means that the same truth is expressed in a different manner. Truth is unconditioned, independent of the subject.

There are five elements to the consideration of the hermeneutical aspect of the movement from the sources to dogma.

First, whatever is received is received according to the mode of the receiver. There are two receptions that are relevant: the first in ancient times, when the developments occurred (whether in the first centuries or in the Middle Ages), and the second in the moderns, who examine and pass judgment on the development.

Second, what is this 'according to the mode of the receiver?' The human mind is one and requires unity with itself. It is not a public forum into which everybody and anybody enters and everything has access. This is obvious even from the example of hearing. The noises of a busy street are not attended to, but the voice of my friend speaking is heard because what my friend is saying is understood. Every apprehension is a selection, every selection is an ordering, and every ordering both reflects and prepares the way for judgment. To deny this is to espouse the principle of the empty head, which is simply a myth regarding objectivity. *Quot homines, tot sententiae*; there are as many opinions as there are human beings. A new apprehension in matters that are fundamental is related to the conversion of a human being.

Third, reception in general is a matter of what Piaget calls assimilation and adjustment or accommodation. There are, of course, instances of no reception, of rejection, as in the case of both Jews and Greeks. When Christianity was preached to the Jews, many rejected it. So also when St Paul preached Christ to the Greeks on the Areopagus. And there are instances of insufficient accommodation, as with the Judeo-Christians, who wanted to keep certain purely Judaic elements, and the Gnostics.

The ancient reception of the word of God is complex. There is the aspect of tradition. 1 Corinthians 15.3, 'I handed on to you what I myself received.' 'Let nothing new be added to what has been handed down.' There is the aspect of truth: the word of God is not to be contradicted. But it was contradicted by heretics, first by Judeo-Christians, Gnostics, and Marcionites, and then in a more determinate fashion by adoptionists, Patripassians, Sabellians,[26] and Arians.[27] The ways of affirming (e.g., Tertullian in the terms of naive realism) are traced in the prolegomena to the dogmatic portion of the treatise on the Trinity. Athanasius teaches us that the Nicene solution was that the same things are said of the Son as of the Father, except for the name 'Father.' 'Homoousion' is not speculation regarding the essence of the Son. It is a rule about predication. It stands not in the essential order, which is concerned with the 'quid sit' question, but in the existential order, whose concern is 'an sit,' the order concerned with 'Is, Is not,' with 'Is the same, is other,' with 'Is the same in one respect, different in another respect.'

Fourth, as for the modern reception of the ancient reception, it is now admitted that in fact there is dogmatic development. Vincent of Lerins's *Quod semper, quod ubique, quod ab omnibus* is not final. If it were, it would open the door to anachronism and archaism.

Understanding development requires both an objective aspect and a development on the part of the subject. The subjective development is absent in extrinsicism, which fastens on the 'objectively true'; in perceptualism, whether that of Scotus and Gilson or that found in historicism; in essentialism, with its concentration on nexus and synthesis rather than on *positing* the nexus, on affirming and denying; in the idealism of Kant and Hegel; in intending only metaphysics; and in positivism, whether the theoretical positivism that denies metaphysics and knowledge of what is first and ultimate, or the practical positivism that prescinds from philosophical questions. Method clarifies and differentiates common sense, science, philosophy, and theology. The judgments about dogma – that it is obscure, minimally religious, and aberrant – stand in need of investigation. Development itself is not simple but complex. Development is twofold. Not only do the doctrines develop; the very notion of dogma, the dogmatic mentality, develops. The study of development has to be concerned both with what the ancient authors knew they were doing and with what they did even though they didn't know they were doing it. This is, of course, opposed to the principle of the empty head.

Fifth, there is the connection of the dogmas. Given the development of one, the development of another can be expected to follow. From the consubstantiality of the Son we moved to the consubstantiality of the Holy Spirit. But if three are consubstantial, how are they distinct? Eventually the

26 See ibid. 82–89.
27 See ibid. 136–71.

movement to processions occurs. Then, is it really one and the same that is born of the Father and born of Mary? Are there two distinct natures, properties, operations, wills in Christ? Is there a third order, the supernatural, in addition to the divine and the human? What about the concrete, sensible, historical, social, cultural order of things? What is to be said about the church, the sacraments, the liturgy, preaching? Is there some one human science that can be said to be normative, and that helps us link these doctrinal matters with other sciences?

More on the Hermeneutical Aspect (10 December, 51300DTL060)

We have seen the four aspects of dogmatic development: objective, subjective, evaluative, and hermeneutical. We have been discussing the hermeneutical aspect. We have treated two dimensions of this aspect. There is an ancient reception in the movement from the New Testament to the dogmas of Nicea, Constantinople I, Ephesus, Chalcedon, and Constantinople II and III. And there is a modern reception as attention turns to understanding the development of dogmas themselves; here there is located the noblest task of the theologian. There is also a third dimension to be discussed: the practical, having to do with preaching.

Hermeneutic process has been understood in several ways. Romantic hermeneutics is used most in interpretation of works of art. Applied to theological literature, it would put on the mind of the author and so think and speak like Isaiah, Paul, John, Arius, Athanasius. Such an approach ends up with a pure multiplicity of descriptive terms. 'The Hebraic mentality' and similar terms are taken as ultimate. The possibility of theology performing its noblest task vanishes.

Classical hermeneutics adheres to the rule *quod ubique, quod semper, quod ab omnibus.* The nouns and verbs may differ, but truth is eternal. Concepts are formed on the basis of a thing itself, otherwise they are not true. Things do not evolve, nor do concepts. Truth is one, errors are many. Conclusions deduced from the truth are added. Such an approach is anachronistic or archaic. It is anachronistic when concepts of later writers are transferred to earlier ones, so that it discusses Paul as though he thought in the light of Nicea, Ephesus, Chalcedon, Constantinople, or so that John knew what the Council of Nicea said as well as Basil did. It is archaic when, realizing that Paul and John did not think this way, it regards the later developments as aberrations. Catholics tend more to anachronistic interpretation, and Protestants to archaism.

In general, both romantic and classical hermeneutics rule out development. Romantic hermeneutics may perhaps say that there is a leap, but it does not understand the process; classical hermeneutics asserts that there is no development.

There is a *via media*. It appeals to the transcendence of truth and to the plurality of contexts, in order to guarantee true continuity.

The transcendence of truth: as true, truth is in the subject, precisely as what is known; but as transcendent, it is not dependent upon the subject; it is not what seems, what appears, what is thought, what is judged probable; it is what *is*. The truth of a judgment as true transcends the subject from whom it proceeds and attains the unconditioned. The transcendence of truth is the necessary premise for avoiding mere multiplicity. Evidence has been grasped as sufficient. Anything less is not sufficient for an unconditioned, while nothing more can be demanded. The unconditioned is in the subject, but it does not depend on the subject. The structure of the movement to the truth may be formulated in the syllogism 'If *A*, then *B*; but *A*; therefore *B*,' whether *A* is a proposition or an experience, and whether the connection is a condition of possibility or the movement from data to concept. See *Insight*, chapter 10.

The pluralism of contexts: I am now seated and can say that I am seated. I get up and I can say that I had been sitting. The same truth is expressed but in another context. Geometrical transformations are another example of the same truth transferred to another context. A more difficult example is the movement from the *quoad nos* to the *quoad se*. A physical science begins from perceptible observations. It also measures and then compares its measurements and arrives at a law, e.g., $s = \frac{1}{2}gt^2$. Theological examples would be found in arguing for continuity between the God of Abraham, Isaac, and Jacob and the God of the philosophers, or showing the continuity between the presentation of the divine missions in the New Testament (*quoad nos*) and in question 43 of the first part of the *Summa* (*quoad se*).

What has been called the noblest task of theology is the transition from the original context to another context and the construction of the new context. The two contexts are compared. There is an order in which the new context is gradually constructed. First, there is the consubstantiality of the Son. Then a question arises about the consubstantiality of the Holy Spirit. Then there is the affirmation of the three as consubstantial, but distinct by properties. Next, the properties are affirmed as relations, and those relations are subsistent. They are grounded in the processions. Then the same one who is 'God from God' is also 'born of the virgin Mary.' He has two natures, properties, natural operations, and natural wills. As the context continues to develop, there is an affirmation of the supernatural order. Etc., etc. Thus does a new context come to be, but the same truth is expressed as is found in the scriptures. There is an order to the construction of the context. The construction of a new context provides the first approximation to the dogmatic task. As the construction of the new context proceeds, the manner of argumentation changes. The new context begins to pose its own questions, not found in scripture.

There follows a historical order of development. Its general, lines are more or less pure: Trinitarian theology, Christology, soteriology, theology of grace and the virtues, theology of the sacraments, theology of the church. Systematic thinking begins to show the interdependence of these developments both with one another and with what is said in scripture.

The Validity of New Contexts (11 December, 51400D0L060)

The question moves to the validity of the new context. There is no solution to this question in romantic hermeneutics, where differences are not grasped, simply the leap from one context to another. Contexts become like islands in the sea, with no map to indicate their relative positions. Only descriptive names are employed: the Semitic mentality, the Hellenistic mentality, the Egyptian mentality, the gnostic mentality, prophetism, Paulinism, and so on.

On the other hand, in classical hermeneutics there is no problem, because there is grasped only an identity. There is no new context, and so no problem. Concepts do not proceed from understanding in such a way that as understanding grows, concepts are perfected. They proceed from things, which do not change. Truths are eternal. All that changes is the linguistic garment in which they are expressed.

Our question is about what is new. The validity of the older context is presupposed. We are concerned especially with the explanatory aspect of the new, in the new context. We are not concerned with proving individual theses but with the general methodological question of possible validity.

There are two steps to be taken in answering this question: analysis of transition in general, and application of the analysis.

The analysis of the process in which a new context is constructed has five aspects. The first is the fundamental distinction between common and proper notions and principles.

Proper notions and principles arise from understanding the intelligibilities of various kinds of things, and so in a process that is moving towards understanding determinate natures. They do not have philosophic generality, but are the proper principles of physics, chemistry, biology, psychology, or human studies. In theology, the proper principles and notions have to do with the understanding of the mysteries: the psychological analogy for the Trinity, the consciousness of Christ (not prescinding from the question 'What is consciousness?'), the satisfaction of Christ, the nature of grace, the organization of the church.

Common notions and principles are grounded in the structure of the mind: experience, understanding, judgment; the questions 'quid sit' and 'an sit'; they are the conditions of the possibility of any investigation. They are the notions and principles that express the mind itself in its very exercise.

Second, both common and proper principles and notions develop, but in different ways. The evolution of the proper principles and notions results in the systematic part of theology, which we will discuss later. But for the moment we are concerned with the dogmatic part. There is a process of discovery, which is the part that uncovers the elements that are to be explained. Here there is a certain diversity of opinion because of the diversity of data. But there is a movement towards unity, a movement from diversity to unity. And this movement itself develops.

The common principles and notions develop in a movement from *exercite* to *signate*, from practice to reflection on practice. At first, they are employed but they are not articulated. Everyone says 'is' but very few think about being. The notions are present *exercite* and implicitly in every use of the mind, but as the sciences and philosophy develop, and with the assistance of more complete reflection, these principles and notions are more completely and more accurately articulated. This progress can itself continue to grow. For example, there is a more accurate acknowledgment of the principle of contradiction today. A perfect articulation would anticipate all possible difficulties; until then, development should occur.[28] The possibility of more accurate formulation remains. In this more complete and more accurate articulation there are found certain invariants, but they are found not in what is said but in the very structure of the mind. There is the question 'Quid sit,' promoting one from experience (matter) to understanding

28 There is a reference to Breton's contribution to *La crise de la raison dans la philosophie contemporaine.* See above, p. 27, note 40.

(form); and there is the question 'An sit,' promoting one from understanding (form) to judgment (existence, operation). These principles and notions express our rationality.

The third aspect is that there is a dialectical process concerned with the common principles and notions. That is, the development itself is dialectical. The dialectic is grounded in the conflict between the common principles as they are exercised and the same principles insofar as they are made explicit, between a man precisely as human and his philosophy. One is always a human being, and only sometimes a philosopher. And it may be that the philosopher does not quite grasp the human being that one is.

There are typical conflicts, as represented in the various perennial philosophies. Materialists, empiricists, positivists, pragmatists attend to the element of experience, to experiential objectivity. Relativists, immanentists, idealists, essentialists attend to the element of understanding, to coherence, to normative objectivity. They demonstrate the presence of intelligence in the materialists, contrary to materialist doctrine. For them judgment is constituted by the composition of ideas. But Newton and Einstein composed their ideas in hypotheses prior to judgment. Or perhaps judgment is conflated with decision, *Entscheidung*. Bultmann is quite familiar with intelligence, but misses the third step in the process.[29]

Realists (not pseudo-realists) distinguish experience, understanding, and judgment.

This kind of conflict resides in the philosopher, the theologian, the scientist himself, as a conflict between what one does in fact and what one says one is doing. The dialectic at play here is not a theoretical but an existential problem. Dialectical conflicts are resolved by conversion. The question is personal. There was a time in Augustine's life, lasting several years, in which nothing could be acknowledged to exist except bodies. Tertullian never transcended this problem. To say that a theologian prescinds from philosophical questions is to say that the theologian does not use his human mind.

Fourth, the common principles constitute a heuristic structure through which the proper matters are investigated. One begins from data, raises the 'Quid sit' question, goes on to successive theories, faces the 'An sit' ques-

---

29 Lonergan refers to Bultmann's *Glauben und Verstehen*. See Rudolf Bultmann, *Glauben und Verstehen: Gesammelte Aufsätze* (Tubingen: J.C.B. Mohr, 1954, 1961).

tion, and issues successive judgments. It is this structure that provides unity and continuity between the successive theories.

Thus: What is fire? The phenomena provide the data. The 'what is it?' question follows, and any proposed answer is an attempt to articulate the 'nature of' fire. Aristotle said it was one of the four elementary substances. A second theory explained it in terms of 'phlogiston.' Lavoisier showed it to be a process of oxidization. These answers display a wide diversity. But they are able to be set against one another precisely because they are answers to one and the same question. The question itself is an indeterminate knowledge. And so even in regard to proper notions and principles, unity and continuity is a function of the heuristic structure.

Again, what is a person? Augustine said a person is what there are three of in God. The Father, the Son, and the Holy Spirit are three. Three what? Not three gods, not three Fathers, not three Sons, but three persons. 'Person' is the answer to the question 'Three what?' Then Boethius, Richard of St Victor, and Thomas provided definitions of person. The definitions were followed by metaphysical theories regarding the constitution of persons: Scotus, Capreolus, Tiphanus, and so on. Then psychological questions were raised, as the person came to be acknowledged as the subject of consciousness. And finally there were the phenomenological questions having to do with intersubjectivity and interpersonal relations.[30] All of these are valid contributions to the notion of person. They are the several stages in the evolution of the same structure.

Fifth, the common principles and notions constitute a transcendental heuristic structure, independently of the proper principles and notions. All the fundamental notions are defined from an analysis of the structure of the mind. The heuristic structure is manifest in questions such as, Is it or is it not? Is it the same or is it distinct? Is it such, is it similar, is it similar under the same respect? These questions enter into fundamental dogmatic questions in theology.

The same structure is applied to the determination of what is proper, and so there is sought an understanding of the mysteries, the questions of systematic theology. The structure is manifest in fundamental dogmatic questions, e.g., whether Christ is God, and in the questions of systematic theology.

The same heuristic structure constituted by what is common is distorted by the absence of intellectual, moral, and religious conversion. The same

30 At this point, the date shifts to 17 December.

premises, understood in a realist, an idealist, and a positivist sense lead to realist, idealist, and positivist positions. The solution does not occur through proof or demonstration, but through conversion.

The constitution of the heuristic structure, its application to proper areas of research, and its distortion all develop over time, but in different ways.

The constitution of the structure develops through reflection on the mind itself. Intelligence becomes more manifest to itself, through more complete articulations of its invariant structure. Everyone asks the 'What' question, reaches some understanding, and then reflects. We have immediate experience of this, and it is only from this that we can explain what understanding is.

Applications to various proper domains develop through better understanding of the various domains themselves.

Distortions of the heuristic structure occur as the various perennial philosophies recur under different forms. Along with more complete reflection on the mind itself there occur more subtle distortions. Tertullian is easily refuted, but the same fundamental position as it arises today is more difficult to discern and transcend. It may be admitted that the spiritual is more real than the corporeal, for example, but it is still maintained that knowledge supposes the distinction of knower and known, that it is a kind of vision. That is the same position as Tertullian's. Again, psychology texts hardly ever use the words 'understanding' and 'insight.' There is a lack of conversion: religious, moral, and intellectual.

So much for the analysis of transition. There remains the question of the validity of the construction of the new context. Here there are six points.

First, the dogmas of the Greek councils, of Nicea, Constantinople I, Ephesus, Chalcedon, and Constantinople II and III, and the classic symbols such as *Quicumque*, are responses to questions that are put as a result of the transcendental heuristic structure, that is, questions concerning not what is proper, the understanding of the mysteries, but the common notions themselves. Is the Son is the same as the Father? Here we have the issues of Patripassianism, Sabellianism, and Adoptionism. Again, Nicea's doctrine is not about *ousia*. Whether the Son is consubstantial to the Father has to do with predication. The question is answered in Athanasius's statement that 'the same things are said of the Son as are said of the Father, except the name Father.' Again, there is the question about distinction. Basil's dilemma was that if he distinguishes the persons, he risks tritheism, but if he teaches that God is one, he risks Sabellianism. His response is 'one substance and three hypostases,' where the meaning of 'hypostasis' becomes clear only from the context. The hypostases are distinct by their properties, and the properties are affirmed as relational, where the relations are grounded in processions. The procession of the Holy Spirit, for the Greeks, because of the emphasis on the divine monarchy, is understood as from the Father through the Son, whereas for the Latins, with the emphasis on one *ousia*, the Father and the Son are one principle, and the Spirit proceeds from the Father and the Son. The problems of Apollinaris and Theodore of Mopsuestia, Cyril of Alexandria's question whether the one who is 'God from God' and the one who is 'born of the virgin Mary' are the same or different, the various responses to the Monophysite and Monothelite controversies: all of these questions are reflections of the transcendental heuristic structure.

Second, in the Greek dogmatic development there arose Christian realism. The Greek dogmas themselves are grounded in a process of intellectual conversion. Nicea is a third possibility: not that of Tertullian, and not that of Origen, that is, not naive realism with its spiritual matter and not essentialist realism with its different essences. There are three possible realisms: one that is referred to experience, another that is referred to ideas, and the third, the one that prevailed at Nicea, that is referred to affirmation and denial. Medieval developments are grounded in the Greek dogmas.

Third, this Christian realism cannot be identified with any one Greek philosophy. It is a product of the same human mind, of course, but its position is something original, something new. Aristotelian thought would not arrive at the hypostatic union. There was a human body animated by an intellective soul in Christ, yes, but for Aristotle this is what would constitute a person. Aristotle's metaphysics is modified by Aquinas, precisely because of the dogmatic positions. The Word assumed an animated body, yes, but not a person. Aristotle's philosophy had to undergo a fundamental modification. Again, Origen is Platonic, Tertullian is Stoic, but dogma is neither. Religious conversion encourages intellectual conversion, not immediately, and not in everyone, but slowly and very effectively. Slowly it becomes clear that there are three tendencies: materialism and positivism; relativism, idealism, and essentialism; and realism. The fundamental critical problem is solved in the very process of dogmatic development.

Fourth, the use of this transcendental structure brings about a newly constructed context. The fundamental conceptuality, the very mode of speaking and thinking, simply is not to be found in the New Testament. It results from the use of the transcendental structure. A movement occurs from thinking of God in relation to the people of Israel to thinking of God in relation to all people, the God who created heaven and earth, who is transcendent and omnipotent, the creator of all, infinite, perfect.[31] The Son, as God, is transcendent, but is distinct as Son, where the distinction is relational. And so on and so forth: there is a series of transitions from context to context.

Fifth, this new context is present *exercite* in the Old and New Testaments, both on the side of the subject and on the side of the object. On the side of the subject: the biblical authors had and used minds; they experienced, they understood, they judged. On the side of the object, the Old Testament paid express attention to the Law, and the New Testament to the word of the gospel, the word of the kingdom, the word of preaching. It distinguished between what is said in an imperative way, the word of God as law, and what is said in narrative fashion, the word of God as gospel. There is the kerygma, the apostolic tradition, the tradition of the church, the baptismal confession, the preaching, hearing, and accepting of the word of God. Matthew 5.39: 'Let your speech be Yes, Yes, and No, No.' Galatians 1.8: 'Even if an angel from heaven proclaimed a different gospel ...' The transition is from the implicit to the explicit. Faith resides in the apprehension of the word of God. It does not reside in experience. 'Blessed are those who have not seen.' Nor does it reside in understanding.

Sixth, the foundation of a possible transition lies in the transcendence of the true. Because the true is unconditioned, it is not tied to a context. It can be uttered in another context, even if it is uttered in a different way. Experience depends on the dispositions of the subject. Understanding depends on already acquired habits. Judgment is a matter of 'is.' It is about something precisely insofar as that something does not depend on me. The unconditioned has no conditions in the subject. It is not tied to a context. Certainly what is true is said in a different way in a different context, but there is had something that can be said in that different context. The truth is independent, and it is precisely for that reason that it can be posited in another context. This is the fundamental solution to the hermeneutic question. Without this there is no possibility of solution. The context of the gospel, where it is said of Christ that he thirsts, that he weeps, is far from the context of the Council of Chalcedon, where there is talk of his human nature. But the true can be validly transposed from one context to another. A brief answer to our question is that the newly constructed context is valid because what is explicitly present in dogma was already operative in prac-

31 Lonergan refers here to Jean Daniélou, *Message évangélique et culture hellénistique aux IIe et IIIe siècles* (Paris: Desclée, 1961).

tice and implicitly in the Old and New Testaments, both subjectively and objectively, and because the true is validly transposed from one context to another, precisely because of the transcendence of the true itself.

These considerations constitute the first approximation to the argument of dogmatic theology. The argument should focus on the moment in which such a development took place. There is genuine continuity through a multiplicity of contexts. What has been called the noblest task of theology consists in the transition from one context and the construction of the new context. There is an order in which slowly the new context is constructed: consubstantiality of the Son, consubstantiality of the Spirit, distinction on the basis of relational properties, recognition of relations as subsistent, and so on.

But while this is the first line of argumentation in dogmatic theology, it must also be recognized that the general lines of development become more and more interdependent.

Transcendental Method (7 January 1964, 51500D0L060)

We have distinguished specialized methods, that is, those of positive, systematic, and dogmatic theology, as corresponding, respectively, to experience, understanding, and judgment. We now consider the transcendental or foundational method, that which manifests the intention of being. We have already illustrated the use of the transcendental method. We have considered the transcendentals: being, one, true, good (1) as objects, in contrast with the predicaments or categories, and (2) from the side of the subject, in terms of the intention of being in every subject who is thinking about anything.

The intention of being may be schematized as follows, from below:

          judgment
is it? is it so?
          understanding
what is it?
          experience

This structure obtains both in ordinary understanding and in the sciences. It also obtains in reflection on the subject, since it indicates what I am doing as I am operating and as I am constituting myself. The structure on the side of the subject is the foundation of knowledge of what is on the side of the object.

Transcendental method has critical, foundational, and methodical aspects. The critical aspect: do not say what you are not able to know; the foundational aspect: know precisely what you are saying by reducing your affirmations to their origin in the structure; the methodical aspect: one who knows the structure knows exactly the operations by which we learn and know. The structure is found in every rational subject. It is implicit and found in practice in the gospels and in the martyrs. Its application is explicit in some of the Fathers and in the councils. It is found explicitly as it is in itself in some theologians. And it is disengaged on the side of the subject by modern methods. But what is found in practice in everyone is applied differently by different authors. Tertullian's application is quasi-materialist. Origen's is essentialist. Athanasius's is realist. The problem of conversion arises and is manifest in Augustine. Aquinas expresses it in terms of *homo immersus in sensibilibus*.[32] The structure provides some help in understanding how the dogmas might be implicitly present in scripture, namely, in the sense that the authors of the New Testament had minds and used them. But directly the structure grounds the Greek dogmas and the transition to the new context. The scriptures tell us that Jesus wept; the new context tells us of his human nature. It employs new categories that tell us of a divine person in a human nature, of one who, because he was divine, transcended the limits of nature. Thus, there is an opening onto the developments having to do with the supernatural.

Further precision is necessary, however. What we have said about the transcendental structure is philosophical. But theology is not grounded in reason alone but also in faith, which transcends natural reason. In this way perhaps we can understand what Vatican I says about the *via media* between traditionalism and fideism, on the one hand, and semirationalism, on the other. In DB 1795–96 a distinction is drawn between principles and corresponding objects. To reason there correspond what can be known naturally. To faith there correspond mysteries hidden in God. And to reason illumined by faith there corresponds an understanding of the mysteries. This is a third principle, and it gives rise to a most fruitful understanding of faith. There is a proportion here, an analogy: philosophical transcendental method is to reason as theological transcendental method is to reason il-

---

32 Lonergan's notes mention also Sorokin's three cultures, and align the ideational with symbolic theology, the idealistic with the medieval, and the sensate with modernity. See Pitirim A. Sorokin, *Social and Cultural Dynamics*, 4 vols. (New York: American Book Company, 1937–41). See below, p. 136.

lumined by faith. Thus, we are provided with the conditions of possibility of knowing, both in general and in theology.

The intending intention of being – experience, understanding, and judgment – gives us the broad lines of all that can be understood, but it also provides the elements that will be found in every method, including theological method. When applied to theology, there will correspond something to be experienced in theology, something to be understood in theology, something to be affirmed in theology.

The intending intention of being (*intentio intendens entis*) is distinct from the intended intention (*intentio intenta*). It is *noēsis, pensée pensante*, rather than *noēma, pensée pensée*. It is the dynamic openness of the human spirit, open to all things, ready to ask about all things. It is opposed to all obscurantism, which without any reason would immediately exclude at least some forms of questioning. And as open it is potency to faith, to those truths that exceed created intellect. It is dynamic in that it is a drive for fulfillment, manifested by wonder. We are not stupid as we experience. And when this openness reaches understanding, it reflects and is critical. Rationalism would allow it to be open only to what can be achieved by the natural use of reason. But this negation is not included in the intending intention itself but is added by one who has reflected on it. The supernatural is included in the transcendental, for it is being; it just exceeds what natural reason is able to attain on its own. The transcendental intending intention regards everything, not of course as known or even as knowable, but as intended. It is a conscious dynamic emptiness, like hunger in an empty stomach.

When we say it is open to all things, we are speaking of its finality. On finality, see 'Finality, Love, Marriage.'[33] Horizontal finality regards only what pertains to a given nature but vertical finality, which is what we are speaking of and which some deny gratuitously, is toward a perfection that transcends a given nature. Things are ordered beyond their essences. The intended intention is the true, and the true regards all beings, all true things. The true is known formally in judgment. Otherwise it is extrinsic, truth in the air, as in the syllogism of extrinsicist faith: What God reveals is true; but God reveals mysteries; therefore, the mysteries are true. The syllogism is valid for extrinsicists, but if truth is in the mind, then the minor has to be distinguished: true in the divine mind, yes; true in a created mind, sub-

---

33 Bernard Lonergan, 'Finality, Love, Marriage,' in *Collection* 17–52.

distinguish; in the created mind of a believer, yes; in the created mind of a nonbeliever, no. And distinguish the conclusion accordingly. Moreover, it is not as if every truth is knowable. Some are knowable, and others are believable, especially those that cannot be known naturally. These objects are not attainable in the order of *natura pura*, but in the real order, with the help of God's grace.

Rationalists, again, will rule out truths that a human mind cannot know naturally. They are non-committal with regard to truths that are perceived by God. They close the openness to truth, in proportion to human capability. In the state of *natura pura* such a stance would not be culpable, but in the present order of reality that closure is erroneous. The faithful do not attain supernatural objects without grace, but with grace that can reach some understanding. The intending intention towards being is of itself transcendental. It regards all things as desired, but not as attainable without help. Knowledge of the nature of God is desired but not attained naturally. But to accept this, one most acknowledge vertical finality.

Theological Data, Understanding, and Judgment
(8 January 1964, 51600DOL060)

The light of faith does not increase the dynamic openness itself, but the field of those things that are formally true.

We move, then, to the question of what is experience in the field of theology. Faith is from hearing (*fides ex auditu*). Therefore, there are data in the theological order. What are they?

Data in general are the matter about which questions are asked, in which an act of understanding happens, from which abstraction is made (the here and now of individual matter), and to which one returns when one weighs evidence. Data correspond to the empirical level of consciousness. They are the materials that are presupposed in all inquiry, understanding, and judgment. Data remain when all inquiry, understanding, and judgment vanish.

Data are different in different fields of knowledge. In the natural sciences, data are what are given to the eyes, ears, touch, smell, taste. They are without any intelligible information. The power of the natural sciences lies in the fact that their data are apparent to all. Is my hand white? A comparison with a white sheet of paper is sufficient to answer the question. The display itself is an empirical argument.

In the human sciences, the given (*datum*) includes meaning and meant in a very broad sense. Some understanding is required in the very apprehension of the data. The meaning is the understanding that the human race has or has had, whether it be about a school, a council, a tribunal, a book, or whatever, in this or that cultural milieu. Hence the importance of phenomenology, where insight is involved in making the data available, and of hermeneutics (even of romantic hermeneutics), and of the historical sense. These are fundamental in the human sciences, where there is a matter of the intelligibility that belongs to the data themselves.

This is not, of course, a matter of scientific understanding, which is deeper and broader and systematic. It is an understanding that belongs to the data as they are understood in their very constitution as data. Ordinary intelligibility is constitutive of the data. In economic or psychological science, laws are added that do not pertain to the constitution of the phenomena in any primary way, but there is a primary and ordinary intelligibility that is constitutive of phenomena as such. It is secondarily that scientific understanding may enter into the common apprehension of data, in accord with *die Wendung zur Idee*, the displacement towards system. Thus, economic conceptions may enter into our ordinary conceptions. Nonetheless, even then the apprehension is still almost never properly scientific, but a matter of vulgarization, popularization, simplification.[34] The primary and ordinary understanding has to do with the common sense of a region. What is meant is uttered in ordinary language, but even the theoretical order is not without some reference to the commonsense realm.

Next, theological data also have meaning, but in addition they possess truth. Their meaning is the meaning of a divine word. The question of theological *loci* is really a distinction among theological data: thus, the scriptures are the word of God, the councils clarify the scriptures, the Fathers and the theologians attest to the tradition, and so on. The problem of contemporary theology in large part consists in the fact that we consider the data of theology differently from the way they were considered in the past, because of historical consciousness. We understand the historical process and interpret documents and councils and everything else on that basis. Positive theology is what gives us the meaning in these various sources. But

---

34 References in the handwritten notes and/or in Thomas Daly's notes include: gold standard, free trade, democracy, *ancien régime*, clericalism, communism, Catholicism, the way the technical doctrine of the Trinity enters into ordinary life through the Sign of the Cross, the 'Glory be to the Father,' the creed, and so on.

because of the truth component in the data themselves, theology differs radically from the human sciences.[35]

So much for experience in theology. What about theological understanding? We may distinguish the understanding attained in positive theology, the understanding available in dogmatic theology, and the understanding intended and sometimes attained in systematics. The understanding of positive theology is the understanding of individual documents and authors. Dogmatic theology operates on the assumption that to understand the history of a doctrine is to understand the doctrine. The understanding is of the doctrine as a response to questions that have arisen in such and such a place and at such and such a time and for such and such reasons. And systematic understanding is the mediate, imperfect, analogical, and obscure understanding of the mysteries that was intended by Vatican I.

Now understanding may be direct or inverse. In direct understanding, something is positively understood about the thing itself. In inverse understanding, one understands that there is no inquiry to be made into something, either because it lacks intelligibility or because it possesses an intelligibility beyond our ability to attain. There are thus three fields, as it were: the field of excess of intelligibility, the field of intelligibility proportionate to human understanding, and the field of lack or absence of intelligibility. Inverse insight is involved in understanding the mysteries of faith, but inverse insight is not peculiar to theology. It is found in all the sciences.[36] In theology there is the excess of intelligibility regarding the mysteries, so that the only understanding we may attain of them is analogical. But there is also the lack of intelligibility in sin.

There remains the question of judgment as it is found in theology. Judgment is transformed in theology. When reason judges naturally, judgment proceeds from the grasp of sufficient evidence. Evidence is sufficient when all conditions for the judgment are fulfilled. When are all conditions fulfilled? When there are no further relevant questions. Knowing when there are no further relevant questions pertains to wisdom. There is wisdom proper to various fields, and in accord with this wisdom one is able to say that a certain conclusion will not be changed by further evidence, is beyond the influence of other fields, and so on. But the wisdom proportionate to

---

35 In Daly's notes, there is reference to *De Deo trino*, that is, to what is now available in *The Triune God: Doctrines*.

36 A reference is made in the notes to the examples of inverse insight in the first chapter of *Insight*.

theology belongs to God alone. It can be mediated to us through the infallible magisterium of the church, and it is for this reason that the theologian judges in such a way that he submits his judgment to the judgment of the church. But theology, a habit having to do with God and with all things in relation to God, does exist, and one does judge precisely as a theologian, at times perhaps with fear and trembling, but if one does not do so, one is like the servant who hid his talent in a napkin and buried it in the earth.

More on Judgment in Theology (15 January 1964, 51700D0L060)

Judgment, again, proceeds consciously, with rational consciousness, from the grasp of sufficient evidence, or from the virtually unconditioned, from the connection between the conditions and the conditioned once one experiences that the conditions are fulfilled. It depends on wisdom, which orders everything. Thus, the better the order of things is known, the better one judges. Specialization is wisdom in a qualified sense, grasping things in their interdependence in a given field. But one can be an expert in one field without knowledge in others, so that specialization and wisdom can be at odds with each other. Strict specialization weakens judgment unless there has been a good general education before specialization.

In theology judgment enters into the field of mystery. The proportionate and capable wisdom for theology is divine wisdom alone. The derived, instrumental wisdom of prophecy, of the assistance of the Holy Spirit, and of the magisterium is not promised to theologians. They have neither proportionate nor derived wisdom, simply as theologians, but they always do have the light of faith, and possibly wisdom as a gift of the Holy Spirit, and the habit of theology which is a certain wisdom, a certain total vision regarding God and all other things in relation to God.

Because theological judgment is concerned with the mysteries, it functions in the supernatural order. One who is dealing with the mysteries, the supernatural order, must know the teaching that has been received in the church. Hence, the theological notes are helpful. A theologian should not consider himself to be a private person. He is a member of the Body of Christ performing a function in the Body of Christ. He judges as a member of the Body. He belongs to the life of the church. He has an influence on others through what he says or does not say.

As far as specialization is concerned, we may note that it favors the consideration of all the data individually, which is an excellent thing, in that it is always most useful to know the positive data. But it also favors endless divisions and subdivisions, which is hard to reconcile with wisdom. Unless it is linked with a very solid basic course, it can have an influence upon the wisdom of a given judgment. It also favors a positivist tendency, with its inclination to reject the possibility of any valid comprehensive conspectus, or any metaphysics or epistemology. The positive sciences tend to dismiss wisdom as well as systematic theology.

The theologian must judge, then, though not in place of the church or in such a way that he arrogate to himself the function of inquisition, so as to condemn others and disrupt the community. But let the theologian really be a theologian. Unless he can trust his own mind and in fact does trust it, he can do nothing. Often he judges unconsciously, and by his prejudices he is brought to a conclusion that he had not considered. There are always these tendencies to rash judgment as well as tendencies to inertia. And he must consciously take his place between these tendencies.

Perhaps the largest field for exercising theological judgment at the present time has to do with the problems raised by new kerygmatic and catechetical problems. There is a new class of theologically uneducated people, often quite erudite in other fields. The way to explain to them is not the same as the way one would explain to the masses, but neither is it the way one would talk to those who are well versed in theology. Nowadays education is almost universal, so that we have a multitude of people neither uneducated nor really educated. The function of developing judgment is of the greatest importance. A Catholic who judges as a member of the Body of Christ thinks socially. And so we should also be familiar with the sociology of knowledge, a field that perhaps has not yet been treated by any Catholic.[37]

Functions of Transcendental Method in Theology (15 January 1964 bis, 51800D0L060)[38]

So much for general comments on the transcendental aspect of theology. We turn now to the function of a transcendental theological method. We

---

37 The notes mention Karl Mannheim, *Ideology and Utopia: An Introduction to the Sociology of Knowledge*, trans. Louis Wirth and Edward Shils (New York: Harcourt, Brace, 1949); Werner Stark, *The Sociology of Knowledge: Toward a Deeper Understanding of the History of Ideas* (London: Routledge & Kegan Paul, 1958); and Robert K. Merton, *Social Theory and Social Structure* (Glencoe, IL: The Free Press, 1957).

38 A second set of notes dated 15 January.

have distinguished positive, systematic, and dogmatic methods. What is the function of transcendental method in their regard?

First, it makes explicit and thematized what otherwise remains implicit and experienced only. The operations are always present, but they are not always considered. The positive, systematic, and dogmatic methods are practiced, but greater advertence to the operations occurs when explicit transcendental considerations are introduced. This is anything but superfluous. Insofar as one attends to the basic operations, one also attends to the areas in which the fundamental problems arise and understands them better. This is not something that is learned in a book and left there or relegated to oblivion. For the person is changed through transcendental reflection. The change promotes theological questions and theological investigations to a higher and more profound level.

Second, a transcendental theological method exercises a critical and foundational function: critical in that it eliminates basic errors, and foundational in that it establishes the foundation for making progress and firming up what is true. Reason illumined by faith is, first, reason. Reason is not merely philosophical, as if theology were only about faith. There is a distinction but not a separation. Faith is received in the possible intellect. The supernatural order is included in the transcendental field. The operations of a theologian are not about some subsistent thing called faith, but occur in a realm of faith that is in the intellect. Theology is an integration of faith in the intellect. Otherwise, we have simply a theology of the ghetto.

Third, reason progresses, and so the integration of theology with reason must similarly progress. Otherwise, it will simply disappear. The traditionalism of the nineteenth century is to be rejected. As Gilson said very well, in God to conserve and to create are the same thing, a comment that points to the true meaning of conservatism.[39] It is reason, not a mythic mentality, that faith illumines. Every science, philosophy, or theology that makes progress that seems to offer something new is overcoming some element of myth. Perceptualism is a mythic notion of knowledge: knowing is seeing, judgment sees the correspondence between the thing and the mind. This mythic mentality is the basis for two philosophical tendencies: naive realism positively, and idealism negatively. Human knowledge is structured, as we have seen, and objectivity has the same structure: experiential, normative, and absolute. Reality, too, is structured in an isomorphism with the struc-

39 No reference is provided for this comment.

ture of knowledge: potency, form, and act, in the central and conjugate orders. Unless one attends to fundamental questions concerning reason, there is no hope in the church for systematic theology. There will be endless fruitless disputes down through the centuries. Dogmatic theology will not last long either, if systematic theology disappears, for it is involved in the same questions. The Greek councils will be the next to go.[40]

The methods that we have distinguished – positive, dogmatic, and systematic – are united as parts of one body of knowledge, even as they are distinguished in accord with their contrasting specialized exigencies. Every development occurs through differentiation and integration. The distinction of methods points to a fundamental development. Patristic theology focused on the dogmatic, medieval theology on the systematic, and modern theology on the positive. Transcendental method unites them. Where a differentiation is called for but does not occur, we find unilateral tendencies. Examples are various. Some would reduce theological method to saying what Augustine said, or what Thomas said, or what Pius XII said. Others would identify theology with preaching; and then students who do not find in their professor a great preacher will find him saying many useless and superfluous things. Again, some would identify theology with history, so that only biblical, patristic, and medieval theology are taught.

Further on the Theological Functions of Transcendental Method (21 January, 51900D0L060)

Transcendental method makes the operations explicit and thematized, so that you do what you do with fuller conscious advertence.

It also is critical, in the sense that it eliminates the possibility of contradictions between what one does and what one says. For example, a theology that understands itself as reason illumined by faith will not make the positivist mistake (whether the positivism be theoretical or practical) of regarding reason as nothing. It will not espouse the mythic mentality of a positive or negative perceptualism, with the endless and fruitless questions and disputes that such a view spawns. It will avoid the difficulties of rationalism, semirationalism, liberalism, modernism, and conclusions theology.

---

40 Several comments appear in the notes about alternative views: rationalism, semirationalism, liberalism, modernism, and conclusions theology. See the next entry, below.

Transcendental method is also foundational. Everything else is reduced into its elements. It is immediately given. It is not avoided except through some sort of performative contradiction between what one does and what one says. The structure of the intending intention, again, begins with experience, in various patterns (aesthetic, practical, intellectual, and so on). One asks the question for intelligence, 'What is it?' Direct and inverse insight are employed in answering such questions, whether in philosophy or in science or in common sense. Then the question for reflection, 'Is it so?' follows with regard to one's formulation of one's understanding. Reflective understanding, grasping the sufficiency of evidence or the lack thereof, issues in the judgment 'It is' or 'No, it is not.' Again, too, there is a similar composition in the notion of objectivity and in the isomorphic metaphysical structure. Experiential objectivity is the given as given, corresponding to potency. Normative objectivity governs the process from experience to judgment, through principles of contradiction and sufficient reason. At the level of understanding, the corresponding metaphysical element is form. And absolute objectivity is reached with the grasp of the virtually unconditioned as it grounds and issues in judgment, the knowledge of act. We may even align with these steps the types of culture mentioned by Sorokin and corresponding ages in theology, so that ideational culture corresponds to act and is found in patristic theology, idealistic culture corresponds to form and is found in Scholastic theology, and sensate culture corresponds to potency and is found in modern positive theology.

Fundamental transcendental method, then, makes theology conscious of itself. It also makes theology a united enterprise. Just as reason is the principle of philosophy (there *are* essences), of the sciences (reaching understanding of essences), and of common sense (concrete practical matters), so reason illumined by faith is the principle of theology, whether dogmatic (the mysteries *are*), systematic (reaching some understanding of the mysteries), or positive (concerned with the concrete). These three are united in the one person of the theologian by the fundamental transcendental method.

The three dimensions also have an internal connection. Understanding the history of a doctrine is intimately connected with understanding the doctrine itself. A doctrine is not understood apart from its context and its development. And so dogmatic theology and positive theology are connected. Again, understanding a doctrine is connected with understanding the matter about which the doctrine is formulated. And so dogmatic theology and systematic theology are thus also connected. The principle of the unity can itself be reduced to the intending intention. Positive theology declares what is believed, and it does so in accord with social, cultural, and historical differentiation. Dogmatic theology declares what is universally believed. And systematic theology understands the reality that is believed to be.

This unity of theology has itself developed, along with the development of methods. In general, all development occurs through differentiation and integration. In differentiation, the separate elements or stages become more perfect. The work is divided. This concentration on the elements leaves out a consideration of the whole. After differentiation, there appears to be nothing but an incoherent congeries. But integration provides that which was lacking, to make the entire enterprise a whole. Prior to differentiation, there was a global whole, but after differentiation, integration restores the interdependence of the elements in a new way. It is at this point that the problem of method in theology is recognized for what it is.[41]

More on Differentiation and Integration
(22 January 1964, 52000D0L060)

The dynamic unity of theology is a matter of the development of methods.[42] Development in general has two moments: differentiation and integration. Differentiation is a prerequisite, but it arrives at a critical moment when integration is required. It is then that the problem of method in theology is recognized.

Of the three parts of theology – dogmatic, systematic, and positive – the dogmatic part of theology developed first. It coincides with the development of the dogmas themselves. From the common apprehension there results the *Wendung zur Idee*, the displacement towards system, and the transition to the literal meaning, in the absolute sense of that term. That is, 'literal sense' here is not a hermeneutical term used to mean 'the mind of the author,' whether or not the author himself or herself had a literal mentality

---

41 The two final pages of this item spell out a bit how this integration takes place. What they add is also presented in the next item.
42 At this point Lonergan lists several relevant bibliographical items. In order, they are B. O'Leary, 'The Renewal of Moral Theology,' *Continuum* 1:3 (1963) 310–18; John B. Cobb, Jr, *Living Options in Protestant Theology* (Philadelphia: Westminster, 1963); Hans-Georg Fritzsche, *Die Strukturtypen der Theologie: Eine kritische Einführung in die Theologie* (Göttingen: Venderhoeck & Ruprecke, 1961); and James M. Robinson and John B. Cobb, Jr, *The Later Heidegger and Theology* (New York: Harper & Row, 1963).

in the strict sense or a mythical mentality; in fact, metaphorical sense is earlier than literal: compare 'effulgence of his glory and very stamp of his being' with 'homoousion.' The movement is more and more towards a manifestation of the transcendental intention in the development. Those who deny the dogmas are also excluded from the communion of the church. As a consequence of this dogmatic development, there now exist schismatics and heretics. But a further consequence is that there takes place in the church an integration between doctrine and life, as witnessed in the liturgy with its explicit Trinitarian and Christological dimensions.[43] The dogmas, moreover, render the mysteries clearly mysterious; whence there emerged the unique character of Byzantine Scholasticism.

Distinctions such as that between person and nature gave rise to the need for speculation in theology. With this need the systematic part of theology emerged. If the dogmas rendered the mysteries clearly mysterious, Anselm asked about the most difficult questions: the Trinity, grace, the virginal conception, why God became man, etc. He showed that questions truly exist, but his solutions lacked a positive basis. Abelard in his *Sic et non* laid the possibility of a positive foundation, but also showed that questions are not solved by authority, that the authorities do not always agree with one another. There emerges the method and the technique of the *quaestio*, with its presentations of the reasons for and against, its argument for a definite solution, and its responses to the objections. The technique is manifest in a very clear way in *De veritate*, q, 24, a. 12, where Aquinas changes the position he had adopted in the commentary on the *Sentences*. By the time of the *Summa theologiae* the technique itself has become rather stylized. But the need for coherent solutions to the questions is clear, and in the *Summa* the series of questions is itself ordered according to an explicitly adopted order of teaching, where the solution to one problem depends on the solution to others and where one begins with the questions whose solution does not depend on the solution of anything else. The need for a system emerged, and the theologians turned to Aristotle.

Around the year 1230 there emerged an ontological distinction between the natural and the supernatural orders. Grace is above nature, faith above reason, charity above good will, merit before God above human praise, and eternal life above prosperity in this world. This distinction laid a methodo-

---

43 There is a reference here to Pope Damasus's adding the 'Gloria Patri' to the psalms in the liturgy of the hours.

logical foundation for theology. Vatican I turned to this distinction to solve problems raised by the semirationalists. But there *are* two elements, and nature itself must be acknowledged, the realm or field in which human reason knows things that have their own proper intelligibility. This distinction marks the essential difference in the approach of Aquinas over against that of Bonaventure.

There are defects in this medieval movement, however. First, it was ahistorical. Conceptions were treated not according to their historical genesis but logically and atemporally. Second, it had no critical foundation, and so disputed questions tended to be raised endlessly and without any resolution. Decadent Scholasticism resulted. Third, we may speak of a division of the subject. As the Greeks separated theory and praxis, so Christians separated contemplation and action. The moderns were to make a threefold distinction: the interiority of the existential subject conscious of self, the world of community, and the field of theory that was developed as much as possible in natural science, mathematics, and logic. Theory as regards human affairs is the enlightenment of the concrete subject precisely as a subject of the historical process, while theory as regards natural objects tends to be instrumental and to head towards the domination of things. Because Scholasticism had no application to practical living, it gave way to the *devotio moderna*, to pietism and Protestantism, and eventually to positive theology.

The emergence of positive theology was also the beginning of the explicit turn to method. In positive theology the sources appear as a result of the invention of the printing press, of readily accessible printing. Editions appeared of the scriptures, the Fathers, the councils, the theologians, and positive studies were made of these texts. The origin and development of positive theology is still not well examined.[44]

Even with the development of positive studies, theology still did not really acknowledge the modern world. Positive renewal remained a medieval phenomenon. The modern world is based on modern science, which requires a philosophy that is capable of controlling the sciences, and on

44 Several comments are made without explicit indication of how they are related: Controversies with Protestants, apologetics against the rationalists, Scholasticism avoided, the Carmelites at Salamanca with their preservation of Scholasticism, Gallican theology and positive studies, the extensive positive bibliography in Xiberta, *Introductio in Sacram Theologiam*, the movement to increase the study of positive sources in seminaries, *Deus scientiarum Dominus.*

historical consciousness.[45] Natural things have properties and are known through them. But man reveals himself to himself, in his very watchfulness and intentionality. Nature is governed by specific laws, but man by transcendental laws, which become determinate through knowledge and freedom. We come to be through our knowledge and our freedom. The juridical order extends to the intentional, which is always present in man. It is when he acknowledges this that he emerges from nature. His institutions are his own creation. We continue to function in them only as we wish. We can change them. And this historical consciousness requires an adaptation in philosophy.

A further distinct character of modernity is the emergence of the masses and of the mass mind, studied through the sociology of knowledge.

Positive studies and recognition of the modern world are connected, then, but they are also distinct. There has yet to emerge among Catholics, however, a clear distinction between positive studies and modern philosophy. Those who reject positive studies do so because they are afraid of a fundamental critique. The methodological part is beyond their horizon. There has developed a type of tardy conventionalism, books with notes and bibliography as demanded by positive methods but still without any acknowledgment of the modern world. Modernity has been met with either fear or fundamental incomprehension.

The present situation concerning method admits of several divisions. These are admittedly being proposed a priori. They have not been made on the basis of a full investigation of authors.

There are those who do not clearly distinguish between positive studies and methodical exigencies. Some reject positive studies because they fear methodical considerations. Some accept positive studies, but the methodical exigencies remain beyond their horizon: these are the people who engage in the tardy conventionalism just mentioned. Others, finally, accept positive studies, without exaggerations, but perhaps also without a clear apprehension of the problems that they raise.

There are others who do distinguish between positive studies and methodical exigencies. But they despair of a solution and either yield to con-

---

45 A reference is made to Robert Johann's comment in *America*, December 1963, p. 795 to the effect that with man's emergence from nature the world becomes unstuck. This clears up the source of a reference to Johann on p. 384 of Bernard Lonergan, *Early Works on Theological Method 1*, vol. 22 in Collected Works of Bernard Lonergan, trans. Michael G. Shields, ed. Robert M. Doran and Robert C. Croken (Toronto: University of Toronto Press, 2010).

ventionalism in positive studies or to an urbane skepticism that despairs of any deeper effort.

Futurists break continuity with the past and leap into an entirely new theology, while simplicists restrict themselves to what is useful, necessary, and practical: the liturgy, biblical studies, homiletics, without any Hellenism or Scholasticism. On this view, the dogmas are not to be pressed. They were the product of a Hellenistic exigency. Method is just philosophy, nothing more. Scholasticism is a medieval aberration, scarcely religious.

Our position is that development consists in differentiation and integration. I have taught differentiation. My studies of Aquinas represent the positive part, my *Divinarum personarum* the systematic, and my *De Deo Trino* the dogmatic, while *Insight* presents the fundamental critical thought that is required.[46]

Integration has two aspects, objective and subjective. In the objective aspect, the objects of the differentiated parts differ only modally. In positive theology there is sought an understanding of the history of a doctrine about some reality; in dogmatic theology there is sought an understanding of the doctrine about the same reality; in systematic theology the reality itself is understood; in the critical methodological review of all this there is sought an understanding of oneself understanding the history and the doctrine and the reality. And in a new variant of positive theology there is sought an understanding of others as they understand the history and the doctrine.

The subjective aspect of the integration is a function of the fact that the human condition is itself structured and is the font of integration. Here the notion of mediation is helpful. Aristotle's logic displays mediation in that the first principles are mediated through evidence, while the other premises are mediated through the principles. Again, Christ is the mediator between God and human beings. In Hegel we find a universal application of this notion.[47]

---

46 The Thomist studies, of course, are *Grace and Freedom* and *Verbum*, that is, the first two volumes in Lonergan's Collected Works. *Divinarum personarum* was to be revised and become *De Deo Trino: Pars systematica*, now available as *The Triune God: Systematics*, vol. 12 in the Collected Works, and what here is called *De Deo Trino* became *De Deo Trino: Pars dogmatica*, now vol. 11 in the Collected Works, *The Triune God: Doctrines*.

47 Reference is made to 'Niel,' that is, to Henri Niel, *De la médiation dans la philosophie de Hegel* (Paris: Aubier, 1945). See the opening paragraphs of 'The Mediation of Christ in Prayer,' in *Philosophical and Theological Papers 1958–1964* 160–63 for clearer exposition on Aristotle and Hegel on mediation.

We may distinguish mutual mediation, self-mediation, and mutual self-mediation. In mutual mediation, a functional whole is constituted by mutually mediating parts.[48] In self-mediation, the whole has consequences that change the whole.[49] Mutual self-mediation is a function of interpersonal relations. Mediation in general, mutual mediation, and self-mediation can be illustrated in mechanical, organistic, and gnoseological examples.[50] Here we are concerned primarily with mutual mediation. Thus, in a watch 'the balance wheel controls itself and all the other moving parts, including the mainspring; and the mainspring moves itself and all the other parts, including the balance wheel. This is a mutual mediation.'[51] In the organism, 'the respiratory system supplies fresh oxygen not merely to the lungs but to the whole body. The digestive system supplies nutrition not merely to the digestive tract but to the whole body. The nervous system supplies control not merely to the nervous system but to the whole body. And the muscles supply locomotion not merely to the muscles but to the whole body. The result is something that has fresh oxygen and is nourished, is under control and is moving, because you have a number of immediate centers, and from each center there flows over the whole the consequences of that center.'[52] In knowledge, we find mutual mediation in the structure. The experiential dimension provides facticity, the intellectual clarity and order, and judgment truth and certitude. The whole of knowledge is true through judgment, clear through understanding, factual through experience.[53]

Theology too exhibits mutual mediation. The whole of theology is given its facticity through the positive part, its clarity and coherence through sys-

---

Other references are taken from this same paper, to fill out what is mentioned in Lonergan's and/or Daly's notes. In mediation in general, 'we can say of any factor, quality, property, feature, aspect that has, on the one hand, a source, origin, ground, basis, and on the other hand, consequences, effects, derivatives, a field of influence, of radiation, of expansion, or that has an expression, manifestation, revelation, outcome – we can say that this factor, quality, property, feature, or aspect is immediate in the source, origin, ground, or basis, and on the other hand is mediated in the consequences, effects, derivatives, outcome, in the field of influence, radiation, expansion, in the expression, manifestation, revelation.' Ibid. 162.

48 Ibid. 165.
49 Ibid. 167.
50 See ibid. 163–74.
51 Ibid. 165.
52 Ibid. 165–66.
53 This example is not provided in 'The Mediation of Christ in Prayer.'

tematics, and its certitude in dogmatics. And it is critically grounded by transcendental method.

Thus, we have the twofold aspect of integration: modally on the part of the object, and mediation on the part of the subject, where integration occurs through the mutual mediation of the parts.

Integration and the Uses of Theology
(28 January 1964, 52100D0L060)[54]

Integration can also be understood from a consideration of the various uses of theology: expository, constitutive, sapiential, edification of the members of the body of Christ, and apologetic extension of the body of Christ. We begin with the sapiential, the integration of theology with other disciplines.

There is a relation between theology and philosophy that is clarified by these transcendental methodical considerations. If theology is reason illumined by faith, then philosophy prepares for an integration of the two within theology itself.

As for the relation of theology and the sciences, it takes place through their respective methods, not as an integration of theology and various scientific conclusions. Scientific conclusions are in flux, but scientific method is stable. The methods of both the sciences and theology develop slowly, and so a relation to science is prepared by theological method itself. The structure of knowledge disclosed through the transcendental method is the ground of scientific method.

The relation of theology and the empirical human sciences is complex. In the medieval period, the integration of theology and philosophy was *eo ipso* an integration of theology and science, since the sciences were simply an extension of Aristotelian metaphysics. Today the human sciences are not integrated through philosophy alone, any more than are the natural sciences. They are empirical. They consider man as he is, but often fail to recognize that such a consideration must have a theological component, for man as he is is man as he is affected by original sin, as he is offered grace, and as he either accepts or rejects the offer. These factors are not treated in philosophy, and so any integration of the human sciences will

---

54 The first three pages of this item simply repeat essential elements in the previous item, with no new developments. These pages are not included in this reconstruction.

have to turn to theology. Philosophy also cannot mediate the relation of theology and the human sciences. There is needed a more direct connection between the two.

The relation of theology with literature and the arts is prepared by the patterns of experience. Scripture itself is a literary work or set of works.[55]

Finally, there is the relation between theology and history. In addition to what has already been said about this relation in speaking of the human sciences, we may add that if theology has to do with God and all else in relation to God, human history is included in the 'all else.' This is particularly emphasized in chapter 20 of *Insight*. What we have been calling dialectic is implicitly grounded in history, with its threefold approximation of progress (no one sins), decline (the social surd), and redemption through the law of the cross, where evil is overcome not by evil but by good.

Also related to integration are the functions of theology that have to do with theology and the life of the church, whether the internal edification of the members of the body of Christ or the apologetic extension of the body of Christ. The life of the church requires not only philosophy and natural ethics but also reason illumined by faith. Some of the truths of philosophy and ethics may be certain, but they are also abstract and can lead to antinomies. What happens in the concrete? We find that problems are solved in the concrete by the light of revelation and in no other way. A strictly philosophical account of human reality has to do with man as he would be in a state of pure nature, and that state does not exist. In the light of the gospel, though, and perhaps in place of what might be more pleasing from a natural and seemingly reasonable point of view, some of these questions can be answered.[56] John XXIII's invitation to open the windows applies also to theology, which itself can open windows that more narrow perspectives

55 Reference is made here to the spring 1963 course on method, with the notions of the analogy of meaning and the meaning of meaning. While these expressions do not occur in Lonergan's notes for that course, clearly the ideas are present there. See also Lonergan's lecture 'The Analogy of Meaning' in *Philosophical and Theological Papers 1958–1965*, a lecture given at Thomas More Institute, Montreal, on 25 September 1963, that is, just prior to the present course. Many of the ideas from the spring course are repeated in the lecture, with the new language regarding the analogy of meaning. See also below, the material beginning on 29 January 1964.

56 It is interesting that in Daly's notes Lonergan indicates at this point that the question of religious liberty, which was being debated at the Second Vatican Council at the time, may be 'ad rem' at this point. This does not appear in his handwritten notes, which do, however, refer to the council at this point.

would leave closed and so exclusive of new possibilities.[57] Practical specialists commonly do not see anything beyond their own narrow horizons.

As for apologetics and integration, there is the question of fundamental theology. As presently understood and taught it has to do not with the foundations of faith but with the reasonableness of faith in accord with some conceptual system. This creates extrinsicism, logicism, and conceptualism. Apologetics should be present in every theology treatise, in the sense that every treatise needs something that orders theology so that it is clear to others, that is, so that they may understand what we are saying, not according to a distorted subjective way of receiving what we are putting forward but with, as it were, open windows.

We move now to a fuller investigation of the systematic dimension of theology.[58] The understanding that is sought in theology is different in the different parts. Positive theology would understand the history of a doctrine, dogmatic theology the strict dogmatic element, and systematic theology that which the dogma refers to. As dogmatic theology and positive theology are distinguished, so the systematic part is similarly distinguished from the dogmatic. The differences are correlated too with the levels of consciousness in the subject, with positive theology correlative to experience, systematic theology correlative to understanding, and dogmatic theology correlative to judgment. The three are obviously interrelated. Unless something is understood about the reality itself, virtually nothing is understood about the words that are used to talk about the reality. But dogmatic theology uses understanding and experiencing while attending especially to judgment, while systematics uses experience and judgment but attends especially to understanding. Systematics seeks an understanding of those realities that dogmatic theology affirms. Dogmatic theology begins from revelation, the 'prior' with respect to us, while systematics begins with those things without which other things will not be understood.

This leads us to speak about a distinction between the order of discovery, which is an analytic resolution to causes, slowly moving to certitude, and the order of teaching, composition, synthesis, which is hypothetical and probable in its understanding of what one holds to be true. Actually, there are

---

57 In Daly's notes, though not in Lonergan's handwritten notes, there is reference here to Piaget on the moral development of children.
58 Reference is made in Lonergan's notes here to *Divinarum personarum*, chapter 1, and to *De Deo trino: Pars systematica*, which in class he called the 'proxima editio,' the recent edition.

five opposite notes according to whether we begin from what is prior with respect to us or from what is prior with respect to themselves. If we begin from what is prior with respect to us, (1) we follow the order of discovery, which (2) proceeds to causes or ultimate reasons (3) in the analytic order, which is temporal in that it gradually discovers the causes; (4) this is the way of certitude, (5) beginning from the most concrete data, what is obvious to all. If we begin with the *priora quoad se*, (1) we are following the order of teaching, which (2) proceeds from the causes or reasons to the realities; (3) this is the order of composition, and it is not a temporal order but proceeds through logical immediacy, (4) according to the way of probability, (5) starting from what has to be understood first before anything else can be understood, that from the understanding of which everything else follows.

These orders are thus inverse orders with respect to the same material. Thus, with respect to the Trinity, the order of discovery moves from the divine missions as they are presented in the New Testament, that is, from the sending of the Son and of the Holy Spirit, from what is prior *quoad nos*, to the divine processions, to what is prior *quoad se*; but Aquinas, in questions 27 to 43 in the first part of the *Summa theologiae*, follows the order of teaching and begins with the *quoad se*, the eternal processions understood in accord with a psychological analogy, and ends with the *quoad nos*, the missions. The systematic part begins where the dogmatic part ends, and vice versa.

The questions raised in the systematic part are interconnected. The solution of one question depends on the solution of others. For Aquinas wisdom orders the questions, understanding grasps the solution to the first question, and science or knowledge ('scientia') grasps the remaining solutions, which are derived from the solution to the first question. In speaking of understanding, I am not speaking about concepts or about judgments, about nouns and verbs and propositions. Understanding precedes definition, and it makes one able to say the same thing in different ways and to provide multiple illustrations. Knowledge, 'scientia,' is an increase, an extension, of understanding. And wisdom is a synthetic overview of all understanding and knowledge in a given field.

Nonetheless, in order to express ourselves we must form concepts, and these must be systematic concepts expressed in technical terminology if we are going to express the connections between the various elements. Theology did not on its first attempt achieve the order of its materials. There is a history to the genesis of any treatise, as is evidenced by the differences in the Trinitarian theologies in the various works of Aquinas. Only with the

Summa theologiae did he reach the systematic way of proceeding. Moreover, a treatment that has been done perfectly does not necessarily last forever. There is decadence. A poor understanding of the first step is the root cause of the decadence, as is manifest today in what follows from a poor understanding or misunderstanding of the psychological analogy for understanding the processions. If the first step is misunderstood, the solutions derived from it are incomplete, and in fact unsatisfactory. Thus, a new series of problems is born, leading to new treatments, different ways of misunderstanding, diverse kinds of decadence.[59]

The systematic part of theology is to be differentiated from the methodical or transcendental aspect. The latter has to do with the general notions and principles, the transcendentals themselves and the operations through which they are pursued, whereas the systematic has to do with a certain proper intelligibility, namely, the intelligibility of the mysteries of faith. It seeks an understanding, however mediated, analogical, and imperfect it may be, of this dimension of reality. The psychological analogy, for example, is the answer to the question 'What is divine procession?' There is a nature to be understood, and systematics concerns itself with that kind of question.

Meaning and Horizon (29 January 1964, 52200D0L060)

We move now, and finally, to consider two fundamental notions, meaning and horizon. These will be our topics in the last classes of the course.

We begin with meaning.[60] The question 'What is meaning?' cannot be answered except by signifying something. Therefore, in some manner meaning is a closed world; it explains itself, in a manner similar to what Aristotle says about color and light in *De anima*. Color is made visible by light. But what is light? If you don't know, Aristotle says, there is no answer.[61]

There are two ways of coming at the question. The synthetic way would compose a meaning from its elements, beginning with cognitional theory. And the analytic way would begin from a concrete whole and derive the ele-

---

59 On this material, see also Lonergan, *The Triune God: Systematics* 26–29.
60 It seems clear that the lecture 'The Analogy of Meaning' (see above, note 55) is a fuller expansion of the material that Lonergan wrote for this class and the next. The editing here relies heavily on that lecture as a background against which to read the present text.
61 See Aristotle, *De anima*, VI, 2.

ments. The latter is the approach we will take here.[62] We are saying three things. First, meaning constitutes communication; second, in the individual meaning is constitutive of human potentiality, human knowledge, and human life; and third, common meaning constitutes potential community, community of knowledge, and community of obligation.

Our treatment of communication as constituted by meaning has seven aspects: (1) ordinary language, (2) intersubjective meaning, (2) incarnate meaning, (4) affective meaning, (5) artistic meaning, (6) literary meaning, and (7) technical meaning. We are seeking the significance and meaning in each of these.

First, then, ordinary language, that is, the language used in the home, in school, in business, in the newspapers, on television, in politics, and so on. Three elements are noteworthy: an expressive element, found in the optative mood and expressed in the first person, an imperative element, found in the imperative mood and expressed in the second person, and a propositional element, found in the indicative mood and expressed in the third person. These can sometimes be found in a pure state, separately and by themselves, and sometimes in a mixed fashion. They can be found in the immediate and transient communication of ordinary speech and in the mediated and permanent fashion proper to written communication. The importance of ordinary language in human communication is seen in the significance of the name among the Hebrews and Greeks and in the example of Helen Keller in the moment when she first realized the meaning of the signs being made on her hand and proceeded from 'water' to the names of other things. Other examples can be found in Ernst Cassirer, *Philosophy of Symbolic Forms*, vol. 1.[63]

Second, intersubjective meaning is the meaning of mutual presence, encounter, recognition. Written and even spoken language abstracts from intersubjective meaning. The meaning present in the very fact that someone comes to me and I go to him revives all the circumstances of our prior meetings and contains a tacit consent to continue or perhaps to change our

---

62 Note the difference from the categories employed at this point in 'The Analogy of Meaning,' where an approach through cognitional theory is called 'analytic' and is contrasted with a 'descriptive' approach, the latter being what Lonergan follows. In the present notes the descriptive approach is itself called analytic. See 'The Analogy of Meaning' 184.

63 Ernst Cassirer, *The Philosophy of Symbolic Forms*, trans. Ralph Mannheim, vol. 1: *Language* (New Haven: Yale University Press, 1955).

prior relations. Intersubjective meaning contains everything that is revealed through tone of voice, facial expression, smiles, liveliness, silence. It is the presence not just of bodies but of complete beings. The whole person expresses himself or herself through such communication. There is a psychic adaptation of persons to one another according to the relationship: friend, superior, relative, and so on. The mutual interaction reveals the possibility of more or less communication. We avoid topics of conversation likely to offend or upset. There is a mutual development of expression between persons, as they influence each other in a cumulative fashion. Phenomenological studies have been made of such communication, by Max Scheler, in *Wesen und Formen der Sympathie*[64] and F.J.J. Buytendijk, *Phénoménologie de la rencontre*.[65]

Third, there is incarnate meaning. The very life and action of a person express meaning, a meaning which we admire and love, recreate and live, or detest, hate, and flee. In the life of Christ himself, we have the incarnate meaning not only of Jesus but also of Peter, John, Judas Iscariot, Pilate, Herod, Caiaphas; and we have the incarnate meaning of Jesus for all these other protagonists in the story. Every country has its national figures whose very life embodies incarnate meaning.[66]

Fourth, there is affective and symbolic meaning. A symbol is an image suffused with affectivity. The feeling may evoke the image, and the image may evoke the feeling. They occur together, mutually confirming one another. As one grows and intensifies, so does the other. But there are various systems for interpreting symbols. In Freud we have symbols of interpersonal relations in the family, as told through the Oedipus cycle. Jung emphasizes that not all dreams and symbols are the fruit of repression. His archetypal

---

64 Max Scheler, *Wesen und Formen der Sympathie* (Bern: Francks, 1953); in English, *The Nature of Sympathy*, trans. Peter Heath (London: Routledge & Kegan Paul, 1954).

65 F.J.J. Buytendijk, *Phénoménologie de la rencontre*, trans. into French by Jean Knapp (Bruges: Desclée de Brouwer, 1952). In the Daly notes, there is added a comment to the effect that phenomenology is an instance of understanding in phantasms, but there is the danger of lacking a higher regulator; acts of understanding are numerous and easy, and a totality is required or they will be erroneous and incomplete; judgment frequently is overlooked, and phenomenologists will often differ among themselves for this reason, despite the fact that they proceed with great care in their work.

66 As elsewhere, Lonergan mentions in this context the three-volume work of Georges Morel, *Le sens de l'existence selon s. Jean de la Croix* (Paris: Aubier, 1960–61).

symbols point to the transformation of the self and to a deep religious aspiration.[67] More elementary symbols are treated by Gilbert Durand, *Les structures anthropologiques de l'imaginaire*: symbols of terror, of ascending, and so on, based on dominant reflexes such as balance, swallowing, and mating.[68] There is also the application of existentialism to symbols, as represented by Ludwig Binswanger, *Traum und Existenz*[69] and Rollo May.[70]

Next, there is artistic meaning. With its revelation of human potentiality it interrupts ordinary life, the life of the ready-made man in a ready-made world, and manifests the possibility of living differently in another world. It is the expression, indeed the intelligent expression, of such potentiality.[71]

Literary meaning aims at doing in written form what is done by the spoken word. That is, it uses language in such a way that all elements of communication are present. Classical rationalization distinguished between the logical meaning and a transferred or figurative meaning. Meaning that is logically ordered and determined is an ideal that not even Euclid managed to attain. In actual fact the figurative sense is primary, while the proper sense is a rational ideal.

Literary meaning fluctuates between the laws of logical coherence and the laws of the imagination and the senses.[72] Besides using the defined concepts and the implications of propositions, literary meaning also exploits intersubjective, incarnate, symbolic, and artistic meaning, and in the measure that this occurs there emerge the modes of thinking, of operating, that

---

67 Lonergan mentions in his notes vol. 7 of Jung's Collected Works, *Two Essays on Analytical Psychology*. Now available in an edition trans. Gerhard Adler and R.F.C. Hull (Princeton: Princeton University Press, 1972). He mentions also Mircea Eliade, *Forgerons et alchimistes* (Paris: Flammarion, 1956) and *Mythes, rêves et mystères* (Paris: Gallimard, 1957).

68 See above, p. 14, note 17.

69 French translation, Ludwig Binswanger, *Le rêve et l'existence* (Paris: Desclée, 1954), with introduction (128 pp.) and notes by Michel Foucault.

70 Rollo May, Ernest Angel, Henri F. Ellenberger, eds, *Existence: A New Dimension in Psychiatry and Psychology* (New York: Basic Books, 1958); Rollo May, ed., *Existential Psychology* (New York: Random House, 1961); Rollo May, 'The Significance of Symbols,' in *Symbolism in Religion and Literature*, ed. Rollo May (New York: Braziller, 1961). The Daly notes include reference to dreams of the night and dreams of the morning.

71 Lonergan mentions Susanne Langer, *Feeling and Form* (New York: Scribner, 1963) and René Huyghe, *L'art et l'âme* (Paris: Flammarion, 1960). The Daly notes refer to '*Insight* on Play and Art.'

72 The remainder of this section is taken from 'The Analogy of Meaning,' which contains all the points mentioned in Lonergan's and Daly's notes.

were analyzed by Freud in his account of dream work. There is a movement from the class concepts of logic towards the representative figure: think of the first and second Adam. Again, from the univocal concept one moves to simultaneous multiple meanings. A word as well defined, as employed logically, has just one meaning, and one proceeds consistently, always using the word in precisely that sense or giving notice to the contrary; but in the measure that the laws of imagination and affect take over, the same word occurs with several meanings at once, and all are intended. Again, instead of the logical law of excluded middle (either *A* or not-*A*), insofar as the laws of imagination and affect take over, there is overdetermination, ambivalence; there is love, but not merely love, also hate, and with respect to the same object. Again, where the logician will prove, the literary thinker will reinforce, he will repeat, he will enumerate, he will give you variations on the same theme, he will build up accumulations that head to a climax. According to the famous phrase of the character in *Alice in Wonderland*, 'When I say something three times, it's true.'

Again, the logical approach is satisfied with the simple negation, It is not so; but the poet posits the object to overcome it, piles up other things against it till it is annihilated. That is the only way imagination and affect can negate. Again, from the single theme, the single level of representation, there is a movement towards condensation, the combination of a whole series of different themes within the same phrase or sentence. This is so conspicuous in Shakespeare, in, for example, the early part of *Macbeth*, when Macbeth states:

> And Pity, like a naked newborn babe,
> Striding the blast, or Heaven's Cherubin, hors'd
> Upon the sightless couriers of the air,
> Shall blow the horrid deed in every eye
> That tears shall drown the wind.

He starts off with pity, a naked newborn babe, which somehow is striding the blast; moves on to heaven's cherubin, horsed on the sightless couriers of the air; and then the horrid deed of murdering the king is blown in every eye, and the eyes start weeping and the wind is drowned. We see here a condensation of a variety of different themes that, from the viewpoint of logical analysis, is very paradoxical but, from the viewpoint of poetic expression, is extremely effective; it fits in with the spontaneous condensations that follow the laws of imagination and affect.

More on Meaning (4 February 1964, 52300DOL060)

There is also technical meaning.[73] Only primitives get along without any technical meanings at all. The build-up of technical meanings has been described by Ernst Cassirer in his *Philosophy of Symbolic Forms* and his *Essay on Man*,[74] by Karl Jaspers in his book on *The Origin and Goal of History*,[75] and by Eric Voegelin in his *Order and History*.[76]

Briefly, the ancient high civilizations – Egypt, Mesopotamia, Crete, the valleys of the Indus and the Hwang Ho, the Mayas in Central America, and the Incas in Peru – developed the mechanical arts of irrigation, architecture, tools, and the organizational arts of bookkeeping, the state, armies, navies. But at the summit, they were locked in myth. They would be completely intelligent with regard to anything that was practical. The king was Son of God, ruler of the cosmos, and ruler of the state.

The breakdown of these ancient high civilizations resulted in a breakdown of the myth. By revelation in Israel and by the *logos* in Greece, there developed something that met the questions that the myth had met in its own way. Plato's early dialogues depict Socrates asking the Athenians, What is temperance? What is fortitude? What is virtue? What is justice? What is knowledge? While the Athenians knew perfectly well what all these things were, they could not answer Socrates because he had a new gimmick. He wanted universal definitions, definitions that applied *omni et soli*, to every case and to no other. He was introducing a technique of thought, and to introduce that technique was a breakthrough from the hold of imagination and affect upon human thinking. Aristotelian ethics worked out the answers to Socrates's questions, the universal answers, the universal definitions, but these answers were technical. The technical word, technical thinking, was developed particularly in that Greek milieu.

The transition to technical meaning involves a differentiation of con-

---

73 The first part of this section, too, is based on the corresponding section in 'The Analogy of Meaning,' again because that lecture contains much that is given in Lonergan's and Daly's notes in a more schematic fashion.

74 Ernst Cassirer, *An Essay on Man: An Introduction to a Philosophy of Human Culture* (New York: Doubleday, 1954).

75 Karl Jaspers, *The Origin and Goal of History*, trans. Michael Bullock (London: Routledge & Kegan Paul, 1953).

76 Eric Voegelin, *Order and History*. Lonergan's notes refer to 3 vols (i.e., *Israel and Revelation, The World of the Polis,* and *Plato and Aristotle,* Baton Rouge, LA: Louisiana State University Press, 1956–58).

sciousness, a new type of subject that differs from the old as Thales differed from the milkmaid. Thales was gazing at the stars and did not see the well at his feet, and the milkmaid laughed: how on earth can he expect to know anything about the stars when he cannot see a well right at his own feet? But still, Thales had become a different type of psychological subject from the milkmaid. There was a prior period when every subject was just like the milkmaid. This development involves a differentiation of worlds. Eddington speaks of the two tables in his office. One was brown and hard and solid, made of wood, containing drawers, useful; and the other was mostly a vacuum – here and there there were electrons and protons floating about, but you could not *imagine* what they were. This development involves also a different language. When the chemist or botanist or depth psychologist starts talking to you, he is talking another language, a technical language, a language invented to describe a different world for a different subject. This development also creates a different society. The man who spends his day doing modern physics and then goes home to his wife and children is migrating from one world to the other. There is a different type of development of understanding, a different type of inquiry and investigation, from that of common sense, one with its own rules, its own criteria, its own laws. There is a movement from 'We both understand what is meant, so why waste our time trying to define it?' to definition; from proverbs, which fulfill the same sort of function as rules of grammar – rules with lots of exceptions, but it is worthwhile paying attention to them – from proverbs to principles and laws that must hold in absolutely every case or else they are completely worthless; from seeing the point to logical deduction and detailed verification.[77]

77 In 'The Analogy of Meaning' Lonergan concludes his treatment of these
   seven instances of communication with the following paragraph: 'I have
   been speaking of meaning as constitutive of human communication, and
   I considered some seven ways in which that meaning takes form. There is
   meaning in everyday language, and if you write out the language you are
   omitting an awful lot, you are omitting the intersubjective element where
   there is meaning that is not conceptual, not verbal, but still very real, very
   vital, and very effective. There is incarnate meaning, which is the intersubjective meaning raised to a pitch of intensity – the meaning of the cruci-
   fix or the meaning of the hero. There is the affective meaning of the symbol,
   whether you think of the Freudian or Jungian symbols or the nonclinical
   symbols studied by Durand. There is the meaning of the work of art, which
   is a breakaway from the ready-made meanings of a ready-made life. There

The fundamental problem in all this is to distinguish between the first intention and the second intention as constitutive of order. The first intention proceeds from the transcendental element in man and determines the true and the good. The second intention begins where all this becomes a social reality, where objectification takes place, where we may distinguish what happens for the most part and what happens rather seldom. The totality of human life is penetrated by intentionality. Economics and politics are the fruit of understanding, judgment, and decision. Institutions are constituted by human intentionality, and they do not change unless we change them.

There is a difficulty in determining meaning. The empirical sense differs because of human constitution, and so there is a problem of knowing human reality. An example is the difference in the meaning of democracy in the United States and in Great Britain.[78]

---

is literary meaning and technical meaning. All are forms of human communication. In all of them there is the constitution of the communication as such by meaning. Remove the meaning and the thing ceases to be what it is.' While his own notes for the 1964 class proceed to discuss material that is very similar to what follows in 'The Analogy of Meaning,' the Daly notes indicate that he took a different direction at this point. Thus, the remainder of this treatment of meaning relies exclusively on the Daly notes. It is not as clear as what is contained in the remainder of 'The Analogy of Meaning,' but our intention here is to present as accurate an account of the actual course as we can. Lonergan's own notes may be found on www.bernardlonergan.com at 53200DOL060.

78 Here the Daly notes meet Lonergan's later development in 'The Analogy of Meaning,' where he writes: 'That constitutive meaning of the institution is something that is specifically human, and because those meanings change and develop, because they reveal their inadequacies and need to be perfected, they constitute the history of ideas, of doctrines, of concepts, of meanings. The United States is a democracy, and England is a democracy, but they are not democracies in exactly the same sense. The Englishman, by his parliament and his institutions, does not mean something that corresponds point to point with what the American means by his democracy. They are two different democracies, and the differences are constituted by the common meanings to which two peoples are committed. Similarly in the family, there is the meaning of the family, and it is the meaning that the members of the family apprehend and are committed to that is realized in the family. One can set up a normative idea of the family, a normative idea of the state, a normative idea of the church, but they are abstractions. They are not the concrete reality that is constituted by the meanings known and willed by the persons involved. Consequently, for institutions to be known in their concreteness, in their individual reality, they have to be studied in their

There are two ways of effecting meaning in the concrete: by considering the steps and by considering the processes. The steps are, first, sensations, imagination, and affects, second, the order of understanding, third, the rational order, and fourth, self-consciousness and decision. Sensations, imagination, and affects provide the material element in human living, but also anticipate the spiritual order and concretize it by interpreting it for the psyche. The order of understanding consists of inquiry, understanding, conception, and word as communication of understanding. The rational order is concerned with the absolute, the true, and decision is concerned with the good. The structure of meaning is present in these. A meaning is cognitively complete through the true, but even more complete through decision and greater self-realization.

The process of meaning moves from identity to objectification. It begins with identity, where meaning in act is the meant in act. At the point of insight, the intellect in act is the understood in act. But there is also distinction. Direct understanding yields to concepts, and reflective understanding to judgment, where what is, independently of me, is known. There is a similar process from identity to objectification in deliberation and decision.[79]

An elementary conclusion is that meaning is not a small dimension of human living. It is not restricted to terms, theses, reasons, objectification, even though it is found there. It is found beyond these. These are but a part. And the part can mistakenly be taken for the whole, as Newman argued in *The Idea of a University*. When that happens, what lies beyond the restricted meaning remains unknown, the whole is mutilated, and what remains is distorted. The living subject is clarified and intensified by objectification, no doubt, but it is the source of all these others. Love is lived before it is analyzed, and there is meaning in the living. People may not be able to define love, but they know it.[80]

---

histories. To change those meanings is to change the reality. The reality of the family becomes a different thing when divorce becomes a common possibility. You have changed the meaning, and changing the meaning changes the reality because the meaning is constitutive of the reality.'

79 In the Daly notes we have 'identity in weighing [the evidence] – stripping – deliberation.'

80 Further reconstruction of this lecture would be tentative at this point. The terms in Daly's notes that would seem to complete this lecture are the following (translated into English by Michael Shields): 'Common meaning is constitutive of society, of culture. Many difficulties: that which is, that which ought to be. Only that which is falsifies. That which ought to be = pure ethical, juridical vision.

Horizon (5 February 1964, 52400D0L060)

We conclude with a discussion of a basic heuristic notion: horizon. The merit of Hegel's philosophy is attention to the intimate meaning of the subject and to the objective historical meaning of a society and its evolution. But this philosophy also radically errs, especially under the influence of Kant, in that while Hegel clearly perceived the naiveté of perceptionism he did not arrive at the notion of being as everything about everything or at the notion of objectivity as absolute affirmation. He also omits consideration of the supernatural order.

Horizon is the circle that limits the field of one's vision. The notion of horizon is defined by the two correlatives of the pole and the field. To every different pole there corresponds a different field, and to every different field there corresponds a different pole. The pole is the subject as determined in such and such a way, while the field is the totality of objects which this subject de facto approaches. The diversity of fields is a function of the diversity of subjects. Literally, the horizon is *ho horizōn kuklos*, the bounding circle that limits one's vision. When the notion is taken psychologically, there is a luminous area, an adequate field of knowledge, interest, perseverance, and absorption; a shadow area where things are more vague and not very exciting or interesting; and the outer darkness where nothing is known and one does not care.

The notion of horizon differs from the habits treated in Scholasticism. The formal object of a habit is the formality under which the object is attained; if the formality is different, the habit is different. But the notion of the pole and the field is more concrete, since it involves the whole subject and the totality of objects. It is also more empirical, in that it involves the subject as he or she de facto is, not merely as one ought to be. It is more psychological, in that it touches on one's interest and perseverance. And it is more compendious, since it includes the totality of the subject and the object.

A distinction should be drawn between absolute horizon and relative horizons. Each person has an absolute horizon. They draw a line, and what is beyond that line does not exist or cannot be known. No inquiry should be made about it and no value attributed to it. Others may feel differently but they are in error, and indeed in a serious manner. They reject the grace of God and resist the Holy Spirit. They yield to illusions and are deceived by falsehoods. They hold on to views long rendered obsolete. They are governed by images and feelings, not by reason and reality. They employ ideology.

Relative horizons are a function of different people living in different worlds. Priests, lawyers, doctors, professors, politicians, workers, businessmen each acknowledge the existence and value of the others and of their worlds, but know little about them and care less. This is not at all an absolute rejection. The move from one relative horizon to another occurs, not by conversion but by development, education, experience, by psychological, social, and historical evolution. But the move from one absolute horizon to another is a matter of conversion, whether religious, moral, or intellectual. Religious conversion moves one towards the supernatural. Moral conversion moves one from egoism to absolute values, the good. Intellectual conversion is a matter of adopting the correct philosophical positions on knowing, being, and objectivity.

Psychological development was studied by Aristotle in terms of the acquisition of habits. But Piaget has studied natural operations, their differentiation, the combination of differentiated operations, groups of combinations of differentiated operations, and groups of groups of such combinations. With him it is always a question of the acting concrete subject, and his judgments are experimentally verified. In psychological development, there are the three stages of the world of immediacy, the world mediated by meaning, and the mediation of the instruments of mediation. The world of immediacy is what is attained by the senses. The world mediated by meaning is the larger world brought to us by imagination, language, numbers. The mediation of the mediators is accomplished by the study of language, mathematics, and logic. From this standpoint, the fundamental psychological problem is that the really real is that immediate world of the child. The psychological horizon is constituted by what I can do, know, and will promptly, easily, and with delight.

Social development is understood in terms of the notion of the human good.[81] The social horizon has to do with the good that is possible here and now or with the future good that may be attained through the mediation of what is here and now. There is eliminated what is merely ideal and merely possible. Attention is paid to the good that may proximately be attained in a given social milieu.

81　Lonergan's notes contain a variant of the familiar schema of the human good. See above, p. 29. Daly's notes would seem to indicate that Lonergan did not cover either social development or historical horizon in his lecture but moved directly from psychological development to horizon as a heuristic notion. With regard to social horizon and historical horizon, Lonergan's notes contain only what is found in this and the next paragraph.

The historical horizon is a function of the differentiation or lack of differentiation of consciousness. Consciousness may be differentiated accidentally, as it were, in terms of theory being distinguished from praxis; it may be differentiated in orientation as mysticism becomes distinct from magic; but modern differentiation is a function of existential interiority discriminating theory from common sense.

And so we come to horizon as a heuristic concept. Every human being is conceived as determined by a horizon, by such and such an absolute horizon and by certain relative horizons. What horizon is absolute in this particular author? What horizon is relative? This allows us to distinguish comparative, organic, genetic, and dialectical methods. Comparative method is employed in order to find the relevant questions themselves. Organic method determines the mutual coherence and dependence of elements, so that when one element changes, there is a reaction that eliminates other dimensions or that adapts to the change. Genetic method finds a series of adaptations to new organic combinations. And dialectical method finds contradictory oppositions between absolute horizons, whether in different human beings and groups or in conflict within the same person between the transcendental orientation of human nature and one's actual horizon.

3 De Notione Structurae[1]

Reverendissimi professores, carissimi in Christo fratres:

Quam maxime non solum me delectat, sed etiam me honorat praesens occasio. Non enim qualiscumque est locus, neque qualecumque est tempus. Non qualiscumque est locus, cum Aloisianum ubique cognoscatur – 'in

1 Verba facta a Patre Bernard J. Lonergan, s.i., die festo Sancti Thomae Aquinatis, 7 martii, 1964, in Collegio Aloisiano apud Gallarate iuxta Mediolanum.

3 The Notion of Structure[1]

I am not only extremely delighted but indeed honored to be here on this occasion. This is, after all, no ordinary day, nor is this an ordinary place, for the Aloisianum has a worldwide reputation – 'Its voice has gone out to the

1 A lecture delivered in Latin at the Collegium Aloisianum, Gallarate, Italy, on the feast of St Thomas Aquinas, 7 March 1964 (since transferred to 28 January). The lecture thus was delivered about one month after the completion of the previous item, the fall and winter course on 'De methodo theologiae.' A transcription of the tape recording of the lecture was printed in the student journal of the college, *Apertura* 1/2 (May 1964) 117–23. This Latin transcription was reproduced as an appendix to the doctoral dissertation of Luigi Patrini, *La Metafisica di Bernard Lonergan* (Università Cattolica del Sacra Cuore, Milan, 1968) 176–97. In 1989 Michael G. Shields made another transcription, with notes, from a cassette recording of the lecture (Cassette tape 383, Lonergan Research Institute Library; item 8300A0L060 in the online Lonergan Archive at www.bernardlonergan.com), as well as an English translation, which appeared in *Method: Journal of Lonergan Studies* 14/2 (1996) 117–31.

   This translation has been revised for the present publication and footnotes have been provided, filling out in a few cases the references Lonergan gave as he spoke. These notes, therefore, are all editorial. In the Patrini edition, the lecture is divided into numbered sections, 24 in all; we have not followed this numbering, but instead have inserted titles for the main divisions of the talk.

   The whole lecture has some similarity to 'Cognitional Structure,' written later in the same year for *Spirit as Inquiry: Studies in Honor of Bernard Loner-*

fines orbis terrae exivit sonus eius'[2] – tum propter conventus philosopho-
rum eximiorum qui singulis annis huc veniunt, hic disputant, hic disserta-
tiones prelo mandant, tum propter magnum illud inceptum, quod media
mechanica et electronica ad opera Sancti Thomae plenius accuratiusque
scrutanda adhibet atque indices nova ratione compilatos praeparat.[3] Non
qualiscumque est locus, neque qualecumque est tempus, cum diem festum
agamus S. Thomae Aquinatis studiorum ducis, hocque meum vobiscum
colloquium in eius honorem vergere debeat.

Omnino ergo convenit ut ex ipso Sancto Thoma ordiar, et illud tamquam
thema elegi perpendendum atque quoad fieri potest penetrandum, quod
ipse in commentariis *In Boethium De Trinitate*, quaestione quinta, articulo
tertio, conscripsit.[4]

[1 Some Preliminary Observations on Abstraction]

Antequam ipsa verba quae considerare volo legam, aliqua forsitan utiliter
praenotentur. Quaestio in illo articulo est de abstractione mathematica, et

ends of the earth'[2] – not only by reason of the annual meetings of outstanding philosophers who come here to engage in discussion and submit their dissertations for publication, but also on account of the massive project being undertaken here of using mechanical and electronic means to facilitate a more thorough and accurate study of the works of St Thomas and to draw up new indices to them.[3] And of course, since this is a very special day, the feast day of St Thomas Aquinas, our intellectual mentor and guide, it is only right that my talk here today should pay homage to him.

It is therefore altogether fitting to take St Thomas as our starting point, and accordingly I have chosen as a topic for us to consider and, as far as possible, to understand, the thought of Aquinas as set forth in his commentary *In Boethium De Trinitate*, question 5, article 3.[4]

[1 Some Preliminary Observations on Abstraction]

Before reading this passage itself, however, some preliminary observations may be helpful. This article deals with the question of mathematical ab-

---

gan, ed. Frederick E. Crowe (Chicago: Saint Xavier College, 1964) 230-42, and republished now in Lonergan, *Collection* 205-21. But it also reflects considerations raised especially in the spring 1963 course 'De methodo theologiae,' the first item in this volume.

2 The quotation is from Psalm 19.4. In the Catholic liturgy these words are applied to the apostles, and Lonergan's application of them to the Collegium Aloisianum evoked much hearty laughter.

3 The reference here is to the work of Robert Busa. Fr Busa was still active at Gallarate, and had put all the works of St Thomas on to a compact disc (CD-ROM). The fruit of his pioneering work has made possible the present easy availability of all of St Thomas's writing on the Internet, at: http://www.corpusthomisticum.org/iopera.html.

4 The question in article 3 is: 'utrum mathematica consideratio sit sine motu et materia de his quae sunt in materia.' See Thomas von Aquin, *In Librum Boethii De trinitate quaestiones quinta et sexta*, ed. Paul Wyser (Fribourg: Société Philosophique; Louvain: Nauwelaerts, 1948) 36, lines 9–10; Bruno Decker, *Sancti Thomae de Aquino Expositio super Librum Boethii De trinitate* (Leiden: Brill, 1955) 179, lines 6–7. An English translation of the entire article is available in St Thomas Aquinas, *The Division and Methods of the Sciences: Questions V and VI of His Commentary on the* De Trinitate *of Boethius translated with Introduction and Notes*, 3rd rev. ed. Armand Maurer (Toronto: Pontifical Institute of Mediaeval Studies, 1963) 25–39.

solutio variis gradibus procedit, et de istis gressibus prioribus agitur. Scilicet, incipit S. Thomas dicendo, 'Oportet videre qualiter intellectus secundum suam operationem abstrahere possit.' Et distinguit proinde duplicem operationem intellectus: primam operationem in qua quaeritur 'Quid sit?' et intelligitur et definitur; et deinde secundam operationem in qua quaeritur 'An sit ?' et evidentia ponderatur et iudicatur. Et dicit quod secundum secundam operationem non tam de abstractione agitur quam de separatione. Deinde circa primam operationem dicit quod 'intellectus potest abstrahere ea quae secundum rem separata non sunt; non tamen omnia, sed aliqua.' Et illud 'non tamen omnia' pertinet ad nostrum thema. Scilicet, vos optime scitis de abstractione, et noluerim aliquid iis addere; sed de iis quae non separantur secundum intellectum, quae comprehenduntur, quae simul intelliguntur, ea sunt ad quae attendere volo.

Dicit ergo quod id quod intrinsece ordinatur ad aliud sine illo alio intelligi non potest. Habetur abstractio vel haberi potest abstractio 'si unum ab altero non dependeat, secundum id quod constituit rationem naturae, tunc unum potest ab altero abstrahi per intellectum, ut sine eo intelligatur.' Et dat exempla. 'Littera potest intelligi sine syllaba sed non e converso.' Nemo enim potest dicere quid sit syllaba nisi de litteris cogitat.' '... et animal sine pede'; si tollitur pes, manet animal, 'sed non e converso.' Pes enim non iam est pes si tollitur animal. '... sicut albedo potest intelligi sine homine, et e converso.' Haberi potest albedo, et cogitari et intelligi potest, etiam si nihil dicatur de homine, et similiter de homine si nihil dicatur de albedine.

Isti casus possibilis abstractionis est quasi principale in illo articulo, quia agitur de abstractione, sed alius casus etiam meretur attentionem, et illum alium casum volo nunc considerare.[5]

Primo legam incisum: 'Quando ergo secundum hoc per quod constituitur ratio naturae et per quod ipsa natura intelligitur, natura ipsa habet

straction; the solution is given in various steps, and it is these prior steps that our topic is concerned with. St Thomas begins as follows: 'We must consider in what way the intellect is able to abstract according to its own operation.' And he goes on to distinguish two intellectual operations: the first operation in which the question 'What is it?' is asked and the thing is then understood and defined, and the second operation in which the question asked is 'Is it so?' and the evidence is weighed and a judgment made. He then points out that the second operation is not so much a matter of abstraction as of separation. Next, with regard to the first operation he says that the intellect 'is able to abstract those things that in reality are not separate – not all of them, however, but some of them.' It is this 'not all of them, but some' that I propose as our subject today. Now, you are all quite knowledgeable about abstraction, and so it is not my intention to add anything on that point; what I want to do is to look at those things that are not separated in the mind – that is to say, that are comprehended, that are understood together.

Aquinas, then, is saying that what is intrinsically ordered to something else 'cannot be understood apart from that other.' Abstraction is possible, he says, in this way: 'As long as one thing does not depend on another according to the way they are naturally constituted, then it can be abstracted from the other by the intellect and so be understood apart from that other.' And he gives examples: 'A letter of the alphabet can be understood apart from a syllable but not vice versa,' for no one can say what a syllable is without thinking about letters; and again, 'An animal can be understood apart from a foot.' The foot may be removed, but the animal remains, 'but not vice versa,' for a foot is no longer a foot if the animal has ceased to be. Yet 'whiteness can be understood apart from a man and vice versa'; for whiteness can exist and be thought of and understood even if nothing is said about a man, and the same holds for man even if there is no mention or thought of whiteness.

These instances of possible abstraction are the main point in that article because abstraction is the issue; but the other case is also worth noting, and it is this case that I should like to consider here today.[5]

First, let me read the passage: 'Therefore, when a nature, in accordance with that which constitutes its essential meaning and through which

---

5 After *casum*, 'case,' the final three or four words are indistinct on the tape, but the sense is clear.

ordinem et dependentiam ad aliquid aliud, tunc constat quod natura illa sine illo alio intelligi non potest.'[6] Si hoc ipsum per quod natura intelligitur intrinsece ordinatur ad aliud, sic fieri non potest abstractio, praecisio ab illo alio, et tamen res vel natura intelligatur. Et dat exempla: 'Sive sint coniuncta coniunctione illa qua pars coniungitur toti, sicut pes non potest intelligi sine intellectu animalis,' quia pes intrinsece ordinatur ad animal; 'sive sint coniuncta per modum quo forma coniungitur materiae, sicut pars comparti vel accidens subiecto, sicut simum non potest intelligi sine naso; sive etiam sint secundum rem separata, sicut pater non potest intelligi sine intellectu filii, quamvis illae relationes inveniantur in diversis rebus.'[7]

Fons praecipuus quo utitur S. Thomas in ista analysi invenitur in septimo libro *Metaphysicorum* Aristotelis, ubi Aristoteles disserit de partibus materiae, de partibus formae, et de partibus definitionis.[8] Invenitur in commentario S. Thomae a lectione nona ad duodecimam.[9] Et debemus perpendere breviter exempla quae adhibet S. Thomas ut videamus in quo consistit illa necessaria connexio ita ut unum sine alio intelligi non possit.

Non pars sine toto. Et dat partes organicas: non pes sine animali. Aristoteles dixit quod oculus seorsum sumptus est oculus aequivoce dictus; nemo videt per oculum qui est extra corpus. Similiter digitus mortuus est aequivoce dictus; nemo potest aliquid facere cum digito separato.

Non forma sine materia. Anima humana est forma quaedam et definitur 'actus primus corporis organici,' vel 'actus primus corporis potentia vitam habentis.'[10] Quod includitur in definitione alicuius omitti non potest in consideratione illius quin desinat cogitatio de ipsa re. Si omittitur a notione animae ista intrinseca habitudo ad corpus, non iam habetur anima sed

it is understood, is ordered to and dependent upon something else, then clearly that nature itself cannot be understood apart from that other.'[6] In other words, if that by which a nature is intelligible is intrinsically ordered to something else, you cannot abstract or prescind from that other and still understand that nature or thing. He gives the following instances: '... whether they are connected in the way that a part is connected to the whole, as in the case of a foot that cannot be understood without an understanding of animal' because a foot is intrinsically ordered to an animal; or 'whether they are connected in the way in which form is connected to matter, as a part is to its corresponding part or as an accident is to its subject. Snubness, for example, is unintelligible apart from the idea of nose; and this can be so even if the two things are separated in reality, as in the case of "father," which cannot be understood apart from understanding "son" even though those relations belong to different individuals.'[7]

The main source which St Thomas draws upon for this analysis is to be found in the seventh book of Aristotle's *Metaphysics*, where Aristotle discusses the parts of matter, the parts of form, and the parts of definition.[8] You will find it in Aquinas's commentary, lectures IX–XII.[9] Let us now briefly consider the examples he uses, to try to determine the sort of connection that is required if one thing is unable to be understood without the other.

A part cannot be understood without the whole. He takes organic parts, for example: a foot cannot be understood without an animal. Aristotle says that an eye that is removed is an eye only in an equivocal sense, since one cannot see with an eye that is outside one's body. Similarly, a lifeless finger is only equivocally a finger, since no one can do anything with a severed finger.

Form is unintelligible apart from matter. The human soul is a form, and is defined as 'the first act of an organic body,' or 'the first act of a body that is capable of life.'[10] A consideration of any particular thing must include whatever is contained in its definition, or else all thinking about it becomes impossible. If intrinsic relation to a body is omitted from the notion of soul,

---

6 *Quando ergo secundum hoc ...*: Wyser 38, 30; Decker 183, 6.
7 *... sive sint coniuncta ...*: Wyser 38, 34; Decker 183, 7.
8 Aristotle, *Metaphysics* VII, 10–12, 1034b 20–1038a 35.
9 Thomas Aquinas, *In VII Metaphys.*, lect. 9–12, §§1460–1565.
10 Aristotle, *De anima*, II, 2, 412b 5 and 412a 21. See also Lonergan's discussion in *Verbum: Word and Idea in Aquinas*, vol. 2 in Collected Works of Bernard Lonergan, ed. Frederick E. Crowe and Robert M. Doran (Toronto: University of Toronto Press, 1997) 32–33.

substantia separata, angelus. Angelus est forma subsistens sine habitudine ad corpus; praecise quia anima habet intrinsecam habitudinem ad corpus est anima.

Non pars sine comparte. Elementa fundamentalia in systemate Aristotelico et iterum in systemate S. Thomae definiuntur non propria definitione, sed per quandam proportionem mutuam: sicut oculus comparatur ad visum, ita auris comparatur ad auditum. Et haec est comparatio materiae ad formam uti dicit in nono *Metaphysicorum*, lectione quinta, numero apud Cathala millesimo octingentesimo vicesimo octavo et sequenti.[11] Et similiter sicut visus comparatur ad videndum, auditus comparatur ad audiendum. Quid sit auditus si non est ad audiendum? Intrinsece habet habitudinem ad audiendum, et similiter visus intrinsece habet habitudinem ad videndum. Et oculus, quid sit oculus? Oculus se habet ad visum sicut corpus se habet ad animam. Est intrinseca quaedam habitudo, et unum sine altero intelligi non potest. Quid sit oculus? Est organum visus, et alia definitio tradi non potest.

Non accidens sine subiecto. Meministis sine dubio longiorem dissertationem Aristotelis de simo. Simum et concavum idem dicunt, cum una tamen exceptione: simum est concavum, sed concavum non qualecumque, sed in naso. Sine naso non habetur simum. Accidens non potest separari a subiecto, secus tollitur ipsa ratio accidentis. Si ponitur definitio circuli et nihil dicitur de superficie plana, non habetis definitionem circuli. Accidentis esse est inesse, secundum ipsam notionem essentialem accidentis: habet intrinsecam habitudinem ad aliud. Hac de causa accidentia eucharistica, quamvis actu non insint alicui substantiae, tamen manent accidentia, non fiunt substantiae. Ratio substantiae et ratio accidentis non dependent ab actuali inhaerentia, vel actuali absentia inhaerentiae, sed ratio accidentis pendet ab ipsa essentia eius quod est accidens; secundum definitionem accidens invenitur in alio sicut circulus in superficie plana. Si quis dicit circulum esse locum punctorum aequaliter distantium a centro, et nihil dicit de superficie plana, definitio non est bona; qualiscumque linea ducta super sphaera esset circulus secundum illam malam definitionem.

Non relativum sine correlativo, sicut non intelligitur pater sine intellectu filii. Et notate, agitur de intelligentia. Non dicit quod mortuo filio pater

you no longer have a soul but a separate substance, an angel. An angel is a subsistent form without any relation to body; what makes a soul a soul is precisely the fact that it has this intrinsic relation to a body.

Again, a part cannot be understood without a corresponding part. Fundamental elements in the Aristotelian system and again in St Thomas's are defined not by a proper definition but by some mutual proportion: as the eye is to sight so the ear is to hearing. And this is the proportion of matter to form, as St Thomas points out, *In IX Metaphys.*, lecture 5, §1828 and following.[11] Likewise, as sight is to the act of seeing, so hearing [*auditus*, the faculty of hearing] is to the act of hearing [*audiendum*]. What is the nature of one's hearing [*auditus*] if not in order to hear? It has an intrinsic relation to the act of hearing. In the same way sight is intrinsically related to seeing. And the eye, what is an eye? An eye is to sight as the body is to the soul. There is an intrinsic relation between them, and one cannot be understood without the other. What is an eye? It is the organ of sight, and no other definition can be given.

An accident cannot be understood without a subject. You will all remember, I am sure, Aristotle's lengthy disquisition on snubness. The adjectives 'snub' and 'concave' mean the same, but with this one qualification: 'snub' means 'concave' – not anything concave; however, but a concave nose: no snubness without a nose! An accident cannot be separated from a subject, for otherwise it would no longer be an accident. If in a definition of a circle there is no mention of a plane surface, you do not have the definition of a circle. The existence [*esse*] of an accident is to exist-in [*inesse*], according to the essential idea of accident. It has an intrinsic relation to something else, and that is why the Eucharistic accidents, although not actually inhering in a substance, still remain accidents – they do not become substances. Accident as such and substance as such do not depend upon actual inherence or actual non-inherence, but the basic notion of accident flows from the essence of what accident is; and according to its definition, an accident is that which is found in another, as a circle is found in a plane surface. To say that a circle is a locus of points equidistant from a centre and say nothing about a plane surface would not be a good definition of a circle, since any line drawn on a sphere would be a circle according to that faulty definition.

Again, a relative term is unintelligible without its correlative. 'Father' cannot be understood without understanding 'son.' And note that this is a

11 Thomas Aquinas, *In IX Metaphys.*, lect. 5, §§1828–29.

non exsistit! Non agitur de esse. Non dicit quod nominato patre nominatur filius. Optime nominamus patrem sine nomine filii, et saepissime hoc facimus; sed non intelligitur pater sine intellectu filii. Agitur ergo de intelligentia et de iis qui simul intelliguntur vel non intelliguntur.

Ergo sicut fit sermo de abstraction, scilicet, de iis quae seorsum intelliguntur, ita etiam fieri potest sermo de comprehension, scilicet, de iis quae simul intelliguntur. Et sicut comprehensio est eorum quae simul intelliguntur, ita etiam structura est eorum quae simul intelliguntur. Habetur tamen distinctio inter comprehensionem et structuram, quatenus comprehensio est ex parte subiecti cognoscentis et structura est ex parte rei cognitae. Elementa scilicet comprehensio simul plura intelligit, et illa plura simul intellecta faciunt structuram: non seorsum intelliguntur.

Iamvero vobis loqui volo non de structura in abstracto, secundum generalissimam rationem structurae, sed, modo magis particulari et concreto, de tribus structuris.

[2 The Structure of the Thing Known]

Primo, de structura rei cognitae – per modum introductionis, quia ibi habetur structura vobis optime cognita. Deinde de structura cognitionis, quae est similis structurae rei cognitae. Et tertio de structura obiectivitatis, quae facit coniunctionem inter primam structuram et alteram: cognoscimus rem propter obiectivitatem cognitionis. Et quia loquimur de structura cui correspondet comprehensio, non loquimur de omni cognitione, vel de omnibus rebus, vel de omni obiectivitate, sed de iis tantummodo rebus quas comprehendere possumus; ideoque non de iis rebus quas comprehendere non possumus, quas tantummodo mediate, analogice, imperfecte cognoscere possumus. Ergo non erit sermo de structura angelorum, vel non erit quaestio utrum sit structura in Deo, quia ea cognoscimus non tamquam obiecta propria nostri intellectus hac in vita, sed tantummodo per analogiam quandam, per viam affirmationis et negationis et eminentiae. Et similiter non de qualibet cognitione, sed de nostra cognitione, quam proprie cognoscere

matter of *understanding*: it doesn't mean that a father ceases to exist when his son dies! It is not a matter of existence. Nor does it mean that if the father is named so too is the son. It is an excellent thing we do when we address the Father by name yet without naming the Son, and we do this very frequently; still, 'father' is unintelligible apart from understanding 'son.' The point at issue here, therefore, is understanding – the understanding of those things that are understood together and those that are not.

Accordingly, just as we can speak about abstraction, that is, about understanding one thing separately from another, so also we can speak about comprehension, that is, about the simultaneous grasp of those things that are understood together. And just as there is this comprehension of things that are understood together, so also is there a structure to the things understood together. The difference, however, between their comprehension and their structure is this, that comprehension is on the part of the knowing subject while structure belongs to that which is known. Comprehension is the understanding of several elements together, and those several things as understood together exhibit a structure: they are not understood separately one from another.

Now, it is not my intention to speak to you about structure in the abstract according to some very general notion of structure, but rather, more concretely, about three particular structures.

[2 The Structure of the Thing Known]

There is, first, the structure of the thing known – just by way of introducing the topic, since this structure is well known to you here. Next, there is the structure of knowledge, which is similar to the structure of the thing known. Third, there is the structure of objectivity, which links the first two structures: we know reality because of the objectivity of our knowledge. And since we are dealing here with that structure to which comprehension corresponds, we shall not be referring to all knowledge or all things or all objectivity, but only to those things which we can comprehend, and therefore not about those realities which we cannot comprehend, but can know only mediately, imperfectly, and by analogy. Thus, we shall not speak about the structure of angels, nor shall we ask whether there is any structure in God, for these realities are not the proper objects of our intellect in this life, but are known only by some analogy – by way of affirmation, negation, and supereminence. By the same token, we shall not speak about any and all

possumus; et non de qualibet obiectivitate, sed de obiectivitate nostrae cognitionis, quam proprie cognoscere possumus.

Primo ergo de structura rei cognitae. Uti scitis, secundum Aristotelem res materialis componitur ex hac materia et ex hac forma, et idem docet S. Thomas. Sed praeterea, uti iam diximus, materia est materia per habitudinem ad formam, et forma materialis est forma materialis quia apta nata est informare aliquam materiam: unum sine alio intelligi non potest. Quamvis sint formae separatae, tamen sunt formae alterius generis. Ergo istae duae faciunt structuram. Si progredimur ultra Aristotelem et intramus in doctrinam S. Thomae, invenimus etiam quod essentia et esse contingens faciunt structuram: unum sine alio intelligi non valet. Omne esse finitum est actus essendi alicuius essentiae, et omnis essentia ordinatur ad esse: unum sine altero non intelligitur. Sermo potest fieri de uno quin de altero fiat sermo, sed intelligentia unius sine intellectu alterius non habetur. Sed essentia est eadem ac forma et materia, ideoque habemus structuram magis complicatam. Esse et essentia faciunt structuram, sed ipsa essentia est, ut ita dicam (sit venia verbo) structurata: componitur ex forma et materia. Vel si modo magis generali volumus loqui, possumus dicere quod habetur in re cognita structura ex potentia, forma, et actu – actu secundo. Ergo structurae non limitantur ad duo tantummodo elementa; structura aeque bene componitur ex tribus, si sunt tres quae nisi simul non intelliguntur. Praeterea habetur radicalis quaedam differentia inter elementa alicuius structurae et totum quod structuram habet; unde aliqua admiratione addiscitur in primo anno philosophiae de comprincipia entis: ipsa non sunt, sed iis aliquid est. Materia non est, forma non est, esse non est, sed iis aliquid est. Materia non est res, forma non est res, esse non est res, res non componitur ex tribus rebus. Habetur tantummodo una res, et tamen illa tria non sunt nihil. Ipsa non sunt, sed iis aliquid est. Ipsa res secundum analysin metaphysicam componitur non ex rebus sed ex principiis quibus sunt res. Insisto in illa differentia quia eandem differentiam inveniemus in cognitione, et eandem differentiam inveniemus in obiectivitate. Rem optime cognoscitis circa analysin rei, sed forsitan non omnes iam cogitastis de possibilitate alicuius similis in ipsa cognitione et in ipsa obiectivitate.

Antequam relinquam rem cognitam, primam structuram quam consideramus, per brevissimum quoddam momentum cogitemus de re scientifice

knowledge but about our knowledge, knowledge that we can have in the manner proper to us; nor about any sort of objectivity, but about the objectivity of our knowledge, which we can know in a proper way.

First of all, then, the structure of things we know. According to Aristotle, as you know, a material thing is composed of this matter and this form, and St Thomas teaches the same. But also, as we have just said, matter is matter by reason of its relation to form, and a material form is a material form because it is meant to inform some matter: one cannot be understood without reference to the other. Although there are such things as separate forms, they are an altogether different kind of form. These two, therefore, matter and form, make up a structure. If we go beyond Aristotle into St Thomas's doctrine, we learn that essence and contingent existence also form a structure: neither one is intelligible without the other. Every finite existence is the act of being of some essence, and every essence is ordered to existence: one cannot be understood without the other. You can talk about one without talking about the other, but there can be no understanding of one without understanding the other. But essence is the same as form and matter, and so we have a more complex structure. Existence and essence form one structure, but essence is itself structured: it is composed of form and matter. In more general terms, we can say that the object known has a structure made up of potency, form, and act – second act, that is. Structures therefore are not limited to two elements only; a structure can just as well be made up of three, if these three are only intelligible when taken together. Moreover, there is a radical difference between the elements of any structure and the whole which possesses that structure; hence our wonderment when, in first-year philosophy, we learn that the principles of being do not themselves exist but are that by which something exists. Matter is not a thing, nor is form a thing, nor is existence a thing, nor is a thing made up of three things. There is only one thing, and yet those three are not nothing. They themselves are not, but by them something is. In its metaphysical analysis a thing is not itself composed of things but of principles by which things are. I am laying great stress upon this difference, because we shall find the same difference in our knowing and again in objectivity. I am sure you are quite knowledgeable about this analysis of a material object, but perhaps not all of you have thought about the possibility of something similar in knowledge itself and in objectivity.

Before leaving the first structure we want to consider, the structure of the things we know, let us take a few moments to consider things as

cognita. Omnes cognoscimus res optime, sed, sicut dixit Eddington,[12] habuit in sua camera non unam tantummodo mensam sed duas. Una erat visibilis, coloris obscurioris, solida, talibus dimensionibus et ita porro: id quod ab omnibus cognoscitur. Sed alia mensa, quodammodo non erat alia, et tamen quodammodo erat totaliter alia, quia non erat solida, erat maxima ex parte vacua, consistebat electronibus, quae imaginari non possunt, non erat fixa in loco at sese agitabat continuo, et ita porro. Tamen de rebus prout scientifice cognoscuntur, sive consideramus scientiam hodiernam, sive scientiam post decennium, sive scientiam post saeculum, sive scientiam in illo fine beatitudinis scientificae ubi omnia prorsus phaenomena intelliguntur – in omni casu quid habetur? Habetur theoria, verificata, in multis individuis. In quantum habetur theoria habetur ea per quam cognoscitur forma in rebus; in quantum habetur verificatio habetur ea per quam cognoscitur esse in rebus; et in quantum theoria verificatur in multis individuis habetur id per quod cognoscitur materia.

Eadem est structura in rebus scientifice cognitis et in rebus metaphysice cognitis – quod videtur mirum.[13] Quaenam est differentia? In metaphysica procedimus secundum intentionem finis. Et intendimus finem quando quaerimus, 'Quid sit?' et intendimus finem quando quaerimus, 'An sit?' Et secundum quod quaerimus, 'An sit?' exspectamus responsum, et illud responsum erit 'Est' vel 'Non est': ponimus esse. Quaerimus, 'Quid sit?' et expectamus responsum, et erit aliqua forma, aliquod obiectum intelligentiae qua intelligentiae, et ergo dicimus formam esse in rebus. Et formae istae sunt in multis rebus; habetur similis omnino forma, et ideo ponimus aliquid quod cognoscitur sensibus: 'residuum empiricum,' ut dici potest alibi.[14]

In metaphysica procedimus secundum intentionem finis, et quia procedimus secundum intentionem finis habemus id quod habetur in scientia hodierna, et post decennium et post saeculum et in fine beatitudinis scientificae. Sed scientifici non procedunt secundum intentionem finis; volunt

known scientifically. We all know things quite well, but, as Eddington tells us,[12] he had in his room not just one table but two. One was visible, rather dark in color, solid, of such and such dimensions, and so forth – what we all know as a table. But the other table, well, in a way it was not another table and yet in a way it was totally different, because it was not solid but mostly empty space, it consisted of electrons, which cannot be imagined, it was not completely stationary but in constant agitation, and so on. What about things, then; as known by science? – whether we are talking about science as it is today, or ten years from now, or in the next century, or in that ultimate state of scientific bliss when absolutely all phenomena will be understood. In every case, what do we have? We have a theory verified in a number of individuals. A theory is that by which a form in things is known; verification is that through which existence in things is known; and insofar as a theory is verified in a number of instances, we have that by which matter is known.

So then, things as known scientifically and things as known metaphysically have the same structure – amazing![13] What then is the difference? Metaphysics proceeds according to an intention of the end, and we know that we intend an end when we ask, 'What is it?' We intend the end when we ask, 'Is it so?' And in asking whether it is so, we expect an answer, and that answer will be either 'It is so' or 'It is not': we are making an assertion about existence. We ask, 'What is it?' and expect an answer, and that answer will be some form, some object of understanding as such, and therefore we say that forms are in things. And these forms are in many things; the form is absolutely the same, and so we posit something that is known by the senses – the 'empirical residue,' as it is referred to elsewhere.[14]

In metaphysics we proceed according to an intention of the end, and because we do so we have what is had by science today and ten or a hundred years from now and in that final state of scientific bliss. But scientists do not proceed according to an intention of the end. They want to attain an end,

12 See Sir Arthur Stanley Eddington, *The Nature* of *the Physical World* (Cambridge: Cambridge University Press, 1928) xi–xv.
13 Some years earlier Lonergan had devoted a special paper to this question. Written for the fourth international Thomistic congress and titled 'Isomorphism of Thomist and Scientific Thought,' it was first published in the acts of the congress (*Sapientia Aquinatis*, vol. 1, 1955); it has been reprinted in *Collection* 133–41.
14 Evidently a reference to Lonergan, *Insight*. See the index under 'Empirical residue.'

attingere finem, volunt actu intelligere, non tantummodo scire quod habetur aliquid intelligendum, ideoque debent determinate loqui. Et quia valde difficile est determinate loqui, progrediuntur, sperant se aliquando pervenire ad veram theoriam; sed nunc proprius accedere se credunt ad finem. Habetur ergo non solummodo structura in rebus sed structura dupliciter cognita: cognita secundum intentionem finis in metaphysica, et secundum aliqualem adeptionem finis in scientiis; sed eadem habetur structura in utroque casu. Et cum prima structura habeat aliquam habitudinem ad secundam, potest dici heuristica secundae, medium quo invenitur secunda; scilicet, 'heuristica' vult dicere 'id quod facit inventionem.' Quomodo faciunt inventionem scientifici? Quaerendo 'quid?' et 'cur?' et 'quomodo?' ponunt quaestiones quae respiciunt intelligentiam; et iterum quaerendo an revera res ita se habeat, faciunt verificationem.

Ergo consideravimus rem cognitam et invenimus in rebus cognitis structuras et quidem similes structuras, sive consideratur cognitio metaphysica, sive consideratur cognitio scientifica.

[3 The Structure of Knowing]

Nunc aliam structuram, aliud caput aggredimur: structuram in nostra cognitione. Dixi quod inveniemus eandem ambiguitatem in nostra cognitione ac cognosicur metaphysicis[15] circa materiam et formam et rem. Materia non est res, sed pars rei; et forma non est res, sed pars rei. Si aliquis videt, audit, olfacit, gustat, sentit, an cognoscit necne? Forsitan dicetis, 'cognoscit.' Certe dici non potest quod nullo modo cognoscit. Tamen, qui ita experitur et nihil prorsus intelligit, an dicimus eum cognoscere? Potius dicimus eum stupere. Qui experitur quae non intelligit, non tam cognoscit quam stupet. Habet experientias, sed nihil intelligit. Ergo habetur ratio dicendi quod debemus distinguere inter cognitionem generice dictam et specifice dictam. Cognitio generice dicta invenitur in qualibet operatione cognoscitiva; sive sit videre, audire, sentire, sive sit esse conscium; sive sit intelligere, vel definire, vel reflectere, vel ponderare evidentiam, vel iudicare. Omnes isti

of course; they want to actually understand and not just know that there is something there to be understood, and therefore they have to speak in a determinate way. And because it is very difficult to speak in a determinate way, they continue to progress, trusting that eventually they will arrive at a theory that is true; but for the time being they believe that they are coming closer to the end. There is, therefore, not only a structure in things, but a structure that is known in two ways: known in metaphysics according to an intention of the end, and known in the sciences according to some degree of attainment of the end; but it is the same structure in both cases. And since the first structure has a relation to the second, it can be called *heuristic* with regard to the second, a means whereby the second is found. 'Heuristic' means that which is conducive to discovery. How do scientists go about finding what they seek? By asking 'What?' and 'Why?' and 'How?' they pose questions that relate to understanding, and by asking again whether the particular thing is really so, they are verifying.

So then: we have considered things as known and in them have found structures, and indeed similar structures, whether we are considering metaphysical or scientific knowing.

[3 The Structure of Knowing]

Let us move on now to consider another heading, another structure, the structure within our knowing itself. I have already indicated that we shall find the same ambiguity in our knowing as that which is familiar to metaphysicians[15] regarding matter and form and thing. Matter is not a thing, but part of a thing; form is not a thing, but part of a thing. If a person sees, hears, smells, tastes, and feels, does he have knowledge or not? Perhaps you will say he does. Certainly it cannot be said that there is no knowledge here at all. Yet, if someone has these sense experiences but has no understanding of them, shall we say he has knowledge? We are more inclined to regard him as being stupid. One who has sense experiences that he does not understand is one who is stupid rather than one who knows something. He experiences things but does not understand them. This, therefore, is why we say that we must distinguish between knowledge in a general sense and

---

15 *cognoscitur metaphysicis*: an unusual construction, especially in prose. The Aloisianum transcription substitutes *habetur in elementis metaphysicis*, but a personal noun is more appropriate as corresponding to *nostra*.

actus sunt cognoscitivi: aliquomodo ad eos pertinent cognitiones. Pertinent ad eos cognitiones sicut realitas pertinet ad principia entis: sicut materia et forma et esse, ipsa non sunt sed iis aliquid est. Simili quodam modo videre et intelligere et iudicare si seorsum sumuntur, si non simul comprehenduntur, si prescinditur a structura, ipsa non sunt cognitiones, sed quibus fit cognitio. Similiter, si quis experitur atque intelligit, an cognoscit? Si nullo modo attendit ad iudicium, ad evidentiam, potius fertur mentalitate mythica; non potest facere distinctionem inter astronomiam et astrologiam, inter chimiam et alchimiam, inter historiam et legenda, nisi facit iudicium. Experitur mythicus, intelligit mythicus, gaudet sua intelligentia quam maxime, sed defectus est in iudicio. An cognoscit? Potius non. Qui experitur et intelligit, sed dubitat, an cognoscit? Non dicimus idem esse cognoscere et dubitare. Qui dubitat nondum cognoscit, anceps haeret, tamen experitur, intelligit, habet pulcherrimam theoriam quam exponit per integros libros. An cognoscit? Ipse non est certus, dubitat. Ergo habentur in cognitione partes. Si iudicat et male iudicat, an cognoscit? Dicimus quod errat; non idem est errare et cognoscere.

Ergo in ipsa cognitione habetur aliquid simile ac in analysi rerum metaphysica. Habetur cognitio proprie dicta, proprie humana, cognitio quae invenitur solum in homine, non in animalibus, non in angelis. Est cognitio composita: habetur elementum experientiale, habetur elementum intelligentiae, habetur elementum iudicii, sed si tollitur unum ex iis tollitur cognitio specifice humana. Qui intelligit sine experientia, quid facit? Fingit. Optime intelligit ea quae imaginat sed ipsas res non intelligit; debet facere verificationem utrum data sensibilia sint eadem ac ea quae ipse imaginatione repraesentat. Vel qui iudicat quin quaestionem intelligat, an vere iudicat? Videtur quod non. Ista tria sibi cohaerent: non habetur cognitio humana, specifice humana, ea cognitio humana quae tractat de obiecto proprio cognitionis humanae, nisi simul intrant elementum experientiae, elementum intelligentiae, et elementum iudicii. Et ita habemus in cognitione triplex illa structura quam etiam invenimus in rebus metaphysice cog-

knowledge in a specific sense. There is knowledge in a general sense in any cognitional operation, whether it be seeing, feeling, hearing, being conscious, understanding, defining, reflecting, weighing evidence, or judging. All of these are cognitive acts and all of them contain knowledge in some way or another. Knowledge belongs to them as reality belongs to the principles of being: like matter and form and existence, they themselves are not but through them something is. In a somewhat similar way, if seeing and understanding and judging are considered separately, if they are not comprehended together, if one prescinds from their structure, they themselves are not knowledge but through them knowledge is generated. Likewise, if someone experiences and understands, does he have knowledge? If he pays no attention to judgment, to the evidence, he is rather under the influence of a mythic mentality: he is incapable of distinguishing between astronomy and astrology, between chemistry and alchemy, between history and legend, unless he makes a judgment. A person with this mentality experiences, he understands, and indeed takes great delight in his intelligence, but he falls short in the area of judgment. Does he have knowledge? Not really. Does a person have knowledge if he experiences and understands and yet doubts? We do not say that doubting is knowing. One who doubts does not yet know; he hesitates between 'Yes' and 'No' and yet he experiences and understands, he may even have beautiful theories and write whole books about them. But does he really know? He himself is not certain: he has doubts. Knowledge, therefore, does have parts. If someone judges but judges wrongly, does he have knowledge? We should say rather that he is wrong, he is in error. To err is not the same as to know.

So we see that in knowing there is something very similar to what we found in our metaphysical analysis of things. There is a knowing that is properly so called, proper to human beings, a knowing that is found only in man, not in animals nor in angels. This knowing is a composite: it has an experiential element, an element of understanding, and an element of judging, and if one of these is lacking, you no longer have knowing that is specifically human. What is one doing when he is using his intelligence but not experiencing anything? He is making things up. He understands quite well what he is imagining, but he is not understanding real things as they are themselves. He must verify to see whether there are sensible data that are the same as what he pictures in his imagination. Or take the case of one who judges without having understood the question: does he truly judge? It would seem not. These three are bound up together: there is no human knowing, no cognition that is specifically human, human knowing

nitis et in rebus scientifice cognitis. Neque est valde mirum quia sumus nos qui habemus cognitionem metaphysicam et sumus nos qui habemus cognitionem scientificam. Ipsae structurae sese multiplicant, quia procedunt ex eodem fonte; et illa similitudo structurae nominari potest 'isomorphismus' – ex *isos* et *morphē*: aequalis formae, aequalis structurae.

[4 Structure of the Link between Knowing and the Known: Objectivity]

Tertium caput considerationis. Non solummodo habetur habitudo inter cognitionem et cognitum, sed ista habitudo cognoscitur, et quatenus cognoscitur habetur nota habitudo cognitionis et rei – cognitio;[16] et hoc pertinet ad ipsam naturam cognitionis. Iamvero ista habitudo potest considerari dupliciter: uno modo ut intenta, secundum aspectum finalitatis consciae, et alio modo ut cognita. In nobis inveniuntur non tantum experientia et intelligentia et iudicium sed etiam habentur ea quibus movemur ex uno gradu ad alterum. Quando experimur tantummodo, elucet lux intellectus agentis, et ponimus quaestionem: incipit conscientia intellectualis et ponimus quaestionem, 'Quid?' 'Cur?' Et sic incipimus differre ab animalibus. Ergo fit promotio ex experientia versus intelligentiam in quantum quaerimus 'Quid sit?' 'Cur ita se habeat?' Et postquam intelleximus iterum fit promotio alia quaestione, 'An sit?' 'Utrum res ita se habeat?' S. Thomas permultos libros scripsit, et quid fecit? Respondit ad quaestionem, 'Utrum ...?' Sunt nescio quot millia 'Utrum?' in operibus S. Thomae, sed omnia quae scripsit respondent ad aliquam quaestionem, 'Utrum?' Ergo illa quaestio, 'An sit?' facit gressum ex intelligentia ad iudicium. Sed iterum quaestiones non sunt prorsus diversae, habent aliquid commune, nempe illud 'sit.' Intenditur

that deals with the proper object of human knowledge, unless there enter into it in concert the element of experience, the element of understanding, and the element of judging. And so we have in our knowing that three-fold structure that we also find in things that are metaphysically known and those that are scientifically known; nor is this surprising, since it is we who have metaphysical knowledge and who also have scientific knowledge. The structures replicate themselves, since they flow from the same source; and this similarity the structures have to one another we may call *isomorphism*, from *isos* and *morphē*, 'having the same form, the same structure.'

[4 Structure of the Link between Knowing and the Known: Objectivity]

We come now to the third heading of the topic we are considering. Not only is there a relation between our knowing and what we know, but this relation itself is known, and inasmuch as it is known we have the well-known relation between knowledge and reality – objectivity;[16] and this belongs to the very nature of our knowing. Now this relation can be considered in two ways: as intended, that is, under the aspect of conscious finality, and as known. In our knowing we find not only experience, understanding, and judging, but also the dynamisms by which we are moved forward from one level to another. When we have a simple experience, our agent intellect lights up and we ask questions. Our intellectual consciousness is aroused and we ask the questions 'What is this?' and 'Why?' This is how we begin to be different from animals. Here we are moved forward from experiencing towards understanding as we ask the questions 'What is it?' and 'Why is it so?' And after we have understood, there is a second movement forward when we ask another question, 'Is it?' and 'Is this the way it really is?' St Thomas wrote many books, and what was he doing? He was answering the question *Utrum* ...? 'Whether ...?' I don't know how many thousand *Utrum*'s there are in the works of St Thomas, but everything he wrote was in answer

---

16 [What Lonergan actually said here was *cognitio*, 'knowledge.' But it seems clear from the context that he meant to say *obiectivitas*, since this is the third point or heading of the lecture; see p. 171 above, where he outlines the three structures he intends to consider, and the third-last sentence of the lecture, '... objectivity, which establishes the link between the knower and the known.']

non tantummodo 'quid,' sed etiam 'sit'; non tantum 'an' sed etiam 'sit.' Illae duae quaestiones habent radicem communem – intentionem entis, intentionem esse. Intendimus esse, habetur naturale desiderium intellectus versus esse, quod promovet data sensibilia ad ordinem intelligibilitatis quaerendo, 'Quid sit?' et promovet ea quae intelligimus ad ordinem iudicii quaerendo, 'An sit?'

Nunc autem non tantum intenditur esse, intenditur ens, sed etiam illa intentio de se ipsa quaerit utrum revera bono eventu ad finem suum pervenerit. Et ista quaestio est de obiectivitate. Non tantummodo sponte et natura ad obiectivitatem pervenimus – aliquomodo est verum – sed etiam cogitamus de ipsa obiectivitate nostrae cognitionis quaerendo quid sit obiectivitas. Et primum notandum circa obiectivitatem est quod omnis scientia, omnis philosophia, est quaedam superatio mythi. Et per mythum intelligo id quod est certissimum, maxime obvium, clarissimum omni homini habenti qualemcumque parvum sensum communem, et tamen falsum – sicut quod tellus est plana, et ita porro. Habentur mythi non solummodo in campo scientifico, sed etiam in campo philosophico. Mythus circa obiectivitatem est omnibus notus. In quo consistit obiectivitas? Bene; imaginatione repraesentamus – vel melius, exemplo demonstremus obiectivitatem. Ecce, manus, oculus; oculus videt manum, manus est obiectum, oculus est subiectum; obiectivitas est quod subiectum sese transcendit et pertingit usque ad obiectum. Nihil clarius.

Sed omissa illa obiectivitate quaeramus ex modo procedendi concreto. Et invenimus non unam obiectivitatem sed tres. Primo habetur obiectivitas quae dicitur empirica, quae consistit tantummodo in manifestatione ipsius dati, ipsorum datorum. An manus mea alba sit? quaero. An charta sit alba? Si 'ita' respondisti ad primam quaestionem, non potes similiter respondere ad secundam. En obiectivitatem experientialem, empiricam. Illa obiectivitas est maximum fulcrum in scientiis empiricis. Quando quaestio ita poni potest ut solutio dependeat ex ipsis datis manifestis, tunc contentissimi sunt scientifici. Et omnes ponunt quaestiones ut quantum fieri possit ita eis respondeatur.

Attamen aliud exemplum, alterius prorsus generis, possumus dare obiectivitatis. Et haec est obiectivitas normativa: tu tibi ipsi contradicis, non potest esse verum id quod dicis. Exemplo sit in systematizatione rei math-

to an *utrum* ...? Thus, the question 'Is it?' is a step forward from understanding to judging. And yet, these questions are not totally different: they have *is* as a common element. We are seeking to know not only 'what' but also 'is'; not only 'whether' but also 'is.' These two questions have a common root, the intention of being, the intention of existence. We intend existence; there is in us a natural desire or drive of the intellect towards existence, by which sensible data are raised to the level of the intelligible by the question 'What is it?' and what we have understood is raised to the level of judgment by the question 'Is it?'

Now, we not only intend existence, or being, but this same intention also asks about itself whether in fact it has succeeded in attaining its end. This is the question about objectivity. It is true, in a sense, that we spontaneously and naturally arrive at objectivity in our knowing. But we also think about it: What is objectivity? we ask ourselves. Well, the first thing to be noted about objectivity is that every science, every philosophy, is, so to speak, an overcoming of myth. By 'myth' I mean something that is most certain, very obvious, quite evident to anyone who has the least bit of common sense – and yet is false. That the earth is flat, for example, and such things – that is what I mean by 'myth.' And there are myths not only in the field of science but also in philosophy. There is a myth about objectivity that we all know about. What is objectivity? Well! we picture in our imagination – or better still, let us demonstrate objectivity by this example. Look: here is my hand, here is my eye; the eye sees the hand, the hand is the object, the eye is the subject; objectivity is the fact that the subject transcends itself and reaches to the object. What could be clearer?

Now let us leave aside the notion of objectivity and look at the matter concretely. We find not one objectivity, but three. First, there is objectivity that is called empirical: which consists merely in the appearance of the datum or data themselves. Is my hand white? Is this paper white? If you have answered 'yes' to the first question, you cannot give the same answer to the second! Here you have experiential, or empirical, objectivity. This sort of objectivity is the most important fulcrum of the empirical sciences. When a question is asked the answer to which depends upon the clear evidence of the data themselves, then it is that scientists are most content. And they all ask questions that as much as possible can be answered in that way.

But we can give still another example of objectivity, of a quite different kind. This is normative objectivity. If you make statements that are self-contradictory, what you say cannot be true. Take, for example, the system-

ematicae a Russell et Whitehead excogitata.[17] Necessarium erat aliquod postulatum de gradibus. Et adversarii dicunt quod postulatum Russell est huiusmodi: nulla propositio de omnibus simul classibus est valida; valida non est quaelibet propositio quae simul respicit omnes classes. En postulatum Russellianum, et illud postulatum sibi contradicit. Quia ipsum postulatum est aliqua propositio, et haec propositio simul respicit omnes classes, ergo postulatum ipsum non est validum. Habetur ergo hic contradictio, et si adest contradictio, deest obiectivitas. Est obiectivitas normativa: est obiectivitas quae respicit ipsum usum nostri intellectus. Procedimus ex datis ad conceptus, hypotheses, theorias. Ille processus potest bene fieri secundum normas ipsius intelligentiae, aut non. Si non, deest obiectivitas normativa; si bene, adest obiectivitas normativa. Et illa secunda obiectivitas est alterius prorsus generis ac prima, quae consistit in comparando albedinem manus et albedinem chartae, et fit oculis.

Sed habetur tertia quaedam obiectivitas. Aliquis ad celebrandum festum S. Thomae exit per silvas, et socius ei dicit, 'En magnum canem!' Alius dicit, 'Esne certus quod non sit lupus?' Bene; quid significat illa certitudo? Si habetur certitudo, habetur aliquid absolutum. Et non absolutum in caelis, sed absolutum in hoc asserto particulari et contingenti, 'Hic non est lupus, est tantummodo canis.' Est alterius generis. Contradictio et alia omnia quae pertinent ad obiectivitatem normativam habent aliquam universalitatem intrinsecam; sed hoc absolutum invenitur in particularibus et contingentibus. Et tamen est id quod dat firmitatem omni nostrae cognitioni.

atization of mathematics worked out by Russell and Whitehead.[17] It was necessary to have some postulate regarding the steps. Russell's postulate, according to his critics, goes like this: no proposition that covers all classes together is valid; any proposition referring to all classes together is invalid. That is Russell's postulate, and that postulate is self-contradictory, because that postulate itself is a proposition and it refers to all classes together, and so it is itself invalid. We have, therefore, a contradiction here. And where there is a contradiction, there is an absence of objectivity. This is normative objectivity, the objectivity that regards the use of our understanding. From data we proceed to concepts, hypotheses, theories. This process can properly be carried out according to the norms of intelligence or not. If not, there is no normative objectivity; if so, there is normative objectivity. This second objectivity is of a quite different kind from the first one, which consisted in comparing the whiteness of one's hand with that of a piece of paper, done by simply taking a look.

But there is still a third objectivity. Let us say that someone, enjoying the holiday on the feast of St Thomas, goes for a walk in the woods, and at one point his companion says to him, 'Look at that big dog over there!' And the other one says, 'Are you sure it's not a wolf?' Well, what is meant by certitude in this case? If you have certitude, you have something absolute. And this is not some sort of celestial absoluteness, but the absoluteness of this particular and contingent assertion: 'This is not a wolf, it is just a dog.' It is another kind of objectivity. Contradiction and normative objective have intrinsic universality; but the absoluteness in this case is found in the particular and contingent. Yet it is this that gives solidity to all our knowledge.

17 [Alfred North Whitehead and Bertrand Russell, *Principia mathematica* (Cambridge: Cambridge University Press, 3 vols., 1st ed., 1910–13; 2nd ed., 1925–27). For some further remarks by Lonergan on Russell's postulate, see his paper 'Philosophical Positions with Regard to Knowing' in *Philosophical and Theological Papers 1958–1964*, vol. 6 in Collected Works of Bernard Lonergan, ed. Robert C. Croken, Frederick E. Crowe and Robert M. Doran (Toronto: University of Toronto Press, 1996) 214–43, at 228. For some of Lonergan's other remarks on Whitehead and Russell's work, see *Understanding and Being: The Halifax Lectures on* INSIGHT, vol. 5 in Collected Works of Bernard Lonergan, ed. Elizabeth A. Morelli and Mark D. Morelli, revised and augmented by Frederick E. Crowe with the collaboration of Elizabeth A. Morelli, Mark D. Morelli, Robert M. Doran, and Thomas V. Daly (Toronto: University of Toronto Press, 1990) 254–55, 262–63; and *Phenomenology and Logic: The Boston College Lectures on Mathematical Logic and Existentialism*, vol. 18 in Collected Works of Bernard Lonergan, ed. Philip J. McShane (Toronto: University of Toronto Press, 2001) 41–43, 61, 90–91.]

Ergo obiectivitas videtur esse aliquid compositum. Debet habere elementum experientiale; debet habere elementum normativum; sed ulterius debet habere aliquod elementum absolutum ut assertum ponatur absolute, sine formidine errandi, uti dicitur. Et haec tria simul sumpta faciunt unam obiectivitatem. Obiectivitas normativa est inutilis nisi incipimus ex datis vere manifeste datis. Et ipsa obiectivitas normativa facit nexum inter data et conceptum, inter data et hypothesin, inter data et theoriam, vel quamlibet complexionem conceptuum, uti dicitur. Et quando venit ad iudicandum formula, ut mihi videtur, omnis iudicii est quod attingitur inconditionatum, id quod est virtualiter inconditionatum: quod habet conditiones, sed conditiones implentur. Quomodo scis quod hic non est lupus, quod est canis? Bene. Sunt conditiones quae debent impleri ut sit lupus et sunt conditiones quae debent impleri si est canis. Et secundum quod implentur necne, potes dicere utrum sit lupus an canis; et similiter de omni iudicio. Quando habetur inconditionatum virtuale, conditionatum cuius conditiones implentur, tunc pervenitur ad aliquid absolutum, tunc dicimus, Est.

Breviter ergo resumam ea quae dixi. Non tantummodo abstrahitur unum ab alio; hoc fit secundum aliqua, non tamen omnia. Sunt quae simul intelliguntur, et quae simul intelliguntur, comprehenduntur etiam in se habent aliquam structuram: unum intrinsece ordinatur ad aliud. (Et ista ordinatio potest esse serialis; posui exempla in quibus habentur solummodo tria mutuo ordinata; sed numerus potest extendi.) Et talis structura invenitur in rebus cognitis, sive metaphysice cognoscuntur sive scientifice cognoscuntur. Et similis structura invenitur in nostra cognitione quia in alio sensu dicitur cognitio quando agitur solummodo de sentire, vel solummodo de intelligere, vel solummdo de iudicare. Et aliter dicitur cognoscere quando agitur de istis tribus simul sumptis. Et similiter de obiectivitate, quae facit nexum inter cognoscentem et cognitum. Ipsa obiectivitas cognitionis humanae: sicut cognitio est composita, etiam obiectivitas cognitionis est composita. Habetur obiectivitas experientialis, sicut habetur elementum experientiale in cognitione; habetur obiectivitas normativa sicut habetur elementum intellectuale in cognitione; et habetur obiectivitas absoluta, sicut et habetur elementum rationale in cognitione.

Miror vestram patientiam et gratias omnibus vobis extendo propter honoratissimam invitationem mihi factam a Reverendissimo Patre Rectore, tum etiam propter vestram bonitatem.

Objectivity, therefore, also appears to be a composite. It must have an experiential element and a normative element; but further, it must have an absolute element, so that an assertion may be made absolutely, without fear of error, as the saying goes. These three taken together make up one objectivity. Normative objectivity is worthless unless we begin from data that are really and obviously given. Normative objectivity makes the connection between data and a concept, between data and a hypothesis, between data and a theory, or any conceptual system. And when it comes to making a judgment, the essential note of every judgment, in my opinion, lies in the fact that it attains the unconditioned, that is to say, what is virtually unconditioned: it has conditions, but those conditions have been fulfilled. How do you know that that was a dog and not a wolf? Well, there are certain conditions that have to be fulfilled for it to be a wolf and there are certain conditions to be fulfilled if it is a dog. And according to whether those conditions are or are not fulfilled, you will be able to tell whether it is a wolf or a dog. The same holds for every judgment. When we have a virtually unconditioned, a conditioned whose conditions are fulfilled, then we have arrived at something absolute, and we say, 'It is.'

Let me briefly sum up what I have been saying. We not only abstract one thing from another – that is true in some cases, but not in all. But those things which are understood together, comprehended, also have a structure to them: one is intrinsically ordered to another. (This ordering can be a series; I have given instances in which there are only three elements ordered one to another, but the number can be increased.) And such is the structure that is found in things that are known, whether known metaphysically or scientifically. A similar structure is present in our knowing because it is called knowing in different senses depending upon whether we are referring only to sense experience or only to understanding or only to judging; and it is called knowing in a still different sense when we are referring to all these three taken together. The same holds for objectivity, which establishes the link between the knower and the known. Such is the objectivity of human knowledge: as knowing is a composite, so also is the objectivity of knowledge a composite. Just as there is an experiential element in knowing, so there is experiential objectivity; as there is an intellectual element in knowing, so there is normative objectivity; and as there is a rational element in knowing, so there is absolute objectivity.

You have been admirably patient, and I am sincerely grateful to you all for honoring me by the invitation extended to me by Father Rector, and for your kindness to me on this occasion.

Index

Abelard, Peter, 57, 67, 138
Abstraction: 19, 42 n. 55, 49, 95 and n. 10, 96, 107, 129, 163–71
Act: first a., 28, 37; and judgment, 19, 100, 136; potency, form, and a., 19, 45, 97, 100, 135, 136, 173; second a., 28, 173
Actio: either act or exercise of efficient causality, 51
Adoptionists, 57, 115, 123
Aggiornamento, 87
Agent intellect, 99, 180
Albert the Great, 112
Albright, W.F., 19
Alexandrians, 20
Already out there now, 56
Altaner, B., 22 and n. 29, 92
Anachronism, 69, 70, 71, 116, 117
Analysis: dialectical a., *see* Dialectic; way of, 66, 67, 85, 145, 146
Ancient high civilizations, 36, 40, 152
Anselm, 138
Apollinaris, 124
Apologists, 26
Appetite: natural and elicited, 51–52; natural a. of intellect for God, 53

A priori: in investigating meaning, 12–13; in science, 11
Archaism, 69, 71, 116, 117
Arians/Arius, 54, 57, 83, 108, 117
Aristotle, 10, 19, 22 and n. 32, 24, 25, 36, 37, 92, 93, 95, 106–107, 122, 124, 138, 141 and n. 47, 143, 147 and n. 61, 152, 157, 167 and nn. 8 and 10, 169, 173
Art: as carrier of meaning, 12, 52
Athanasius, 80, 83, 107, 116, 117, 123, 127
Atheism, 47, 90
Attention: and horizon, 28, 29, 30, 37, 38, 39
Aufhebung, see Sublation
Augustine, 35, 36, 47, 68, 88, 112, 121, 122, 127, 135
Augustinians, 22 n. 32
Authenticity, 43, 48, 54, 55, 56, 57, 68. *See also* Inauthenticity
Autonomy: absolute a., 47; and horizon, 36, 40
Avicenna, 19

Basil of Caesarea, 117, 123

nomic, bureaucratic, educational, legal d., 59

Deus scientiarum Dominus, 39, 139 n. 44

Development: and conversion, 39, 40, 41, 59, 80, 82, 157; cultural d., 32, 33, 41, 48, 57, 58, 59, 62, 63, 64, 75, 82 (*see also* Conversion: and cultural development); d. *in fieri*, 33, 34, 35; philosophic d., 54; psychological d., 41, 48, 57, 58, 59, 62, 63, 64, 75, 82, 157; social d., 41, 48, 57, 58, 59, 62, 63, 64, 75, 82, 157; from undifferentiation through differentiation to integration, 16, 20–21, 32–33, 35, 40, 79, 84, 135, 137, 141. *See also* Development of dogmas; Development of theology

Development of dogmas: 7, 54, 57, 70–72, 91, 107, 110, 114, 116, 117, 119, 124, 126, 137

Development of theology, 57, 70–72, 91, 103, 126, 137, 139

Devotio moderna, 138

Dialectic/Dialectical: and common notions and principles, 121; and conversion, 30, 121; and horizon, 32, 158; and irreducible opposites, 26, 27, 48, 59, 158; and judgment, 27, 74; d. methods, 18, 20, 26, 51, 73, 80, 158; and positions and counterpositions, 28, 63

Differences: and comparison, 20, 32; philosophic d., 25; relative d., 64, 75. *See also* Worlds

Differentiation: and adaptation (Piaget), 29, 157; as breakdown of previous integration, 32; and fate of system, 67; and technical meaning, 152; from d. to integration, 16, 20–21, 32–33, 35, 40, 79, 84, 135, 137, 141; of transcendental horizon absolute, 48–49. *See also* Consciousness: differ-

entiation of; Development; Meaning: differentiated

Dilthey, W., 25, 35, 79 n. 83

Discovery: order of, *see* Analysis: way of

Doctrine: history of from New Testament to Nicea, 25; understanding d. and history of d., 6, 7, 8, 66, 82, 91, 131, 136, 141

Dogma(s): connection of, 116; and contexts, 116; development of, *see* Development of dogmas; d. of Greek councils, 123–24, 127; history of, 12; infallibility of, 84; and method, 80, 82; and mysteries, 138; notion of develops, 116; objections against, 111–12, 114, 116; obscurity of, 111–12; orders intellect to God, 112–13; relations of to Scholastic theology and church teaching, 85; and religious spirit, 111–12; and revelation, 85; and sources, 15, 107, 110–17; and system, 81, 84, 86; technical terms in, 79; term of development, understood from development, 91; and truth, 110; as what is to be believed by all, 85, 107

Dogmatic: certitude, 110, 143; communication, 84; definitions, 69; element, 84, 145; end, 6; exegesis, 80, 81; expression, 80, 110; facts, 9; meaning, 108; mentality, 116; method, 107–108, 134; moment, 78; movement, 85, 110, 113; process, 79, 114; questions, 81, 122; spirit, 71; statements, 79, 104; task, 119; theologian, 71, 92, 108–10; theology, 71, 74, 79, 80, 81, 82, 86, 94, 103, 104–10, 111, 116, 120, 126, 131, 135, 136, 137, 141, 145, 146

Dreams: and levels of consciousness, 43; of morning, 17, 149–50 and n. 70

Drifter, 30, 38

Droysen, J.G., 23, 24

of, 53, 58, 61; and religious conversion, 49, 53–54, 56; and unlimited
being, 53, 55
Good: g. absolutely, 52; and being, one,
true, 8, 19, 21, 27, 40, 54, 55, 56, 81,
101, 126; criterion of, 60; human g.,
27, 29, 30, 38, 52, 157; and moral conversion, 49, 54, 55, 157; g. of order,
29, 30, 38, 52; particular g., 29, 30, 38,
52; and value, 29, 30, 38, 52
Grimm, H., 23, 24

Habit: and Aristotle, 37, 157; formal object of, 156; and horizon, 28, 37, 156;
intellectual h., 29; and Piaget, 29, 37,
157; theology as, 132; volitional h., 29
Hegel, G.W.F./Hegelians, 16, 19, 23, 24,
35, 36, 50, 55, 74, 75, 77, 82 n. 87, 99,
116, 141 and n. 47, 156
Heidegger, M., 35
Heresy/heretics, 26, 57, 104, 114, 115,
130
Hermeneutics: classical h., 117, 118,
119; and intellectual conversion,
47; method of, 62; and problem of
knowledge, 76; Romantic h., 79, 117,
118, 119, 130; rules of, 24
Heuristic structure, 13, 82, 100, 121,
122, 123, 124
Heussi, K., 69 and n. 71, 72 n. 74, 73, 74
and nn. 75–76
Hilbert, D., 93
Hippolytus, 20
Historical consciousness, 39, 40, 63, 78,
86, 87, 88, 89, 94, 104, 130, 140
Historicism, 18, 34 and n. 45, 69, 70, 82,
94, 116
History: and correctness, 70; creates
its own experiments, 12; critical h.,
72–73, 74–77; h. of doctrine and understanding of doctrine, *see* Doctrine;
existential h., 72, 75; and existential-

ism, 74; and *Geschichte-Historie*, 75–76;
gnoseology of, 77; and intellectual
conversion, 47; learning art of h., 24;
as lived, understood, and undergoing
crises, *see* Schema; metaphysics of,
77; method in, 72–74; method of, 62;
and minor and major criticism, 21,
22, 23, 24, 25, 26; narrated h., 72, 73;
nature and h., 77–78; object of relatively fixed and relatively fluid, 77;
h. as progress, decline, redemption,
83; and relativism, 69; and theology,
84, 90, 144; and way of analysis, 66;
as written and written about, 77–86,
88. See also *Geschichte*; Historical consciousness; Historicism; *Historie*
Hobbes, T., 60
Holy Spirit, 57, 105, 109, 116, 118, 122,
124, 132, 146, 166
Homoousion, 20, 116, 138
Honestum, 53
Horizon: 27–42 passim, 48–59 passim,
62–66 passim, 74, 80, 82, 128, 140,
145, 155, 156, 157, 158. *See also* Conversion: and development; Development: and conversion
Husserl., E., 75 and n. 80, 88 n. 2, 96
and n. 7
Huyghe, R., 12, 150 n. 71

Idealism, 19, 21, 26, 47, 49, 51, 74, 75,
86, 89, 111, 113, 116, 121, 123, 124,
134
Ideology, 42, 47, 61, 156
Image: and feeling, 149
Immanentism, 35, 76, 121
Implicit-explicit, 13, 15, 42–43, 50, 54,
64, 88, 89, 108, 120, 125, 134. See also
Exercite-signate
Inauthenticity, 31
Incarnate meaning, 12, 14, 15, 148, 149,
153 n. 77